LOST ISLAMIC HISTORY

FIRAS ALKHATEEB

LOST ISLAMIC HISTORY

RECLAIMING MUSLIM CIVILISATION
FROM THE PAST

HURST & COMPANY, LONDON

First published in the United Kingdom in 2014 by
C. Hurst & Co. (Publishers) Ltd.,
41 Great Russell Street, London, WC1B 3PL
This revised and updated version published 2017
© Firas Alkhateeb, 2017
Eighth impression 2021
All rights reserved.

Printed in the United Kingdom by Bell & Bain Ltd, Glasgow

Distributed in the United States, Canada and Latin America
by Oxford University Press, 198 Madison Avenue, New
York, NY 10016, United States of America

The right of Firas Alkhateeb to be identified as the author
of this publication is asserted by him in accordance with the
Copyright, Designs and Patents Act, 1988.

A Cataloguing-in-Publication data record for this book
is available from the British Library.

978-1-84904-689-3 *paperback*

This book is printed using paper from registered sustainable
and managed sources.

www.hurstpublishers.com

For the most important people in my life,
my mother Sanaa, my wife Hadeel, and my sister Huda.

بسم الله الرحمن الرحيم

In the name of God, the Most Gracious, the Most Merciful

من سلك طريقا يبتغي فيه علما سلك الله به طريقا إلى الجنة

"If anyone travels on a road in search of knowledge, Allah will cause him to travel on one of the roads of Paradise."

Prophet Muhammad

CONTENTS

PREFACE

The aim of this book is to provide a short overview of the history of Muslim civilization, from the inception of Islam in the early seventh century to the modern day. To fully and accurately cover the depth and breadth of Muslim history is of course a monumental undertaking, one that perhaps no single volume could ever adequately contain. My goal with this attempt is thus simply to introduce the reader to the general narrative of Islamic history. It is not meant for the specialist or the serious student of Islamic history, but rather for the general reader who hopes to become somewhat more familiar with the subject. I therefore hope that for many, this text will be a jumping off point, from which a more thorough study of Muslim history and civilization will spring. Considering that this is an introductory text, it contains little in the way of original research. The vast majority of it is based on the research of others, whose works are listed in the bibliography and can serve as a valuable starting point for a deeper study of the subject.

I began the Lost Islamic History project in the early 2010s, after I began teaching Islamic history to high school students. Due to the structure of the American educational system (which is woefully light on the humanities in general), most of my students had only the most basic understandings of Muslim civilization. Their textbooks placed much emphasis on the ancient Greeks and

Romans, and then the "rise" of Europe after the Dark Ages through the Renaissance and the Enlightenment, but barely spoke of Muslim, or other non-Western, civilization at all. One small section on the Prophet Muhammad or half a page on the Ottoman Empire in Eastern Europe might be all that most textbooks devoted to the 1400 years of Islamic history.

My Islamic history class thus developed as a response to that deficiency, with my goal being to expose students to the richness of Muslim civilization that they didn't get elsewhere. I aimed to provide an alternative to the presentation of European history as World history, focusing on the rise of Muslim civilization and the many contributions of that civilization to humanity in general. To my delight, the response was overwhelmingly positive. Most of my students were the children of immigrants who had come from various Muslim countries, and thus finally felt a connection with something historical. Naturally, it was much easier for them to identify with historical figures such as Abu Hanifa and Yusuf ibn Tashfin than they ever could with John Locke and Napoleon.

The book *Lost Islamic History* then developed out of my teaching notes. Considering that there was no high school textbook of Islamic history available in English, *Lost Islamic History* became my attempt to fill part of that gap. If people outside of my classroom could similarly get a taste of what they missed in their high school history courses, then this book would serve its purpose.

Since its initial publication in 2014, I've spent more time studying in-depth myself, particularly the Islamic sciences. As such, for this second edition, we have chosen to revise the text and include a new chapter dedicated to the development and history of Islamic thought. As the beating heart of Muslim civilization, Islamic jurisprudence, theology, and spirituality deserve far more discussion than the few pages in this text, but I hope that this new chapter brings some light to the Islamic sciences that the first edition lacked. For this section of the book in particular, I am indebted to Shaykh Amin Kholwadia and the rest of the teachers at Darul Qasim, without whom my understanding of the Islamic tradition would be elementary at best. Thanks must also be given to the staff at Hurst Publishers, who have been incredibly helpful and supportive during the writing and publishing process for both the original text and this updated edition.

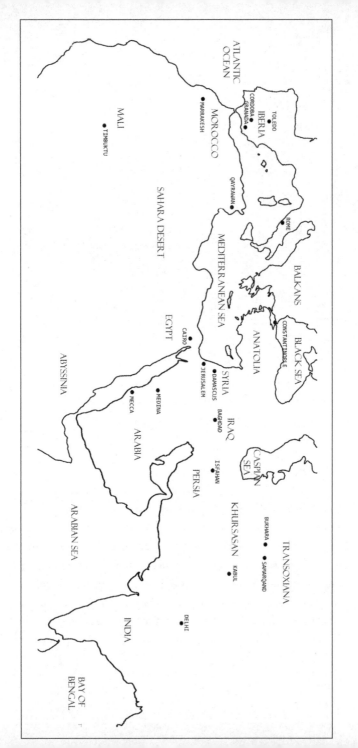

1

PRE-ISLAMIC ARABIA

The dry, mountainous landscape of the Hijaz is not an environment that gives much life. Situated in the western part of the Arabian Peninsula, this land can be described with two words: dry and hot. In the summer, temperatures regularly rise to well over 100 degrees Fahrenheit, with little precipitation. Further east, endless sand dunes mark a landscape devoid of greenery or permanent settlements. Yet it was from this harsh landscape that, in the early 600s, a new movement emerged; one that would change the course of history in the Arabian Peninsula and beyond.

GEOGRAPHY

The Arabian Peninsula covers an area of over 2 million square kilometers in the southwestern corner of Asia. Situated between Asia, Africa and Europe, the land is unique in its connection with all three continents of the Old World. Despite its position, it has been mostly ignored by outsiders. The Ancient Egyptians chose to expand into the Fertile Crescent and Nubia rather than venture into Arabia's deserts. Alexander the Great passed by it in the 300s BCE on his way to Persia and India. The great Roman Empire attempted to invade the peninsula through Yemen in the 20s BCE, but could not adapt to the harsh landscape and thus failed to annex the region.

One could hardly blame outsiders for ignoring the Arabian Peninsula. Its dry climate is barely hospitable, even for the nomads who live there. Monsoon winds bring seasonal rains to the southern coast of the peninsula in the autumn, but these are stifled by the quickly rising landscape and never make it deep into Arabia's deserts. Similarly, rains from the Mediterranean Sea barely touch upon the northern extremities of the Arabian Desert. The result is that the vast majority of the peninsula remains dry year-round. Parched riverbeds known as *wadi*s run throughout the land, yet they are barely recognizable as rivers. When clouds gather and rains fall, they become gushing and powerful waterways, essential for the growth of the seasonal flora that manages to bloom in this dry land. Once the wet season is over, however, the *wadis* return to their usual, dry state, useless as sources of water. More reliable are the oases—small fertile spots surrounded by the vast expanse of the desert. They were capable of serving host to small communities, or as waypoints for travelers, but were hardly enough to sustain an advanced and large society.

THE ARABS

Civilizations tend to be greatly shaped by the environments in which they develop, and the Arabs are no exception. Everything about the life of the Arab was based around the harsh environment in which he lived. Due to the desert's inability to support settled civilization, the Arabs were constantly on the move in search of fertile land for their flocks. One theory of the etymology of the label "Arab" even posits that the word itself comes from a Semitic root meaning "wandering" or "nomadic". The Arabs would spend the summer months around whatever oases or wells they could rely on year after year, trying to make supplies and water last by living on the bare minimum. After months of enduring the summer heat, they would migrate to the south, near Yemen, where rain fell in the autumn and fertile land appeared for their herds. The rain-fed pastures gave their flocks of sheep, goats and camels enough food to live off through the winter months as they pitched their tents and temporarily settled. By the time the rains stopped and the dry season began again in the spring, the Arabs returned to their oases and wells to wait out another summer. This harsh cycle had been the norm for the nomadic Arabs since time immemorial, and it remains in place for the Bedouin Arabs who still live in Arabia's deserts.

In pre-Islamic Arabia, hospitality was of such importance that a guest at the home of an Arab was guaranteed at least three days of total security and protection before he would even be questioned about why he was there. This tradition was further reinforced by the Prophet, who stated that a guest has the right to be hosted for three days.

The desert was not a place to be alone. With so many threats to the survival of the Arabs, community cooperation was essential. Reliance on relatives was the first line of defense against famine and the heat that constantly threatened survival. Families were expected to share resources and shelter, and the concept of pure individualism was strongly frowned upon. As such, the family (and by extension, the tribe) served as the most important unit within Arab society. Groups of families travelled together and were considered a *qabilah*, or clan. Several clans would constitute a tribe, led by a tribal leader called a *shaikh*. Tribal identity and belonging were vital in the pre-Islamic world. Belonging to a tribe brought protection, support and economic opportunities. Tribes would go to battle to defend one of their own, and tribal warfare was unnervingly common before the arrival of Islam. Competition over grazing lands and flocks regularly brought tribes into devastating wars which could last years and extract a heavy human toll on the participants. For the Arabs, struggle was a constant, against both man and nature.

In a tribal, nomadic society like this, artistic expression becomes difficult. The resources and time necessary to complete great sculptures and paintings like the ancient civilizations of Egypt and Greece were almost non-existent. Yet the natural human desire to search for beauty could not be extinguished by the desert sands. Instead it took on a new form: language. Perhaps more than any other language in the world, Arabic itself is a form of artistic expression. Word and sentence structure is fluid, creating many different ways for a person to express the same idea. Poetry thus naturally became the de facto art of Arabia; long, epic poems glorifying tribes and heroism in war were their greatest works of art. The finest poets were revered celebrities in every way. Their words were memorized by the masses and repeated for generations. The seven most magnificent pre-Islamic poems were known as the *mu'allaqat*, meaning "the hanging ones". They were so called because they were hung on the walls of the Ka'ba in Mecca, or alternatively because they were hung in the hearts of all Arabs due to their reverence for the poetic medium.

Despite being an advanced literary society, writing was rare in the Arabian Peninsula. While a written form of the language did exist by the 500s, it was rarely learned. Memorization was enough for the Arabs, who were capable of learning poems that were thousands of lines long by heart so they could repeat them to future generations. Memorization would prove to be a vital skill once Islam arrived in the peninsula in the 600s.

When it came to religion, the pre-Islamic Arabs were almost exclusively polytheistic. Islamic tradition holds that the Prophet Ibrahim (Abraham) and his son, Isma'il (Ismael), built the Ka'ba in the valley of Mecca in ancient times as a house of worship for one God. The Ka'ba was built as a plain rectangular building on a foundation set by the first man—Adam. From this shrine, Isma'il was able to preach the monotheistic message to the Arabs, who adopted him as one of their own. Over the centuries, however, the progeny of Isma'il distorted his monotheistic teachings. Stone and wood idols were carved to represent attributes of God. Later, they would go on to represent separate gods entirely. By the time of the Prophet Muhammad, there were 360 gods in the Ka'ba. The message of Ibrahim and Isma'il was not entirely lost on the Arabs, however. The two prophets were still revered figures in the minds of the Arabs and even some of their basic teachings still held weight in this society. They certainly believed in the God of Ibrahim and Isma'il, called Allah in Arabic. But they believed he was one among many different gods, represented by the idols. This belief system was far removed from the strict monotheism those two prophets had preached, and reflected influence from Sumerian religions to the north. Isolated Christian and Jewish communities existed within the Arabian Peninsula and also revered the prophets, but that was where their similarities ended. The sparse monotheists of Arabia tended to avoid complete assimilation with the polytheistic Arabs, instead creating their own insular communities.

ARABIA'S NEIGHBORS

In spite of being deep in the deserts of the Arabian Peninsula, far from more advanced civilizations, the Arabs were not completely isolated from their neighbors. The Romans had become a regional superpower along the northern borders of the peninsula in the early decades CE. By putting down numerous Jewish revolts in the province of Syria Palaestina, the Romans stamped their control on the area. For the Bedouin Arabs, this meant the presence of a wealthy and strong trading partner to the north. Merchants regularly traversed the western part of the peninsula from Yemen in the south to Syria in the north, trading goods that came from places as far away as India and Italy. The Romans were content to remain in the more hospitable and familiar lands of the Fertile Crescent and let the nomadic Arabs carry on the trade with more distant lands.

To the northeast of Arabia lies the Iranian Plateau. The rise of the Sassanid Dynasty in Persia in the 200s CE ushered in a centuries-long struggle between the Romans and Persians, which would have its effects on the Arabs. The border between the two great Empires fluctuated, but was generally in the Syrian Desert, in the northern part of the Arabian Peninsula. Both the Romans and the Persians attempted to gain the upper hand by using Arab tribes (usually ones that had converted to Christianity) as proxies. Keen to use this conflict to their own benefit, two Arab tribal confederations developed into client states for the great powers. The Ghassanids founded a kingdom in what are now the modern countries of Jordan, Syria and Palestine, where they served as a buffer for the Roman Empire. Similarly, the Lakhmids controlled southern Mesopotamia and served the Persians. Both Arab kingdoms were greatly influenced by their overlords, who spent heavily on keeping their vassals well equipped in the face of the enemy. Yet the constant warfare between the two sides would slowly wear down all four parties. By the early 600s, the Romans and Persians were exhausted by decades of warfare and were weakening behind a façade of militaristic power. The Ghassanids and Lakhmids too felt the stress of war, as they were mere pawns in this constant conflict. Most Arab tribes, however, avoided the external conflict between the two imperial powers. They were more interested in carrying on a profitable trade with the two warring Empires than helping to decide the winner.

To the south of the peninsula was the powerful Kingdom of Aksum in Abyssinia, modern Ethiopia. Based high in the Abyssinian mountains, Aksum was a powerful trading state that connected inland African kingdoms, the Indian Ocean sea routes and the southern part of the Arabian Peninsula. As a crossroad for trade, it had considerable influence on Arab merchants, who dealt with the Aksumites in Yemen. Like Rome, Aksum was a Christian empire that had tension with Persia on numerous occasions. Control of trade routes running through Yemen was a constant source of friction, as both sides sought to turn local leaders into vassals.

In the increasingly globalized world of the early 600s, the Arabs were aware of their neighbors and became affected by events outside the Arabian Peninsula. Being at a crossroads of three powerful states meant being aware of international politics and having the skill to use rivalries to their advantage. Yet despite their precarious location, the Arabs were safe in the depths of the desert. They called their peninsula *jazirat al-Arab*, meaning "the island of the Arabs" due to how isolated its inhabitants were. This isolation proved to be greatly beneficial. The harsh environment meant that none of the surrounding states could invade and occupy Arab lands. The Arabs' traditional cycle of wandering and their way of life was mostly unaffected by regional politics and wars.

In this protected environment a movement would rise in the early 600s that would have huge implications for the surrounding states, and eventually the entire world. It would change the destiny of the Arabs forever, building on and using their unique abilities and doing away with the negative cultural traits that kept them as wandering, warring nomads. Geography, climate, culture and politics together all led to the perfect environment in which Islam could rise to become a world power faster than any other movement, religion, or empire in world history. It would sweep out of the deserts of Arabia into the battered Roman and Persian Empires, conquering territories and assimilating diverse peoples, creating an empire that stretched from Spain to India by the early 700s—the world's largest at the time. This exponential growth in power and civilization would have been unfathomable to the Arabs of the early 600s, who were struggling to survive. Yet all it took was the arrival of a man who came with a revolutionary message and a promise to the Arabs of a new destiny, one beyond the sands of Arabia: Muhammad.

2

THE LIFE OF THE PROPHET

The Prophet Muhammad was born in the town of Mecca around the year 570 CE. He belonged to the Banu Hashim clan, a subset of the Quraysh tribe that controlled Mecca—the trading and religious center deep in the heart of the Arabian Peninsula. About eighty kilometers inland from the Red Sea, it benefitted greatly from the north-south trade routes that connected the Romans in the north and Yemen in the south. Yet, Mecca was far detached from both these places. Hundreds of kilometers of desert surrounding the valley town allowed it to develop independent of any foreign control or influence. Mecca was at once both internationally connected and isolated. But when it came to religion, Mecca was a focal point for the entire Arabian Peninsula. It was the location of the Ka'ba and the annual pilgrimage that attracted Arabs from all over the peninsula. So while Mecca was far away enough to elude imperial control by the Byzantines or Persians, it was central enough to have a major impact on the Arab people. Both of these characteristics would play a major role when Islam began to spread.

EARLY LIFE

Muhammad's early life was marked by hardship and loss. His father, 'Abdullah, died before his birth while on a trading mission in the town of Yathrib, north of Mecca. His mother, Aminah, died when he was six, leaving his respected grandfather, 'Abd al-Muttalib to care for him. Two years later, his grandfather also died and Muhammad came to live with his paternal uncle, Abu Talib. Despite belonging to the wealthy tribe of Quraysh, Muhammad did not grow up amid riches. His status as an orphan and his belonging to the clan of Banu Hashim—considered an inferior branch of Quraysh—meant he was not a part of the ruling class. He did, however, accompany his uncle on numerous trading missions to Syria in his childhood, inaugurating him into the age-old nomadic tradition of the Arabs. His reputation as an honest trader led to him being known by two nicknames: *as-Sadiq* and *al-Amin*, meaning the truthful and the trustworthy. He was thus respected by the Quraysh, and he was regularly trusted with money and business transactions, acting as an arbiter in many cases. By his twenties, Muhammad was an accomplished merchant, working as an agent for a wealthy widow named Khadijah. Eventually, his reputation as an honest and reliable man caught the attention of his employer, and when he was twenty-five, Khadijah proposed to Muhammad, who accepted, despite being several years her junior.

Although being surrounded by a polytheistic idol-worshipping society, the young Muhammad did not get involved in the religion of the Quraysh. The original monotheistic message of Ibrahim and Isma'il was a faint memory to most Arabs, but it still held weight for a few, known as the *hunafa'* (singular *hanif*), meaning "monotheists", who refused to accept the hundreds of stone and wood gods. Muhammad was one of them. Instead of engaging in the idol worship so rampant in society, Muhammad chose seclusion. He made a habit of retreating to a cave atop a mountain about five kilometers from the center of Mecca, where he would sit in silence and reflect on the society and religion that surrounded him in Mecca.

THE FIRST REVELATIONS

According to Islamic tradition, in 610, while sitting in the cave he had come to many times before, Muhammad experienced something new. An angel suddenly appeared to him in the cave, commanding him, "Read!" He responded that he did not know how. Like most people in Mecca, Muhammad was illiterate. Again, the angel demanded he read. Again, Muhammad responded that he was unable to. A third time, the angel demanded he read, and for a third time, Muhammad responded that he was unable to. The angel then recited to him the first verses of the Quran to be revealed:

> *Recite in the name of thy Lord who created*
> *He created man from a clot of blood.*
> *Recite; and thy Lord is the Most Bountiful,*
> *He who hath taught by the pen,*
> *Taught man what he knew not.* (Quran 96)

He repeated the words after the angel, who then informed him that he is Jibreel (Gabriel), an angel sent by the one God and that Muhammad is the Messenger of God. Shaken and scared, Muhammad rushed home, not knowing what to make of the encounter. He was comforted by Khadijah, who believed his account of the encounter in the cave. She asked her cousin, who was familiar with Jewish and Christian scriptures, what this could mean. When he heard of what happened, he immediately accepted Muhammad as the messenger of his time, like Moses and Jesus before him. Consoled by his wife and her cousin, Muhammad accepted his mission as the Messenger of God, and his life as the Prophet began.

The first person to hear of Muhammad's prophethood and accept it was Khadijah, who can be said to have converted immediately upon his return from the cave. He soon began to invite those closest to him to this new religion. His closest companion, Abu Bakr, his young cousin, 'Ali, and his house-servant, Zayd, all respected and trusted Muhammad, and thus immediately accepted him as a prophet. They began to inform those closest to them, and slowly the number of people who accepted Muhammad began to grow. The first attempts at proselytizing were covert. Mecca was, after all, a polytheistic society, and the idea of one God replacing the numerous idols in the Ka'ba would no doubt be seen as a threat. Thus, the early months and years of Islam were marked by the development of a secret, hidden group, fearful of society's reaction to them, but submitting to the ideas of this new religion. They were called Muslims, meaning "submitters". The word Islam itself, from which Muslim derives, denotes submission to God and His will.

"Woe to every scorner and mocker. Who collects wealth and continuously counts it. He thinks his wealth will make him immortal. No! He will surely be thrown into the Fire."

– Quran 104:1–4

At the same time, the core ideas of Islam began to take shape through continuing revelations, which would be shared throughout the community. Strict monotheism, far different from the prevailing religion of Mecca, was the core theme. According to Muhammad, there was only one God. The idols worshipped by the Meccans were nothing more than useless statues of stone and wood, and were incapable of bringing benefit to anyone. The verses also warned of a Day of Reckoning, when all souls would be brought before God to account for their deeds. Those who believed in God and did good deeds would enter an eternal Heaven as a reward. Those who did not would have a place in Hell and would be eternally tormented. But Islam was not just concerned with theology and life after death. The early verses also denounced social ills that were prevalent in Mecca. With increasing prosperity from the trade routes, distinct social classes developed. The wealthy would use their money to fund more caravans that would in turn bring them more wealth. A poor person, meanwhile, continued to be marginalized, doubly so if they did not belong to a powerful clan. The Quran declared such disregard for the poor as detrimental to the establishment of a just social order, and worthy of punishment in the Hereafter. It would be years until the rules regarding society would be laid down, but from early on, it was clear that Muhammad had come not just to change people's religious beliefs, but also society itself.

The early revelations repeated these themes numerous times. The verses and chapters revealed in Mecca, which are found towards the end of the Quran, tended to be short and to the point. This worked well for the nascent Muslim community, which was still unknown to the rest of the city. When around fellow believers, the Muslims would discuss the latest revelations among themselves and teach each other. When around non-Muslims, they had to hide their conversion and beliefs. After all, these new ideas would threaten the established social order of Mecca. Social, economic and tribal equality flew directly in the face of the wealthy and powerful members of Quraysh. Social revolution is rarely welcomed by those in positions of power.

Even if Muhammad had not advocated any change in society, the new beliefs alone were a threat to the economic and social position of the polytheists. Because of the Ka'ba, Mecca was a religious center for Arabs throughout the Arabian Peninsula. Once a year, Arabs would travel to Mecca for a pilgrimage and to honor the hundreds of idols kept around the Ka'ba. This meant big business for the Quraysh. Trade was a natural by-product of the pilgrimage: with people from so many distant lands in the same place at the same time, a natural market evolved which made Mecca a religious, economic and political focal point of Arabia. And as the facilitators of this trade, the Quraysh stood to make huge profits. Muhammad's message, however, denied the importance of the idols, emphasizing the unity of God. Without idols, there would be no pilgrimage. With no pilgrimage, there would be no business. This was not a scenario that was pleasing to the Quraysh, and the early followers of Muhammad knew that. For this reason, there could be no mention of this new religion around the leaders of the tribe. The Muslim community was still small and weak enough that it could not yet come into open ideological conflict with those in positions of power. Especially considering the fact that most of the early converts were those who were considered the lowest class of society. Slaves, servants, and the poor made up a large proportion of the early Muslim community, attracted by the equality of all people before God and the egalitarian nature of the new religion, where wealth and social status did not determine a person's worth.

PERSECUTION

Eventually the size of the Muslim community became too large for the rest of Quraysh to ignore. Previously the Muslims had been able to perform their prayers together in a secluded area on the outskirts of the town. But as their prayer groups grew larger, the chances of them being seen increased. That is exactly what happened as a group of praying Muslims were seen by a group of idol-worshippers, whose immediate reaction was to ridicule the Muslims and their prayer. At first the Quraysh were content to view the small community as an abnormality to be mocked, until they realized the gravity of these new ideas. Monotheism, social justice, equality, and submission to the rule of God were all threatening theories to the Quraysh. In the eyes of many leading members of Quraysh, the solution was to rid themselves of this new religious and social movement by getting rid of the source: Muhammad.

But Arab society still had structure and rules. Although Muhammad was an orphan, he was still under the protection of his uncle, Abu Talib, who was the leader of the Banu Hashim clan of Quraysh. Abu Talib himself refused to accept Islam, but his dignity and respect for Arab social customs demanded that he protect his nephew. Furthermore, age-old Arab customs dictated that if Muhammad was killed, his clan would have permission to go after his killers, and thus civil war could break out on the streets of Mecca. So Muhammad himself could not be harmed, but the protection that he enjoyed was not extended to his followers, many of whom were not protected by any clan or family. The Quraysh decided to threaten and persecute them, in the hopes of discouraging others from joining the new religion. Muslims were thus regularly harassed and deprived of the same rights as polytheists in Mecca. While Muhammad himself had protection, he was powerless to stop the oppression of his followers.

Quraysh also took steps to prevent the spread of the new religion outside of Mecca. A group of Muslim refugees who escaped to Abyssinia were promised protection by its Christian king, the Negus. The Quraysh sent emissaries after them, hoping to convince the king to give up his protection and send the Muslims back to Mecca to be persecuted. When the Negus heard Muhammad's cousin Ja'far recite verses from the Quran about Islamic beliefs regarding Jesus and Mary, he refused to forsake his fellow monotheists, and the Quraysh had to go back to Mecca without the refugee Muslims. But even if Muslims had not escaped to distant lands, Islam could still spread beyond Mecca. Thousands of Arabs visited the city each year, and if some of those visitors heard Muhammad's message and saw Quraysh's inability to stop his unorthodox ideas, the status of Quraysh as one of the leading tribes in the peninsula would begin to wane. Alternatively, the visitors would believe Muhammad, accept his religion, and take it back to their homelands, spreading Islam outside of Mecca, and making it harder to stop.

All of this led to the extreme measures taken by the Quraysh. In 617, approximately seven years after the first revelations, the Quraysh decided to implement an all-out boycott on Muhammad's clan, Banu Hashim, to whom many Muslims belonged. No one was to enter into any business transactions with them, nor marry anyone to a member of the clan. They were even forced into exile in a barren valley just outside of Mecca. This had disastrous humanitarian effects on the Muslim community. Persecution brought hunger, social isolation and economic woes to the Muslims, and even the non-Muslims who happened to be part of Banu Hashim, such as Abu Talib. The few Muslims not belonging to Banu Hashim, such as Abu Bakr, 'Umar, and 'Uthman did all they could to supply the persecuted group by circumventing the boycott's rules, although at great personal loss. The boycott was draining on the entire Muslim community, those belonging to Banu Hashim as well as other clans. In the end, the boycott was ineffective in persuading Muhammad to discontinue his preaching, and it was thus ended after just over a year of enforcement. Despite Quraysh's efforts, more people continued to accept Islam. The boycott also revealed the strength of ties in the young community, as those not a part of Banu Hashim were still willing to sacrifice their wealth and safety to help their brothers and sisters that were being persecuted. Here, one of the core concepts of Islam—that loyalty to the religion transcended loyalty to a tribe or family— was on full display.

The boycott was not without its effects, however. Years of being denied food and access to shelter, coupled with physical abuse, took a toll on the Muslims. The persecution probably played a role in the death of the Prophet's wife, Khadijah, in 619. She had been the first convert and had stood by Muhammad through the adversity he had faced at the hands of Quraysh. The emotional support she provided in the early years was indispensable for the Prophet, encouraging him to continue in the face of persecution. The loss was a huge one on Muhammad, but it was not the only loss he had to deal with. Soon afterwards, his uncle who had protected him, Abu Talib, became ill and died. Although he did not accept Islam, he endured persecution like the rest of Banu Hashim and never gave up protection of his nephew. Beyond being another emotional

.nad, the death of Abu Talib had huge implications
, community. Without a strong leader, there was little
.uhammad and the rest of the Muslim community
fro. .ders of Quraysh, who were becoming bolder in their
attacks on the Muslims, verbally as well as physically. Despite his
love for the city of Mecca, Muhammad decided to try to find
another city that would accept him and give him more freedom to
preach his religion than the Quraysh did. The natural choice was
Ta'if, a town ruled by the tribe of Thaqif, sixty-five kilometers to
the southeast of Mecca. He rode out to Ta'if and met with the
three brothers who led the tribe. They unequivocally rejected his
proposal that they accept Islam and refused to grant him any form
of protection. To make matters worse, on his way out of the city
and back to Mecca, a crowd of people from Ta'if gathered to pelt
him with stones and insults, leaving him bloodied by the time he
was safely out of range of the city. Islamic tradition holds that he
was visited by the angel Jibreel, who asked the Prophet if he would
like him to destroy the city of Ta'if between two mountains as
punishment for their treatment of the Messenger of God. The
Prophet replied in the negative, stating that he hopes perhaps one
of their descendants would one day be a believer. This event would
play a huge role in the spiritual connection between Indian Muslims and the Prophet in later centuries.

After losing his family's support, being rejected by neighboring
tribes, and watching his own followers persecuted for their faith,
Muhammad recognized that a radical change was necessary if Islam
was to survive at all. The opportunity for such a change came from
an oasis town 300 kilometers north of Mecca, Yathrib. The two main
tribes of Yathrib, Aws and Khazraj, were engaged in a perpetual
struggle for power that turned deadly in the 610s. Further exasperat-

ing the problem, numerous Jewish tribes also lived in Yathrib and had trouble coexisting with the local Arabs. Muhammad's reputation as a trustworthy and reliable man was already well-known in Yathrib, and it was in 620 when numerous notables from the town travelled to Mecca to seek his emigration to Yathrib to serve as their leader and a mediator of their disputes. Muhammad accepted their offer and encouraged his followers in Mecca to make the journey with him, where the oppression of the Quraysh was absent. Muhammad himself was one of the last to leave Mecca in 622, when he journeyed with his close friend Abu Bakr, barely eluding Quraysh's plans to have him murdered before he could leave. In Yathrib, which was soon renamed *al-Medina al-Munawwarah* (the radiant city), officially known as "Medina" (the city), Muhammad would find security, and the ability to spread Islam away from Quraysh's opposition.

MEDINA

The Prophet's flight from Mecca was known as the *hijra*, meaning "the emigration". It marked a turning point in early Islamic history and is used to this day as the beginning of the Islamic calendar. No longer was the Muslim community a marginalized group and Muhammad a social outcast. The Muslim community would now turn Medina into the first Muslim state, and Muhammad into its leader. The example set by the Prophet in his ten years in Medina would inspire hundreds of years of Muslim politics, social order, and economics.

But life in Medina was certainly not without challenges. Chief among them was the new mix of emigrants from Mecca, known as the *Muhajirun*, and the original residents of Medina, the *Ansar*. The *Muhajirun* were not a single cohesive unit. None of the clans of Mecca converted entirely, so the community of emigrants represented a diverse group of people, on their own without the protection of a clan or tribe. In contrast, the *Ansar* belonged to either Aws or Khazraj, the two embattled tribes of the oasis. Furthermore, there were numerous individuals who belonged to neither group, immigrants from lands as far away as Africa, Persia, and the Byzantine Empire. For many Muslims, where their loyalties should lie was a major question. In response, the Prophet made clear that the old pre-Islamic ideas of loyalty were outdated. Instead, they were superseded by loyalty to the *Umma*, the Muslim nation. In the eyes of Muhammad, it did not matter if a Muslim hailed from Quraysh, Aws, Khazraj, or even the Jewish tribes. Once they accepted Islam, they were part of a new community of brotherhood based on shared belief, not shared ancestry.

"The Jews ... are one community with the believers. To the Jews their religion and to the Muslims their religion. [This applies] to their clients and to themselves with the exception of anyone who has done wrong or committed treachery, for he harms only himself and his family."

– The Constitution of Medina

Muhammad's new political and social order in Medina came to be codified in a text known as the Constitution of Medina. The Constitution detailed that, under Muhammad's authority, Medina would operate as a state based on Islamic law. The *Umma* was to operate as one political unit. Furthermore, Muhammad would act as the city's ultimate arbitrator. Old Arab customs regarding revenge and honor in the face of injustice were eliminated in favor of a structured justice system based on Islamic law. The Constitution gave the oasis's Jews freedom to practice their religion, but they had to recognize the political authority of Muhammad over the city and join the common defense in the case of an attack from Quraysh. Muhammad's nascent political entity in Medina would serve as the model Islamic state for centuries of Muslim governments, particularly with regards to the treatment of non-Muslim minorities.

The nature of the continuing revelations changed to match the change in circumstances for the Muslim community. Verses and chapters revealed to Muhammad in Medina tended to be longer than the ones from Mecca, detailing things such as forms of worship, taxation, inheritance, and relations between Muslims and non-Muslims. The Quran provided the generalities of how a Muslim society should operate, and where necessary, Muhammad explained the precise details. His words and actions, known as the *hadith*, were a vital source of guidance and law, second only to God's revelation itself. But the Quran was not only concerned with law and social order. Many of the Medinese verses described the stories of earlier prophets. Stories of Noah, Abraham, Moses, David and Jesus were all described in great detail to Muhammad's followers, making very clear that Muhammad was simply the last in a long line of prophets, and that his message is no different from theirs.

Much of this was aimed at the Jewish community of Medina. On the surface, they shared much in common with the Muslims. They were both monotheistic in a land known for polytheism, they both revered the same prophets, and early on in Muhammad's prophethood, they both prayed towards Jerusalem. As a result, some of Medina's Jews accepted Muhammad as a prophet and converted to Islam. Jewish scriptures speak of a Messiah, and to them, Muhammad was that promised man. But many more rejected

Muhammad. Judaism is unique, in that belief and ethnicity were tied to the concept of a Chosen People. Muhammad's message of egalitarianism and the unity of all Muslims regardless of ethnicity challenged some of the main ideas the Jews believed in. Some probably genuinely believed he was a prophet, but the fact that he was not a Hebrew was problematic for those who followed Jewish theology strictly. The divide between a Jewish community that believed themselves to be specially chosen by God and a Muslim community that advocated the unity of all people would develop into serious tensions between the two faith groups.

THE BATTLES

The Prophet's *hijra* to Medina did not mean the end of conflict with the Quraysh. The *Muhajirun* were still bitter at their treatment by their fellow clansmen in Mecca and the *Ansar* were eager to punish those who had oppressed their new brothers in Islam. But the Muslim community had not yet been given permission to fight by the Prophet. Warfare is, of course, a serious endeavor, especially in the Arabian Peninsula where complex rules regarding honor and vengeance had reigned for centuries. Furthermore, the Quran itself testifies to the sanctity of life and the egregiousness of unjustly taking one. The Muslim community was thus hesitant to act militarily against Mecca, despite the years of oppression they faced at the hands of the Meccans.

But that changed early on in Muhammad's time in Medina. He proclaimed to his followers a new revelation from God, which stated "Permission [to fight] has been given to those who are being fought, because they are wronged. And indeed God is competent to give them victory. [They are] those who have been evicted from their homes without right—only because they say, 'Our Lord is

Allah'" (Quran 22:39–40). These new verses made clear to Muhammad's followers that war was permissible, even obligatory, when Muslims were being oppressed. They also signaled an important aspect of Islam's role in the world: that this religion was not just a set of beliefs about the unseen, but a complete way of life that encompassed everything from prayer rituals to foreign relations to theology. Like they did with other instructions given in the Quran, the Muslim community of Medina was eager to show their worth and follow this new command.

The opportunity came in 624 when the Muslim community mustered a small army of around 300 men to intercept a caravan belonging to Quraysh that was passing by Medina. The Muslims were unable to reach the caravan, but ended up meeting a much larger Qurayshi force that had been sent to protect the caravan. At the Battle of Badr, about 100 kilometers southwest of Medina, the Muslims had their first opportunity to physically fight their former oppressors. Despite being outnumbered, the Muslim army, commanded by the Prophet's uncle, Hamza, managed to rout the Meccans, taking numerous prisoners. The Battle of Badr was of monumental importance for the new community at Medina. It established the Muslims as a real political and military force, while simultaneously lowering the prestige of Quraysh in the eyes of the rest of the Arabs.

The Quraysh were of course not willing to allow such a humiliating defeat to go unpunished. The next year an even larger Meccan army was assembled, with the aim of harassing Medina enough to lower Muhammad's newfound prestige and call into question his ability to protect his followers. The army camped out a few kilometers north of the city, in the shadow of the imposing Mount Uhud, where they could harass the rural farms surrounding Medina. As part of the Constitution of Medina, Muhammad had vowed to protect the city and its inhabitants, and was thus compelled to organize a fighting force to go out and confront the Meccans. There was, however, a group within the city that opposed his plan, believing that their best bet was to leave the rural farmers to fend for themselves and keep the army inside the city to defend it. They were joined by two of the Jewish tribes of the city, who refused to go out to Uhud to battle a superior force. Muhammad was thus forced to march out to Uhud with a considerably smaller army than he anticipated.

The results of the battle were disastrous for the Muslims. The Meccans, led by the brilliant Khalid ibn al-Walid—who would later convert to Islam and lead Muslim armies into Syria—managed to rout the Muslims from the battlefield up onto the slopes of Uhud. Hamza, the hero of Badr, was killed in the fighting and his body mutilated by the Quraysh. Muhammad himself was at one point surrounded along with a small group of Muslims by the Meccans and was injured in the hand to hand combat that followed. The Quraysh, having defeated the Muslim army in battle and believing they had done enough to damage Muhammad's reputation, retreated back to Mecca.

The Battle of Uhud did not manage to end Islam or the Prophet's authority in Medina as the Quraysh had hoped, although it did sow seeds of tension between Medina's Muslims and the Jews, most of whom had refused to honor the terms of the Constitution and join the battle. It was becoming clear that neither the Muslims nor the Quraysh were going to be able to decisively defeat the other on the battlefield. Both sides thus resorted to trying to gain support among the numerous Arab tribes of the region, each hoping to tip the scales against the enemy. The Meccans in particular hoped to gain the support of Medina's Jewish tribes, which seemed willing to dislodge the Prophet from their midst. Five years after the Prophet's *hijra*, the Meccans besieged the city of Medina from the north, and sought the help of one of Medina's Jewish tribes, the Banu Qurayza, who lived on the southern outskirts of the city. It was a calculated gamble for the Jews. The siege looked promising, and by joining with the Quraysh, they could wipe out Muhammad and his followers for good. As it happened, however, the Meccans and their Jewish allies were unsuccessful. Muhammad, advised by a Persian immigrant named Salman, ordered the construction of a trench around the city to thwart the Meccan siege. The Battle of the Trench, as it was called, was a disastrous failure for the Quraysh, who failed to even dent the power of Muhammad in the city. But it was even worse for the Banu Qurayza. They had broken the terms of the Constitution, and thus were liable to be punished according to its terms. An arbitrator assigned to the case ruled against the subversive tribe, ordering that the men who had taken part in the siege be executed while the women and children exiled from the city. Muhammad was setting an important standard with his handling of the Jews of Medina. He made clear that Islamic law had no problem with the presence of non-Muslims living within a Muslim state. For years Medina's Jews had been tolerated. But when they failed to live up to existing agreements and threatened the security of the Islamic state, punishment had to be doled out. Like everything he did, Muhammad's example in dealing with Banu Qurayza would set the precedent for hundreds of years of Muslim relations with non-Muslims.

VICTORY

With his position in Medina secured, Muhammad could finally deal with Quraysh on an equal level. Confident in the stability of the Muslim state and inspired by a recent revelation that promised impending victory, Muhammad set out in 628 with an army of 1,500 towards Mecca. But this was not an army intent on war. They were clothed in the simple two-garment outfit of pilgrims, and only carried travelling swords. No armor, no cavalry and no banners of war were brought along. Muhammad hoped to gain access to Mecca and the Ka'ba peacefully in order to conduct a pilgrimage. He camped just outside the borders of Mecca, at Hudaybiyyah, waiting for permission from Quraysh to enter the sacred grounds.

The Meccans, no doubt baffled by the audacity of the Muslims, just six years after their escape from Mecca, had a difficult decision to make. If they allowed Muhammad and his followers to enter Mecca, they would look weak to other Arab tribes, unable to prevent a barely-armed force from entering their city. On the other hand, their main role in Mecca was to facilitate the pilgrimage for anyone, a duty they took very seriously. In the end, they negotiated a treaty with Muhammad. They agreed to vacate Mecca for three days to allow Muhammad and the Muslims to complete the pilgrimage—the following year. Muhammad would have to return to Medina that year without having visited his hometown. Furthermore, a truce was agreed to. Mecca and Medina (and their affiliated tribes) would refrain from fighting for ten years. Some Muslims were clearly discontented by the terms of the Treaty of Hudaybiyyah, having hoped for immediate access to Mecca or even a complete conquest of Quraysh.

But the treaty provided a welcomed respite from conflict that gave Muhammad the ability to expand Islam far beyond Medina.

Now without the threat of internal dissent and external invasion, he had the freedom to send missionaries throughout the Arabian Peninsula, and even beyond, into the Byzantine and Persian Empires in the north. Bedouin tribes converted en masse, allying themselves with the Prophet. Even Meccans began to convert. Khalid ibn al-Walid and 'Amr ibn al-'As, two of Quraysh's greatest military commanders, left Mecca and joined Muhammad in Medina in the years after Hudaybiyyah. The treaty had failed to give the Muslims immediate control of their holiest site, but it allowed Islam to grow exponentially throughout Arabia, much to the dismay of the hardliners in Mecca, who just a few years earlier hoped to end Islam.

Furthermore, the sanctity of the truce was not completely fulfilled. Just two years after its signing, a tribe allied with Quraysh launched a surprise attack against a tribe allied with Muhammad just outside the borders of Mecca. This constituted a breach of the treaty, which had promised a total peace for ten years. With the treaty now voided, Muhammad could call upon his newfound allies throughout the peninsula in a new expedition aimed for Mecca. This time, however, they would not be travelling as peaceful pilgrims. Muhammad was finally in a position of power. Thousands of Muslims from all over the peninsula were now at his command, bound by alliances and conversions to join his army whenever called upon. At this point, the people of Mecca knew there was no way they could militarily defeat the Prophet. It was Mecca versus dozens of tribes, all united together for the first time in the history of the Arabs. Attempted negotiations between Muhammad and the Quraysh ended in failure, and in early 630, his army of over 10,000 Muslims—brought together from all corners of Arabia—marched on the holy city.

Most Meccans realized that resistance was futile. With the exception of some minor skirmishes, Muhammad's army entered Mecca bloodlessly. His triumphant return to his birthplace was seen by his followers as the final victory of Islam over polytheism, of truth over falsehood. The hundreds of idols surrounding the Ka'ba were destroyed, making the sanctuary a place for Muslim worship dedicated to one God. For many in Mecca, including the leader of the Quraysh, Abu Sufyan, this complete conquest was a sign that their idols were in fact no more than crude sculptures of stone and wood. They submitted to Muhammad, the man they had oppressed, chased out of the city, and gone to war with. Muhammad, in turn, proved to be a lenient conqueror. Most Meccans were left unharmed, a remarkable gesture for a people accustomed to brutal tribal wars that showed no mercy. Once again, Muhammad was setting the example that his prophethood marked the beginning of a new era with new rules and customs. The pre-Islamic period of *jahiliyyah*, meaning ignorance, would forever be left behind.

Muhammad's return to Mecca is remarkable if only because of the circumstances of his life in the preceding years. Just eight years after his escape in the middle of the night from his oppressors, Muhammad returned to his hometown as a victorious leader with an army of thousands. In Mecca, he had gone from a trusted merchant, to an undesirable rebel against polytheism, to a distant enemy, to the benevolent conqueror of his native land. No doubt his rapid accession to power and his ability to break down old tribal rivalries under the banner of unity in Islam were seen as miraculous and signs of his prophethood by many. The Muslims of that era, including those who had suffered through the early years of oppression in Mecca and the ones who only converted upon the city's conquest, thus believed there was something special about Islam. It was guided and protected by God, in their eyes, and they were on a special mission to spread this true religion to the rest of the world. This mindset would play a major role in the way Muslims viewed themselves on the world stage throughout their history.

THE END OF THE PROPHETHOOD

By the time of the Conquest of Mecca, Muhammad was about sixty years old, an old man by the standards of his time. Through his sayings and the continuing revelations of the Quran, the tenets of Islam had been formalized, covering everything from articles of belief, to instructions for worship, to guidelines for Islamic governance. A new social order had been inaugurated, one that left behind tribalism and nationalism in favor of Islamic unity under divine laws. Muhammad codified this in his last sermon, where he declared that "You all descended from Adam and Adam was created from the soil. The most noble in the sight of God is the most pious. No Arab is superior to a non-Arab except by their God-consciousness." His religious and social message was intertwined with a political one that forged a united Muslim empire that spanned the entire Arabian Peninsula, the first time in history that all the Arabs had been united. He even managed to make some inroads among the tribes living on the southern edges of the Byz-antine and Persian Empires, an accomplishment that would not go unnoticed by those two great empires, who would soon take the rapid spread of Islam very seriously.

After his conquest of Mecca, Muhammad returned to his adopted hometown of Medina. He had, after all, promised to lead the Muslim *Umma* from that oasis eight years earlier when Aws and Khazraj invited him. Here, he began to make preparations for a Muslim community that would continue long after his death. He spoke increasingly about the obligations of a true believer, the preservation of the Quran and his example. In early 632, he journeyed to Mecca for a final pilgrimage, the *hajj*. He spoke to thousands of his followers, all equally dressed in simple white robes regardless of their financial status, reminding them of the equality of all people. He cautioned his followers to avoid oppression, treat women with respect and love, and leave behind the old tribal rivalries that had been the bane of Arab civilization for centuries. His Farewell Sermon summarized his prophethood: it was a complete revolution in every sense. In the eyes of his followers, a new order was dawning upon the world, one that would be based upon God's law and inspired by the example of Muhammad.

After the pilgrimage, Muhammad returned to Medina, where the foundation was laid for the continued expansion of Islam. Learned men were sent to distant provinces such as Yemen and the eastern edge of Arabia to teach the recently converted the basics of Islam. Medina, the community in closest contact with the Prophet, would operate as a hub of knowledge about Islam, serving to educate the rest of the Muslim world, even after the Prophet. A military expedition was prepared to trek north against the Byzantines. The Islamic ethics of war, which would guide hundreds of years of Muslim armies, were reiterated.

According to Islamic belief, Muhammad's role was to serve as a messenger for God, delivering God's word, the Quran, and acting as a model for Muslims. After twenty-three years of acting as a prophet of God, his mission was complete. The Quran was finalized and recorded on scraps of parchment, leather, and bone, but more importantly memorized completely by many of Muhammad's Companions. The pre-Islamic tradition of memorizing long poems gave the Arabs the ability to maintain and ensure the preservation of Islam's holy book. Narrations of Muhammad's actions and sayings were also given due importance, and spread throughout Arabia by word of mouth. According to Islamic tradition, one of the final verses of the Quran revealed to Muhammad stated, "Today I have perfected for you your religion and completed My favor upon you and have approved for you Islam as your religion" (Quran 5:3).

Muhammad fell ill in the early summer of 632. He experienced debilitating headaches and a fever, and was soon unable to walk without the help of his cousin 'Ali and his uncle Abbas. When he was unable to lead the five daily prayers in the mosque, he appointed his close friend and companion, Abu Bakr, to lead them in his place. He spent his final days in the house of his wife Aisha, the daughter of Abu Bakr. From a wall adjoining the home to the mosque, he was able to watch the Muslim community follow his instructions to worship God, even in his absence. It was no doubt an emotional time for his followers, who had been with him through the difficult days in Mecca, the fierce battles against Quraysh where he established his authority, and his triumphant bloodless conquest of Mecca. They had looked to Muhammad for guidance and leadership in all aspects of life. His increasing talk of death, and the fact that he was now unable to even rise up to lead them in prayer played heavily on the hearts of the Muslim community.

His final days were spent resting in his home, with his head in the lap of his wife Aisha. Close family members and friends visited, hoping to see some signs of recovery in their leader. But one of the central aspects of Islam was uncompromising monotheism. Muhammad preached that only God is divine; all other creatures, whether they were animals, humans, or even angels would experience death, according to Islamic belief. Thus while they were prepared for his passing, recognizing that Islam would indeed continue after him, Muhammad's followers, deeply emotionally invested in this man that had led them out of the era of pre-Islamic polytheism and tribal warfare, could not imagine life without him. On 8 June 632, with his head on Aisha's lap and his followers gathered in the mosque hoping to hear of his recovery, the first era of Islamic history, spanning the twenty-three years of prophethood, ended as the Prophet Muhammad breathed his last.

3

THE RIGHTLY GUIDED CALIPHS

The death of the Prophet caused an emotional outpouring in the streets of Medina. The Muslims had a very difficult time dealing with the fact that their prophet was no longer with them, with some initially refusing to believe the news. But the death of Muhammad also brought questions of leadership to Medina. For over twenty years, Muhammad had led the Muslim community both politically and spiritually. His direct connection with God meant that society was guided by divine power in accordance with a divine plan. Now that that connection was no more, what would happen to the society that Muhammad had established? Specifically, who would lead the Muslim community after the death of the Prophet?

Before Muhammad was even buried, a group of leading figures from among the Meccan emigrants and the people of Medina gathered to answer the question of leadership. Disagreements between the groups about who should be given authority over the young Muslim state could threaten to divide the community indefinitely. There may have even been some proposals for a two-state solution—one led by a Medinese and one by a Meccan. In the end, 'Umar nominated Abu Bakr to be the political leader of a unified Muslim state based in Medina. Abu Bakr was the natural choice. After Khadijah, he was the first person to accept Muhammad as a prophet and convert to the new religion. He had been with Muhammad during his flight from Mecca. He was even appointed by Muhammad to lead the prayers in the Prophet's Mosque in the final days of his life. Yes, he was from the people of Mecca, but no one—neither the *Muhajirun* nor the *Ansar*—could dispute his qualifications.

ABU BAKR

Abu Bakr took the title of *Khalifat-ul-Rasul*, meaning Successor of the Messenger of God—shortened as *khalifa* (caliph)—in 632. The caliph was not a new prophet. Islamic scripture is clear that Muhammad was the final prophet and no more would come after him. Rather, the caliph's role was to act as a political leader, following the example set forth by Muhammad in his time as the leader of Medina. Thus, the caliph was expected to be someone who is an adept leader, capable of efficiently managing the affairs of the Muslim state, as well as someone who can preserve the religion of Muhammad and inspire people to follow it to the best of their abilities. Abu Bakr's example in doing so would serve as the precedent for later caliphs of how to fulfill these roles.

Establishing continuity with the political goals of Muhammad, Abu Bakr dispatched an expeditionary force to southern Syria to battle with the Byzantines in retaliation for an earlier confrontation between the two sides. The expedition showed that the Muslim *Umma*'s political goals would not stop because of the Prophet's death. But it was not as important as a growing threat coming from the sandy desert to the east of Medina. There, the various Bedouin tribes that had recently converted to Islam began to rebel. Their logic was simple: they pledged allegiance to Islam at the hands of Muhammad, and since Muhammad had now passed, that oath held no weight. Perhaps another reason for their desire to break away from Abu Bakr's government in Medina was the traditional Arab dislike for organized government. For centuries, the Arab tribes had roamed free, without a central government dictating their actions or demanding taxes. They may have begrudgingly accepted such an arrangement under Muhammad, but they would certainly not accept it under Abu Bakr. Coupled with their hatred for organized government was the appearance of numerous people claiming to be prophets themselves, chief among them a man by the name of Musaylima—known as Musaylima the Liar in later historical sources.

"Neither kill a child, nor a woman, nor an aged man. Bring no harm to the trees, nor burn them with fire, especially those which are fruitful. Slay not any of the enemy's flock, save for your food. You are likely to pass by people who have devoted their lives to monastic services; leave them alone"

– Abu Bakr's warfare rules, dictated to his army

The refusal of these tribes to pay the *zakat* tax, an important pillar of Islam, combined with their acceptance of new prophets led Abu Bakr to declare that they had left the fold of Islam and constituted a threat to the religion itself. If groups could decide what aspects of Islam they chose to accept, or could declare themselves prophets and adapt the religion to whatever suited them, the sanctity of Islam itself could be lost amid hundreds of versions. No doubt the examples of previous peoples that were mentioned in the Quran who had altered God-given religion to suit their needs came to Abu Bakr's mind. Those people were reprimanded by God and would be punished on the Day of Judgment for their sins, a fate the pious among the Muslim community desperately sought to avoid. As a result, military action had to be taken by Abu Bakr. He appointed Khalid ibn al-Walid as the commander of an army to be sent east to crush the rebel movement. Khalid was well-known throughout the Arabian Peninsula. He had not lost a single battle he had fought in, both before and after conversion to Islam. His familiarity with desert warfare and mastery of cavalry made him the obvious choice to lead the expedition.

After successfully defending Medina from any possible attacks by the rebels, Khalid led the army eastward to where numerous rebelling tribes were based. Musaylima's forces were no match for the military ability of Khalid: the rebels were routed and Musaylima was killed in battle. One by one, armies loyal to the caliphate spread throughout the Arabian Peninsula, calling tribes back to Islam and battling against those who continued to rebel. By 633, the Wars of Apostasy were over, and the entire Arabian Peninsula was once again united as a Muslim state. Islam had survived its first political challenge, born out of the questions of loyalty to Islam and its political leadership after the Prophet.

The Wars of Apostasy set an important precedent regarding the future of the Muslim world. First, the conflict showed that the spiritual unity of Islam was of paramount importance. Deviations and false prophets would not be tolerated. According to Islamic belief, previous nations that had been called to monotheism and deviated from God's laws were given the benefit of additional prophets sent to straighten them out. The finality of Muhammad's message meant no more prophets would be coming to fix the errors of deviant Muslims. There could be no room for error in keeping Islam as authentic as it was during Muhammad's life. Khalid's military expedition showed that the Muslim world was even ready to take up arms to protect the Divine message of Islam. Second, the political unity of the Muslim world was ensured for the time being. There was only room enough for one leader of the Muslim world. The Arabian Peninsula was situated between two world powers—the Byzantines and the Sassanids. If they were to survive in the international arena, unity was necessary. The Wars of Apostasy confirmed that there would be only one Muslim state—the caliphate—under one Muslim leader—the caliph. Third, and perhaps most important, the authority of the central government was confirmed. To the Arab tribes, unity and acceptance of a central government based hundreds of kilometers away was a foreign idea. The Wars of Apostasy set the tone that subsequent Islamic history would be (ideally) a break from the nomadic, decentralized past of the Arabs. The Arabs were entering a new era in their history, and their government had to reflect it.

Besides reinforcing the continuity of the Islamic state, Abu Bakr's time as caliph was significant for the preservation of the Quran in written form. During the Prophet's life, numerous secretaries were assigned to write down new revelations of the Quran as they came to him. These manuscripts were not compiled into a bound book, but rather existed as fragments scattered throughout Medina. Arabia was, after all, an oral society, and few people could read and write. The written pieces of the Quran were not as important as its the memorization word for word. During Abu Bakr's caliphate, 'Umar suggested that all the various manuscripts be collected, checked against the memories of reliable Companions for accuracy, and stored in a central location, just in case the unlikely scenario that all those who had the Quran memorized would die out. Despite his initial hesitance to do something that the Prophet himself had not done, Abu Bakr went along with the plan and a collection of the Quranic manuscripts was assembled in Medina.

Abu Bakr's caliphate lasted a mere two years—from 632 to his death in 634. In those two years he managed to stabilize the Muslim state after the death of the Prophet and prime it to take advantage of weakening imperial powers to the north. His two years set the precedent for what role a caliph plays in Muslim society and the continuation of Muslim belief after the death of the Prophet. The last precedent that Abu Bakr set was through the nomination of his successor. Rather than choose a relative of his to lead his community after his death—as had been tradition in Arab society before Islam—Abu Bakr chose someone whom he believed was most qualified and capable of handling the job of the caliph. While on his deathbed, he nominated 'Umar ibn al-Khattab as his successor.

'UMAR

Like Abu Bakr, 'Umar was an early convert to Islam. He accepted the religion at the hands of the Prophet in Mecca before the Hijrah, and was with him at all the major battles and events in Medina. There could be no doubting his credentials to lead the Muslim state, and based on Islamic tradition, there appears to have been no disagreement regarding his succession to office. This kind of stability in governance and succession would be sorely missed later in Islamic history.

Unlike Abu Bakr, 'Umar did not have to deal with questions of political stability or the continuity of the religion. The entire Arabian Peninsula was united under his command. The massive military effort that spread throughout the peninsula in the Wars of Apostasy gave the Muslim state the confidence and skills to begin thinking seriously about territorial expansion to the north. Furthermore, the traditional Arab way of life that was confined to the Arabian Peninsula was no longer feasible. For centuries, Arabs had survived through the continual raiding of rival tribes and the subsequent spoils of war. Now that the vast majority of Arabia was Muslim, such raids on neighboring tribes meant contravening Islamic law. The Prophet had spoken on numerous occasions about the entire Muslim population being one *Umma*, or nation. It was inconceivable that that nation would go on through history in constant conflict with itself. Partly to remove chances of inter-Islamic conflict, and partly to provide security to the few Arab tribes that were converting to Islam within Byzantine and Sassanid borders, the Muslim armies turned north, where their greatest conquests would come.

Raids into Sassanid-controlled Mesopotamia already began during the last year of Abu Bakr's life, and continued once 'Umar took power. At first, 'Umar and other leading Muslims probably did not foresee these raids turning into permanent conquests. But a devastating war between the Byzantines and Sassanids that lasted from 603 to 628 left the imperial powers weak and unable to hold off waves of Arab Muslims arriving at their borders. The fertile lands of Mesopotamia and Syria were ready to fall; all that was needed was an organized assault by the Muslims. This would be a new type of war, however. Unlike the campaigns of destruction that the two empires had waged, the Muslim calls for war were combined with the calls for justice and social harmony consistent with the message of Muhammad. When Abu Bakr sent out the first armies, he ordered his forces to secure the safety of women, children and the elderly; to leave monks in their monasteries unmolested; and even to refrain from destroying crops. These rules could not have been more different from what the Arabs engaging in these conquests were used to before Islam. But Muhammad's movement had been revolutionary from the start. Old ideas, traditions and ways of life had to give way to a new order, and that extended to warfare.

Armies were simultaneously sent into Syria and Mesopotamia in 633. Khalid ibn al-Walid, fresh off his victories in the Wars of Apostasy led the detachment headed towards the Persians. Meanwhile, Yazid, the son of Abu Sufyan, led the armies sent to Syria, where he quickly managed to defeat a Byzantine force near Gaza. For the Byzantines, the surprising loss indicated this could turn out to be not a routine raid, but a full-scale invasion. Emperor Heraclius ordered the imperial army to mobilize and prepare to crush the Arabs before they were able to consolidate their victory. The Medina government was aware that this was a possibility, and Khalid was ordered to immediately leave Iraq, where he had already had some success, and travel across the waterless Syrian desert to reinforce the armies there. The combined Muslim forces met the Byzantines at the Battle of Ajnadayn about thirty kilometers west of Jerusalem, where the Muslim armies completely routed the imperial force under the command of the emperor's own brother. The remaining Byzantine troops in southern Syria retreated to the well-fortified cities of Jerusalem, Caesarea and Gaza, leaving the victorious Muslims free to roam the countryside of Palestine.

The Muslim armies under the command of Khalid moved north and laid siege to the ancient city of Damascus, which fell in September 635. The treaty he forged after the city capitulated was intended to allay the fears of the locals. In it, 'Umar promised that their lives, property and religion would be safeguarded from any harassment, so long as a tribute to the Muslim government was paid. This set the tone for the fighting—that it was aimed at the Byzantine government and army, not the civilians. With such guarantees, there would be a much lower chance of rebellions by the Syrian population, which was essential considering that a relatively small Bedouin force was now beginning to occupy a large and diverse province in Syria. The loss of Damascus caused the Byzantine emperor to assemble an even larger force, with the hopes of sending the Arabs back into the deserts for good. Khalid knew his raiding force was no match for the bulk of the imperial army and decided to withdraw south, stalling the inevitable climactic battle between the two sides. Eventually, Heraclius' army caught up with the Muslim force at Yarmuk, along the border of present-day Jordan and Syria, in the summer of 636. The Byzantine force was much larger, better equipped and better trained. But morale was low as numerous rivalries and quarrels caused friction in the ranks. Taking advantage of this and the familiarity the Arabs had fighting in rough terrain, the Muslim force decisively defeated the Byzantines. The Byzantine army was chased off the battlefield and ceased to be an effective fighting force capable of any military action. Emperor Heraclius was forced to concede defeat in Syria, as he had neither the soldiers nor the money to hold off the Muslim invasion. Cities throughout Syria fell one by one, all of them given terms similar to the ones given to Damascus by Khalid ibn al-Walid. By 638, the conquest of Syria was complete. From there, the fight against the Byzantines continued in Egypt, which fell relatively quickly, by 642. Two of the Byzantine Empire's most valuable and prosperous regions had fallen into the hands of a people they had scarcely considered important enough to recognize before Islam.

In 70 AD, the Roman Empire exiled Jews from Jerusalem. It was not until the Muslim conquest in 637 that they were allowed back to the Holy City.

Within a few years, Syria had gone from a land firmly under the control of Byzantine empire to a province of the growing Muslim empire. For the victorious Muslims, the conquest must not have seemed that surprising. After all, they believed that God was on their side so long as they adhered to the religion that He sent down through Muhammad. The examples of Badr and the Conquest of Mecca from the time of the Prophet proved to them that victory was possible in the face of overwhelming odds with God's help. For the Byzantines, the loss of Syria was simply the first domino to fall in the final decline of the successor to the Roman Empire. Imperial armies would never again march through Christianity's Holy Land, nor would they ever again reap the economic benefits of this fertile region. For the locals living in Syria, however, the Byzantine loss did not have much of an impact on daily life. Churches continued to operate, peasants farmed land, and trade caravans passed through as they had before.

To help sort out the civil administration of the region, 'Umar personally travelled from Medina to Syria. One of his first actions in the country was to relieve Khalid ibn al-Walid of his post. This no doubt shocked everyone, including Khalid himself. Among the many possible reasons for forcing Khalid into retirement, Muslim historians in the past tended to settle on 'Umar's desire to remind the Muslim armies that God, not Khalid, was the reason for their victories. If the Muslims could sustain their streak of battlefield victories without one of the greatest generals of all time, it would serve as proof for those with weak faith of the divine guidance and help for their mission. When it came to governorship of the new province, 'Umar appointed Mu'awiya, the son of the Meccan aristocrat Abu Sufyan. He hailed from the wealthy and powerful Umayyad family, which had a major role in the administration of Quraysh before Islam. That lineage of governance would serve Mu'awiya well in turning Syria from a new province to the economic and political heart of the Muslim world over the next twenty years.

While 'Umar was in Syria, he personally attended to the surrender of Jerusalem in 637. He was given a guided tour of the city by the Patriarch Sophronius, an Arab Christian who had risen to become one of the leading figures of the Greek Church in Jerusalem. The terms of the treaty that was signed with the leaders of Jerusalem was similar to others put in place throughout Syria. What is unique about the Muslim conquest here, however, is that the new governors of Jerusalem allowed Jews to come to the city to worship for the first time in over 500 years. Islamic scripture holds the Christian and Jewish religions in special esteem, calling them "The People of the Book". It would not have made sense in Islamic law to allow the Christians freedom to visit their holy sites in Jerusalem while upholding the Byzantine laws preventing Jews from doing so. This precedent of freedom and religious pluralism was based on Muhammad's Constitution of Medina, which 'Umar was of course intricately familiar with. Yet while acknowledging the rights Christians and Jews had in Jerusalem, 'Umar was keen to send the message that this city also belonged to Islam. According to Islamic belief, this was the city to which Muhammad travelled in his miraculous Night Journey from Mecca, where he prayed on the site of the house of worship built by his fellow prophet Solomon and then ascended to Heaven. There could be no minimizing the importance of Jerusalem in the Islamic tradition, and with this in mind, 'Umar set about cleaning the Temple Mount, which the Romans and then Byzantines had let fall into disuse. Upon the Mount he erected the first version of the al-Aqsa Mosque, the third holiest site in Islam.

After the fall of Syria, the attention of the caliph went back to the Sassanid Empire, which had been mostly ignored since Khalid was ordered to move his armies to Syria. 'Umar appointed another veteran of Arab warfare who fought with the Prophet, Sa'd ibn Abi Waqqas, to lead the Muslim armies into Mesopotamia. Despite initial setbacks due to the Arab inability to deal with war elephants, Sa'd's army managed to defeat the Persians at the Battle of Qadisiyya in late 636. The battle saw significant spoils fall into Muslim hands, much of it forwarded to Medina for distribution according to Islamic law, and the temporary defeat of the Sassanid army. If the Muslims really wanted to hold Iraq, however, they would have to take Ctesiphon, the Sassanid capital. Ctesiphon was not a well-defended city; it lay on the plain between the Tigris and Euphrates Rivers, about sixty kilometers north of the ancient city of Babylon. After a siege that lasted about two months in early 637, the imperial city fell to the Muslim forces. The entire Tigris-Euphrates plain was now firmly under the control of the Muslim armies, with the Sassanid emperor and his government fleeing into the Persian highlands. Despite the string of impressive victories, 'Umar forbade his army from pursuing the Sassanids outside of Iraq. In Mesopotamia the land was familiar enough to the Arab tribesmen that traditional military tactics proved useful. In the Iranian Plateau, the Arabs would be unfamiliar with the terrain and could be decisively defeated. Furthermore, the native population there was entirely Persian, unlike in Iraq, and resistance from both the Sassanid army as well as the locals could be expected.

The royal standard of the Sassanids was captured at Qadisiyya and taken to Medina. Rather than keep it as a symbol of Islam's victory over Persia, 'Umar ordered that it be destroyed and its jewels and gold be sold to feed the poor.

'Umar's time as caliph is noteworthy not just for his military conquests, but also his administration over conquered territories. One of the most impressive aspects of the conquests and subsequent incorporation of them into the Muslim empire was the fact that life barely changed for most inhabitants of the conquered lands. The Byzantine and Sassanid armies and aristocratic class left as the Muslims moved in, but the local populations remained untouched. There were only two main changes in the lives of the conquered people. The first was who they paid their taxes to. Whereas previously they had paid taxes (oftentimes oppressively high taxes used to fund the ongoing wars) to the governments in Constantinople and Ctesiphon, now they paid a tribute, in accordance with Islamic law, that was forwarded to Medina. In most cases, this tribute did not exceed the previous taxes, and oftentimes was much less. For an everyday citizen, lower taxes are usually good news, regardless of who collects it. The second major change was the religious tolerance given to certain groups. Monophysite Christians, who differed from the ruling Greek Orthodox on matters of the nature of Christ, were allowed to practice their religion in Syria, a welcome change from the oppressive nature of the Byzantine government. Jews were similarly relieved of official oppression and were allowed to go back to their holiest city, Jerusalem, to worship. In the former Sassanid lands, Nestorian Christians saw increased religious freedom, as the ruling Zoroastrians had routinely restricted their freedoms on suspicions of being secretly allied with the Christian Byzantine Empire. Tensions of course still existed between religious groups, especially since the settled Christians of the Fertile Crescent probably resented the rule of nomadic Semites from the desert, but overall, the egalitarian nature of Muhammad's message helped usher in an era of religious tolerance that had mostly been absent in the Middle East previously.

In economic terms, the conquests brought unimaginable wealth to the relatively simple Arabs. Thousands of silver and gold coins and valuable gems flowed from conquered lands, particularly Iraq, into Medina as part of the spoils of war. In keeping with the precepts of Islamic law, the spoils were considered to belong to the entire Muslim community and were divided among members of the *Umma*, from the earliest converts to Islam to the newest non-Arabs to accept the religion. A huge boom in economic activity ensued in Mecca and Medina, with new houses being built regularly and huge estates being established to provide continued economic growth after the conquests ended. For the first time in Islamic history, immense wealth came into the hands of a Muslim government.

Through ten years as the caliph of the Muslim world, 'Umar had taken the young Muslim state from a desert-based raiding society to a regional power. This rapid expansion coupled with social stability is proof of his incredible capabilities as an administrator and leader, and he has thus gone down as one of the most successful rulers in Islamic history. His reign came to a sudden end in 644 when he was murdered in Medina by a Persian slave who had a personal grudge against the charismatic leader. While on his deathbed, 'Umar appointed a council of six well-respected leaders of the community of Medina to choose his successor from among themselves. They chose 'Uthman bin 'Affan, another early convert to Islam, who unlike Abu Bakr and 'Umar came from the Umayyad clan of Mecca and was a very wealthy and powerful man before accepting Islam. No doubt seeing the success of 'Umar's policies, 'Uthman promised to follow in 'Umar's footsteps and uphold the same practices as the deceased caliph, which led to his appointment in late 644.

'UTHMAN

'Uthman's descent from an aristocratic family played a huge role in his decisions as caliph. The Umayyads had ample experience in administration dating back to the days before Islam, and 'Uthman relied on that experience in his personnel decisions. His cousin Mu'awiya was already the governor of Syria, and was doing an admirable job in transitioning that province from a frontier territory to the backbone of the Muslim state. 'Uthman proceeded to appoint his foster brother, 'Abdullah ibn Sa'd, as governor of Egypt, hoping that Umayyad lineage would serve Egypt as well as it did Syria. Other cousins of his were appointed in Iraq, where they led raids into the Persian homeland, slowly conquering the rest of the Sassanid Empire. There were some allegations of nepotism for the first time in Islamic history, although they do not seem to have been serious enough to hamper the efforts and capabilities of the expanding Muslim state.

During 'Uthman's caliphate, a Muslim embassy was sent to China to establish diplomatic relations between the caliphate and the Tang Dynasty.

Continuing in the footsteps of 'Umar and his emphasis on the military, 'Uthman ordered the construction of the first naval fleet in Muslim history, intended to thwart any Byzantine counterattacks. Governors in Syria and Egypt relied heavily on the expertise of the local Christians in building sea-faring vessels. Christians who had formerly been under the sovereignty of the Byzantine Empire seem to have showed enthusiasm in their work for their new Arab governors, especially considering that many of them belonged to the Coptic Church and other Christian denominations that were not recognized by the Byzantines. The Muslims' willingness to treat them better than the Byzantines must have played a huge role in their loyalty to the caliphate. The result of this was peaceful civil society, and security from external threats, as a Byzantine fleet attempting to recapture Alexandria in 646 was thwarted by Christian sailors in the employ of the caliphate. Besides simply defending its borders, the Muslim empire was able to expand its influence in the Mediterranean, capturing Cyprus and Crete, and raiding as far away as Sicily. Military success also continued on land, as Mu'awiya led his powerful Syrian army into

Armenia against Byzantine rule. The mountainous terrain of Anatolia, coupled with its mainly Greek population, meant a natural border between the Byzantines and the Muslims developed around the modern border of Turkey and Syria. Further east, Muslim armies continued to push into the Persian heartland, under the command of another of 'Uthman's relatives, 'Abdullah ibn 'Aamir. The conquest of the rest of the Sassanid Empire was not as rapid as the conquest of Iraq. Here the society was more homogeneous and connected to the Sassanid government. As a result, the war exacted a heavier toll on the Muslim armies. Still, the completeness of the Muslim victory at Qadisiyya during the caliphate of 'Umar had essentially sealed the fate of the Sassanid Empire. It was simply a matter of time and effort to subdue the rest of the empire. Sassanid Emperor Yazdegerd was never able to fully replace the army he lost in 642, and over the following ten years, the Sassanids were constantly on the defensive. By 650, the Iranian Plateau was secured, and by 651, Khurasan was taken. That same year, the last Sassanid king was found while on the run and executed. Within a decade the Muslim armies had pushed from Iraq to the River Oxus, reaching the edges of Central Asia.

For 'Uthman, leading a rapid military expansion like 'Umar did not result in the same popularity as the second caliph. Trouble began to fester as discontent with his administrative policies, particularly his appointment of fellow Umayyads, began to take shape. Coupled with this, the slowing conquests (in comparison to 'Umar's rapid expansion) meant less booty made its way into Medina, resulting in economic stagnation. 'Uthman's popularity was certainly not as high as his two predecessors, but it would be a stretch to assume a massive revolution was brewing that would remove him from power. Instead, it was a small band of soldiers who would bring violent and chaotic change to the Medinese government.

In 656, a group of soldiers from Egypt came to Medina to protest directly to the caliph regarding his policies and the division of spoils between the army and the civil government in Egypt. He listened to both sides of the dispute and promised to take steps to solve the problems equitably. On their return to Egypt, the soldiers intercepted a letter supposedly written by the caliph to the governor of Egypt ordering their execution. They returned to Medina and besieged 'Uthman in his own house. Despite the mortal danger he was in, 'Uthman refused to order that the people of Medina arm themselves and fight the rebels, and even prevented his cousin Mu'awiya from sending a force from Syria to protect him, lest blood be shed in the city of the Prophet. Many of the remaining Companions of Muhammad opposed this mutiny, but were powerless to stop it. Martial law reigned in Medina and its residents could only watch in horror as the rebels eventually forced their way into 'Uthman's house and murdered him as he sat reading his copy of the Quran. The caliph was dead, and with him so was the unity of the Muslim world.

'ALI

As the kingmakers of Medina, the rebels sough to appoint a new caliph themselves. 'Ali was the natural choice, as he was the most respected Companion still alive, and was related to the Prophet in two ways—as a cousin and son-in-law. 'Ali, holding onto the unwavering honor and justice that many of the closest Companions were known for, initially refused to be appointed by people who had rebelled against the caliphate. He was eventually persuaded by other leading figures in Medina that he was the most qualified and best equipped to bring back peace to the Muslim world.

As it turned out, however, no personality would be able to manage the crisis that the Muslim world stood at the precipice of. 'Ali's most pressing problem was dealing with the murderers of 'Uthman. There was popular sentiment in favor of punishing the rebels. Mu'awiya even insisted that he would not pledge allegiance to the new caliph until steps were taken to punish the people who killed his cousin. But 'Ali, being as pragmatic as his predecessors, knew that to punish them would likely lead to his own assassination, as the rebels still controlled Medina. This would in turn force the Muslim world into a downward spiral of bloodshed that he was keen to avoid. Instead, he moved his capital to Kufa, in the fertile plain of Iraq, where support ran high for the embattled caliph. Many in Medina were disheartened by his resistance to bringing the rebels to justice, and soon a force gathered with the intention of convincing 'Ali to punish them. Led by two fellow Companions, Talha and Zubayr, and aided by the Prophet's widow Aisha, the army departed for Iraq to confront 'Ali.

It is difficult to judge the intentions of 'Ali and his political opponents in their preparations for the coming conflict. On both sides there were people who were close to the Prophet and must have been aware of the severity of fighting among Muslims. Yet both sides believed themselves to be entirely correct in their *ijtihad*, or independent reasoning, regarding the correct course of action in dealing with the rebels. For 'Ali, punishing them was not politically feasible as he believed the best solution was to move on and attempt to reunify the *Umma*. For his opponents, reunification was impossible without fixing wrongs and sending the message that the caliphate could not be violated as it was during the siege of 'Uthman. Both arguments probably had elements of truth in them, but the political divisions that came from 'Uthman's death were too big for even the Companions to solve. Disunity was inevitable.

Eventually, in 656, the supporting armies of the opposing ideas met at a field near Basra, in southern Iraq. Some members of the opposition, including Talha and Zubayr, met with 'Ali before the battle, hoping to avoid bloodshed. A tentative peace treaty was agreed upon by the leaders of the opposing sides, who were loath to see fighting between Muslims just over twenty years after the Prophet had been laid in his grave. Less pious-minded extremists on both sides still urged the soldiers to come to blows with each other, despite the negotiations of their leaders. In the confusion, the two armies finally collided, each believing the other side had started the fighting. The Battle of the Camel, as it came to be known, was indecisive, with both sides taking on heavy losses. Talha and Zubayr were both killed in the mayhem. 'Ali and Aisha escaped the battle unharmed but were disheartened at the first battle between Muslims in history. Aisha retired back to her home in Medina, accompanied along the way by a military escort for her protection, appointed by 'Ali. She dissociated herself from politics until her death in 678.

Despite this bloodshed, 'Ali's hold on the caliphate was still not secure. Mu'awiya had remained neutral in the conflict between 'Ali and the dissenters from Medina, but continued to withhold his allegiance until 'Ali punished his cousin's murderers. 'Ali could not effectively govern while one of the most powerful governors of the Muslim world did not submit to his authority, but he still held onto his position that punishing the rebels was not a priority and was not feasible in any case. This time, to prevent further bloodshed, he agreed to meet with Mu'awiya to settle their dispute through arbitration. The two sides met at a site midway between Iraq and Syria, their respective bases of support, in 658.

Exactly what happened at the negotiations and their outcome is difficult to judge through the fog of history, but it seems that the arbitrators favored a solution that remove both 'Ali and Mu'awiya from power and resulted in the election of a new caliph. When results of the arbitration were announced to the opposing sides, a group of 'Ali's supporters decried the results. Declaring, "Decision belongs to God alone!" and refusing to accept the legitimacy of the arbitration itself, the group condemned 'Ali for allowing his political fate to be decided by mere humans capable of error. Their extreme political position morphed into an extreme religious position, in which they deemed any sinning human to be an unbeliever. After separating from the main body of 'Ali's supporters, they were given the name *Khawarij* (or Kharijites) meaning "the ones who left". The Kharijites went on to terrorize the Iraqi countryside, battling against anyone who disagreed with their fanatical positions. Meanwhile, 'Ali, who had rejected the results of the arbitration as being invalid, decided that his former supporters who had now become the first in history to secede from accepted Islamic theology could not be allowed to go about with their reign of terror. He assembled his army and confronted the opposition in the summer of 658, where the main body of *Khariji* support was destroyed. The movement continued in a more clandestine form, with the aim of removing both 'Ali and Mu'awiya. An attempt to assassinate Mu'awiya in Damascus by the Kharijites was unsuccessful, but they succeed in killing 'Ali. As he prayed the dawn prayers at the mosque in Kufa, an assassin stabbed the caliph, bringing his turbulent reign to a violent end. The caliphate fell to the only man left in the Muslim world with widespread support and the capabilities to be an effective leader: Mu'awiya.

THE ESTABLISHMENT
OF THE MUSLIM STATE

The death of 'Ali at the hands of the Kharijis and the rise of Mu'awiya to the caliphate marks the end of the era commonly referred to as the "Rightly Guided Caliphs". The nature of Muslim government and society fundamentally changed during the nineteen years of Mu'awiya's rule from 661 to 680. Coming to power at a time when disunity and chaos reigned from Egypt to Iran, Mu'awiya's political skill and competence helped prevent the Muslim world from falling into total anarchy—from which it may never have risen. Yet at the same time, some of his policies and actions were controversial, and formed the basis for some of the biggest divisions in the Muslim world today. His reign marks the beginning of the Umayyad Caliphate, when succession to the position became hereditary and stayed in the Umayyad family until 750, when it was replaced by another old family of Mecca, the Abbasids.

MU'AWIYA

Despite the attempts at arbitration, a real solution to the dispute between 'Ali and Mu'awiya never took shape, and the last years of 'Ali's caliphate were marked by de facto division between the realms of Mu'awiya and 'Ali. With the death of 'Ali, however, Mu'awiya was free to extend his control over the areas formerly loyal to 'Ali and reunify the Muslim world under his command. Indeed, he was probably the only man at the time that had enough support to manage such a monumental task. He was incredibly popular in Syria, a province he had looked after as governor for twenty years before the start of his caliphate, and Syrian army formed the backbone of his military. He was not without enemies, however, particularly in Iraq, where popular opinion was in favor of the caliphate being inherited by 'Ali's son, Hasan. Ever the pragmatic statesman, Mu'awiya had no desire to plunge the Muslim world into further warfare over leadership. So instead of mobilizing the army to violently crush the opposition, he negotiated a deal with 'Ali's son in which Hasan would give up any claims to leadership and retire to a life of worship and scholarship in Mecca. Desire among some for rule by the house of 'Ali remained, although under the surface, and it never materialized into a real threat to the reign of Mu'awiya.

The Dome of the Rock Mosque was built in the late 690s as part of the al-Aqsa Mosque complex in Jerusalem. Its design is largely Byzantine, and was partly engineered by Christians.

The caliph also relied upon negotiation and deal-making with other potential opponents. In many ways, Mu'awiya ruled like an

Arab tribal leader from pre-Islamic Arabia, using family relations, an unwritten code of honor and gifts to get his way politically. Having been a youth in Mecca who saw how his father led Quraysh, these old traditions were no doubt ingrained in his political persona. At the same time, however, Mu'awiya began to change the caliphate into something new: a monarchy. He was the first caliph to sit on a throne and the first to pray in an enclosed area in the mosque, protecting him from possible assassins. He no longer followed in the modest and simple footsteps of the first four caliphs. Instead, royalty and court culture became a part of the caliphate as it had been part of the Roman and Sassanid Empires. For the first thirty years after the death of the Prophet, the caliph was simply a first among equals, and numerous anecdotes survive of the asceticism of those first four leaders, such as 'Umar being mistaken for a commoner or refusing the service of bodyguards. Mu'awiya was the bridge between the simple caliphate that came before him and the monarchy that succeeded him. He would walk in the markets of Damascus in his patched clothing as enormous and elaborate mosques were built by his architects.

As part of his overall program to de-emphasize political divisions among Muslims, Mu'awiya chose to focus on expanding the borders of the caliphate. Reminiscent of 'Umar, who focused on outward expansion after the infighting of the Wars of Apostasy, Mu'awiya sent armies to continue the war against the Byzantine Empire by land and sea. The important islands of Rhodes and Crete in the Aegean Sea were occupied by the navy first established under 'Uthman. Buoyed by these victories, the Muslim armies were, for the first time, able to lay siege of the Byzantine capital of Constantinople. The legendary city had been a prize since the earliest days of Islam, when the Prophet promised that eventually a Muslim army would conquer that distant and seemingly impenetrable city. As Muslim armies approached the city for the first time in 674, fulfilling that promise seemed to be within reach. From 674 to 678, the Umayyad armies laid siege to the city's massive walls, but lacked the manpower or technology to conquer the city. Among the casualties of the siege was the elderly Abu Ayyub al-Ansari, a notable Companion of the Prophet who lodged Muhammad in his home when he arrived in Medina. He was buried near the walls of Constantinople, and almost 800 years later would become a mythic legend for the Ottoman armies that eventually managed to overcome Constantinople's walls.

Expansion also continued in North Africa, where the Byzantines still had control west of modern Libya. The fringes of Umayyad-controlled land west of Egypt were governed by 'Uqba ibn Nafi', another Companion originally from Mecca. In 670, he was ordered to advance into Byzantine Africa in conjunction with the ongoing advances into Byzantine territory in the Aegean. 'Uqba's army consisted of 10,000 Arab horsemen who were aided by huge numbers of local Berbers who had recently converted to Islam. Because of the Byzantine preoccupation with other fronts, 'Uqba was able to advance unchallenged into modern Tunisia, where he established the garrison city of Qayrawan. The main threat ended up not being the Byzantine forces, but the local Berbers who had to be slowly subdued before any more advances towards the West could be embarked upon. Following a short period from 675 to 680 during which 'Uqba was replaced as governor of Ifriqya (the province of Africa), 'Uqba continued his westward raids. By 680 the Umayyad armies were well-established enough in North Africa to embark on serious conquests across modern Tunisia, Algeria, and Morocco, collectively known as the Maghreb, to the Atlantic Ocean. 'Uqba's role in these conquests would raise him to a legendary status for North Africa's Muslim population.

After leaving Qayrawan in 680, 'Uqba's army marched generally unopposed through the desert plateau south of the coastal mountain ranges that run along the Mediterranean. Advancing from one Byzantine outpost to the next, 'Uqba's army was able to quickly annex hundreds of kilometers of territory along the coast with relative ease, even as disunity and civil wars raged in the heartland of the Islamic empire. One possible explanation for this seemingly miraculous conquest was linguistic, cultural and religious division between the Berbers of North Africa and the Byzantine rulers. The Byzantines who ruled over North Africa could not be more different from the Berbers under their control. The Berbers were a desert people, closer to the Arab nomads who arrived in the 600s than the urban Latins and Greeks who had administered the area for centuries. Their language shared no history with the Greek used in administration, and few Berbers went out of their way to learn the language of their governors. The lack of common cultural traits meant a constant social divide between the two, and examples of full assimilation of the Berbers into Roman/Byzantine society are scarce.

Religion, however, seems to be a larger factor that led to Berber support for the Arab Muslim armies. Early Islamic accounts speak of entire tribes of Berbers converting to Islam immediately upon arrival. There were certainly divides between North Africans and the Byzantines on issues within Christianity: the main issue was the nature of divinity and humanity. Separatist Christian movements such as Arianism and Donatism openly disputed the official orthodoxy promoted by the Byzantines and may well have caused North Africans to lean closer to Islam. But even if they did not all convert immediately, as early chroniclers claim, the Berbers certainly had practical reasons to rise up against the Byzantines in conjunction with arriving Muslim armies. Thus it was possible for 'Uqba's army to continue gaining momentum as it did through the early 680s until they were able to push into modern Morocco and to the shores of the Atlantic. His legendary words when he rode his horse into the crashing waves of the ocean hint at the deeply religious nature of these conquests: "O Lord, if the sea did not stop me, I would go through the lands like Alexander the Great, defending your faith and fighting the unbelievers!" Whether or not he actually said those words is not as important as the role that heroic image would play in the minds of generations of military leaders that would rise out of the Islamic Maghreb.

CONFLICT OF SUCCESSION

Despite his success in unifying the Muslim world after the troubles of 'Ali's caliphate, one decision Mu'awiya made would make him a controversial character and change the nature of Islamic government for the next 1300 years. He appointed his son Yazid as his successor well before his own death and demanded oaths of allegiance from the notables of Damascus. Muslim historians throughout the ages have speculated as to his reasoning for doing so, especially considering the subsequent opposition that arose to Yazid. However, keeping in mind the historical context of Mu'awiya's time makes it easier to understand why the switch to a hereditary system made sense. Mu'awiya's time as caliph showed the emphasis he placed on political unity and harmony. After the political upheaval of 'Ali's caliphate, Mu'awiya's main challenge was keeping the Muslim world united under one command. Although he largely succeeded, there was no guarantee that all subsequent caliphs would be able to use external threats or political maneuvering to minimize internal divisions. Mu'awiya thus felt that the only way to preserve social unity and harmony was to simply bypass wars of succession and make the caliphate hereditary.

As it happened, however, the choice of Yazid was not without controversy. Unlike his father, he had never known the Prophet, and was thus without the aura that comes with being a Companion. Furthermore, rumors swirled in the holy cities of Mecca and Medina of the sinful life that Yazid led. Alcohol, singing girls and excessive luxuries were to be found in Yazid's presence, a far cry from the pious and simple lifestyle Muhammad had preached. Whether or not these allegations of wickedness were accurate, they were enough for some to revolt, such as 'Abdullah ibn al-Zubayr, the son of the Zubayr who opposed 'Ali. Compounding the problem were the desires of some in Iraq to see a descendant of 'Ali take the title of caliph of the Muslim world. 'Ali's oldest son Hasan had already died in Mecca during Mu'awiya's reign, so support fell to his younger brother, Husayn. This grandson of Muhammad was attracted to the city of Kufa in Mesopotamia by promises of support from its people. Against the advice of 'Abdullah ibn al-Zubayr, who warned him that the people of Iraq will desert him at their first opportunity, Husayn set out to establish a base in Iraq in 680 from which he could oppose the Syrian Umayyads, as his father had done twenty-five years earlier. True to 'Abdullah's prediction, the people of Kufa abandoned their support for Husayn before he even arrived. Yazid had already sent a new governor to the city to root out any opposition and ensure that the population does not rise up in revolt against him, and it appears to be this show of force that persuaded the people to abandon their promises of support. Husayn had been counting on that support and only travelled with about seventy family members and friends, hardly a force capable of overthrowing Yazid. At the plain of Karbala about 80 kilometers north of Kufa, Husayn was surrounded by Yazid's forces, which proceeded to kill the would-be rebel and most of his supporters. The Battle of Karbala would later become one of the founding legends of a new, divergent strain of Islam, the Shi'a.

'Abdullah ibn al-Zubayr's revolt did not fare much better. After the killing of Husayn, popular support throughout the Muslim world was against the Umayyad government. Husayn was, after all, the Prophet's dearly beloved grandson, and killing someone who had the Prophet's blood flowing through him was a shock to many of the more pious-minded. 'Abdullah used this opposition to Yazid to bolster his own revolt against the Umayyads, which he declared in Mecca in 680, after Husayn's death. With such support, 'Abdullah's revolt could not be stamped out as easily as Husayn's. In fact, Yazid was never able to do away with the revolt in the Hijaz and died in 683 without complete control over the Empire. After Yazid's death, it seems that Umayyad control collapsed almost everywhere in the Muslim world. Yazid's successor, a youth who seems to have had no interest in government, only ruled for a few months before his own death. 'Abdullah declared himself caliph, and was given oaths of allegiance by people in Iraq, Egypt, and even the fringes of Syria itself. But through a mix of tribal politics and open fighting, the Umayyads managed to regain control of the caliphate under Marwan, a cousin of Mu'awiya. Under Marwan and his son 'Abd al-Malik, the Umayyads regained control of Syria, Egypt and Iraq, and eventually stamped out 'Abdullah ibn al-Zubayr's rebellion in Mecca by 692. The Umayyads had come back from the brink of extinction to regain complete control over the Muslim empire. This certainly was not the tranquility and harmony

Mu'awiya had hoped for when he appointed his son as caliph, but once the Umayyads were re-established, the period of civil wars between 680 and 692 seemed like nothing more than a small hiccup. In the late 600s and early 700s, the Umayyads continued with a second period of rapid military expansion and economic growth that would rival any period of expansion in Islamic history before or since.

The fact that the Umayyads conquered most of Iberia in just four years with a few thousand soldiers indicates that they received support from the local population.

FURTHER CONQUESTS

Full consolidation of 'Uqba's conquests in North Africa had to be completed before further conquests could be undertaken. The caliph 'Abd al-Malik sent armies to conquer Carthage, the final outpost of Byzantine control in North Africa in 698. With this, the last remnants of Byzantine North Africa disappeared for good, as the former rulers of the land were forced to retreat to Sicily and Greece. Now the Muslim armies were primed for one of the most spectacular and unlikely conquests in history. Legend has it that a former Byzantine official, Julian, appealed to the new Muslim governors of North Africa to punish the Visigothic king of the Iberian Peninsula, Roderic, who had supposedly seduced Julian's daughter while she was under his care. Julian even promised to ferry a Muslim expeditionary force across the strait to Spain to exact his revenge upon the tyrant king. Whether or not Julian really existed, reports of unrest in

Visigothic Spain along with pleas from persecuted Jews and unorthodox Christians must have played a role in the decision to cross the strait and venture into the Iberian Peninsula.

Musa ibn Nusayr, the Umayyad governor of the Maghreb sent a force under the command of Tariq ibn Ziyad, a Berber convert to Islam, who in early 711 landed near a giant monolithic promontory on the south shore of Spain. He established his camp near the mountain, which became known as Jabal Tariq (the Mountain of Tariq), Anglicized as Gibraltar. From this base, Tariq led raiding parties throughout the south of Spain, which proved to be generally successful—especially since Roderic and the main bulk of the Visigothic army was in the north of the peninsula dealing with a Basque rebellion. By the time Roderic was able to march his army south to meet the Muslim forces in the summer of 711, Tariq had managed to bring over an army that numbered around 10,000 soldiers from Muslim North Africa. At the decisive Battle of Guadalete, Tariq's army crushed the amassed forces of Roderic, who suffered from disloyalty in his army's ranks along with the effects of an exhaustive march to meet the Muslim invaders. Roderic himself was killed in the battle, and the underlying weakness of the Visigothic kingdom soon became apparent. Central control collapsed throughout the peninsula. Tariq advanced to take Roderic's old capital city of Toledo within a few months of the battle, and soon afterwards, cities began to fall one by one to the invading Muslims. Tariq's superior, Musa, also crossed over into Spain to aid in the ongoing conquest. Tariq was the conqueror and Musa was the consolidator. As expeditionary forces under Tariq took cities as far north as the Ebro Valley, Musa's larger army followed up to fully establish Muslim rule in conquered areas and set up civil government. In the years from 711 to 715, Tariq and Musa managed to bring the vast majority of the peninsula under Umayyad control. The seemingly improbable conquest of such a large territory by relatively small invading armies (no more than ten to twenty thousand soldiers) was reminiscent of the conquest of North Africa just a generation before.

Many of the early Indian converts to Islam were Buddhists and members of lower castes, who were attracted to the egalitarian nature of Islam.

Further raids to the north into Gaul initially proved to be as successful as the conquest of Spain. The Muslim armies managed to advance into the south of modern France, establishing their rule in Aquitaine and Septimania in the 720s. The climax of the Muslim invasion of Gaul was in 732, when armies under the Muslim governor of al-Andalus, 'Abd al-Rahman al-Ghafiqi, were defeated by the Franks under Charles Martel at the Battle of Tours, in northern France. The importance of this battle has been thoroughly debated by historians. Some argue that a Muslim victory would have led to the eventual complete conquest of Europe and its subsequent conversion to Islam in the 700s. Others downplay the battle, making the point that al-Ghafiqi's advance to northern France was nothing more than a summer raid with no aims at conquest. Whether or not the battle really was that important cannot be determined, but one has to wonder at the implications of what Muslim rule in France and beyond could have meant for European history in the Middle Ages.

What makes Umayyad expansion in the early part of the eighth century so extraordinary is that it was not confined to North Africa and Spain. Simultaneously, on the opposite side of the Empire, Umayyad armies were marching into an unknown land into which even Alexander's armies dared not venture. The impetus was a Muslim trade vessel returning from Ceylon (modern Sri Lanka) that was attacked by pirates based in the northwest corner of India, Sindh. When the king of Sindh, Raja Dahir refused to return the Muslim captives taken from the ship, Umayyad armies were again spurred to action to push the empire's borders even further. Under the command of Muhammad bin Qasim, a young man who hailed from the tribe of Thaqif, based in Ta'if (the same city that according to Islamic tradition Prophet Muhammad chose not to destroy). Although he was in his teens, Ibn Qasim proved to be an able leader under the tutelage of Hajjaj bin Yusuf, the governor of Iraq. He was sent with an army of 6,000 Syrian soldiers across Persia and into the Indian subcontinent in 711, the same year as Tariq ibn Ziyad's foray into Spain. Upon reaching the Indus River, several small communities capitulated to the invading force once given the promise of religious freedom. Aided by Buddhist temple officials, the Muslim army marched from city to city with relatively little resistance. When bin Qasim's force finally met Dahir in battle along the Indus River, the Muslims, along with locals discontented with Dahir's rule, managed to inflict a devastating blow on the Sindhi army. Dahir himself was killed in the chaos of the battle, his war elephants being no match for the flaming arrows employed by the Muslims. Like in Spain, the loss of a major battle and the death of the king led to the complete collapse of local government. Muhammad bin Qasim's forces mopped up the remaining organized opposition within months, and established Muslim rule in Sindh. For the first time, a part of India was under Muslim control, although it would be centuries before Muslims would manage to establish control further into the subcontinent. For the locals living in Sindh, the Muslim conquest did not change their daily lives much. On the advice of his superiors in Iraq, Ibn Qasim extended the same religious freedom to Buddhists and Hindus that was already given to Christians and Jews elsewhere in the Muslim world. Temples and idols destroyed in the fighting were allowed to be rebuilt by the new Muslim governors. Once again, the relaxed terms offered by the conquering Muslims created little discontent with Muslim rule and relative social harmony.

By the mid-700s, the Umayyad caliphate stretched from Spain to India, making it the largest empire in the world just 100 years after the Islamic movement began high up on a mountain in Mecca. While expansion and conquest are usually signs of a powerful and capable government, a plot for the end of the Umayyad dynasty was being planned just as Umayyad armies marched into unknown territories. Where other rebellions against the Umayyads failed, this one would succeed as it capitalized on the many different ethnic groups that were now under Muslim control and their discontent with Umayyad social policies.

The rapid expansion meant that a huge number of peoples came under Muslim control who were not Muslims themselves. The percent of the population that was Muslim in the early to mid-700s is estimated to be around just 10 per cent, the rest being a blend of Christians, Jews, Zoroastrians, Buddhists and Hindus. According to Islamic law, these groups were granted religious freedom and were exempt from military service in exchange for payment of a poll tax, the *jizya*. Muslims on the other hand, were only subject to a land tax and the *zakat*, a mandatory tax meant to be distributed to the poor. Although the *jizya* was usually lower than the pre-Islamic taxes of the Byzantines or Sassanids, it was still higher than the taxes paid by the Muslims. A natural economic reaction to this system would be for non-Muslims to convert to Islam in order to pay less tax. But this solution posed a problem for the Umayyad government: if all the non-Muslims in the empire converted to Islam, it would lead to a huge fall in tax revenue, making further military expeditions (not to mention luxurious Umayyad palaces) financially unfeasible. Consequently, a safeguard to protect revenue was put into place. Non-Muslims who converted to Islam were required to continue to pay the same *jizya* tax they had paid before their conversion. In theory, this would protect the Umayyad caliphate from losing a valuable tax base, and ensure that all conversions would be sincere. In practice, it meant institutionalized discrimination based on race. Since the Arabs had almost entirely converted to Islam before the Umayyad caliphate began, the only people who were converting into the religion were non-Arabs such as Copts, Greeks, Berbers, and especially Persians. They were the only Muslims paying the *jizya*, while their Arab brothers in faith were exempt. The intention of the Umayyads may have been to protect their tax base, but the policy ended up having a racial aspect, keeping non-Arabs at the bottom of society while Arabs rose to the top. From a religious perspective, this directly contradicted Prophet Muhammad's call for unity during the Farewell Pilgrimage, when he famously proclaimed, "No Arab is better than a non-Arab and no non-Arab is better than an Arab."

An attempt was made by the caliph 'Umar ibn 'Abd al-'Aziz to undo the un-Islamic taxation policy during his reign from 717 to 720. Although his reforms were wildly popular with the non-Arabs of the empire, he was distrusted by his own family for his views of equality and was poisoned by the Umayyad clan just two years after taking power. Later Muslims would give Umar II the honorary title of the "Fifth Rightly Guided Caliph" because of his religious-minded reforms, but in the end, his reign would be nothing more than a small hiccup in Umayyad policy. With ever increasing numbers of non-Arabs accepting Islam, dissatisfaction at the unequal tax policy of the Umayyads grew. Riding this wave of discontent, another old family of Mecca rose to take control of the caliphate for themselves: the Abbasids.

THE ABBASID REVOLUTION

The Abbasids take their name from the uncle of the Prophet, Abbas, who was the patriarch of the clan. They had settled in the land east of the Jordan River after the conquest of Syria, and generally stayed out of politics as the civil wars of the 600s raged. But sometime in the early 700s, they began to circulate a rumor that one of the descendants of 'Ali had officially transferred the right to rule to the Abbasids. Why he may have done this, or if it even happened in the first place, is a mystery. From a practical standpoint, it gave legitimacy to the Abbasids. Not only were they more closely related to the Prophet than the Umayyads were, but they could also claim to uphold the desires of those who supported 'Ali's descendants as leaders of the Muslim world. From their base in southern Syria, and later in Iraq, they sent agents east to Khurasan, where the Persian population could be counted on to support a revolt against the oppressive Umayyads. Throughout the 730s and 740s, oaths of allegiance and networks of allies were formulated, far from the Umayyad base in Damascus. With promises of a more equal society under their caliphate and vague assurances that the descendants of 'Ali would play a greater role in Muslim government, which was major desire for many Muslims in the eastern part of the empire, the Abbasids were able to secure backing from a wide spectrum of society. Support came from pious-minded worshippers who desired to see a government more in line with the Prophet's ideals, non-Arab Muslims who resented their second-class status, and loyalists to the house of 'Ali, who believed rule should belong to the Prophet's family.

In 747 the Abbasids formally declared their open revolt, unfurling their distinctive black banners in the skies above the city of Merv, in the far east of the Muslim world in modern-day Turkmenistan. The revolutionaries were led by a mysterious figure known as Abu Muslim. Not much is known about him, but he does not appear to have been a member of the Abbasid family, and was probably ethnically Persian. Under his brilliant political and military leadership, the Abbasid revolution quickly secured control of Khurasan, which was soon to serve as a base for the movement. Abu Muslim sent armies westward, into the heart of Persia, where local Persian Muslims rose up against the Umayyads and joined in revolutionary fervor. What initially seemed like an insignificant expression of discontent in distant Merv now became a danger to the existence of the Umayyad dynasty as Abbasid armies flowed out of Persia and into the Arab world. Kufa, ever a hub of anti-Umayyad sentiment, rose up against its Umayyad governor and expelled him when the black Abbasid banners appeared on the eastern horizon.

Once Kufa was liberated, formal oaths of allegiance could be given to the Abbasid claimant to the caliphate, Abu al-'Abbas. The revolution had a clear goal, widespread support throughout Persia, and now, a leader to unite behind. Everywhere the Umayyads were on the defensive as more people flocked to support the Abbasids. Meanwhile, rousing the Umayyad supporters proved to be a challenge. It had been decades since the last real threat to the Umayyad position, and the Syrian army officers were content to remain on their estates, erroneously thinking the revolution would peter out. By the time the Umayyad caliph Marwan II could muster together the Umayyad forces, the Abbasids had already taken control of the majority of Iraq. In early 750 at the climactic Battle of the Zab in central Mesopotamia, the Abbasid forces completely routed the Umayyad army. Organized resistance to the Abbasids effectively ended after the battle, as Umayyad control collapsed throughout the Muslim world. Now nothing stood between the Abbasids and the Umayyad capital, Damascus. One by one, cities capitulated and accepted Abbasid sovereignty, and one by one, members of the Umayyad family were hunted down and executed. Marwan himself was captured in Egypt, where he was unsuccessful in building an army that would drive back the Abbasids and re-establish Umayyad control.

Only one member of the defeated family managed to escape the revolutionaries. The teenaged 'Abd al-Rahman, a relatively obscure member of the Umayyad family, found a way to escape in disguise to North Africa. Pursued by Abbasid armies from Palestine to Egypt to the Maghreb, and aided only by a slave who had once worked for his family, his legendary journey led him eventually to al-Andalus, where he would establish an Umayyad emirate far from Abbasid reach that would last almost 300 more years.

THE ABBASID CALIPHATE

The Abbasid Revolution of the mid-700s inaugurated the second dynasty to control the caliphate. The revolt was based on the ideas of building a government more in line with Prophetic ideals, giving non-Arabs a more equitable role in society, and giving the descendants of 'Ali some role in leadership. These broad and idealistic promises were necessary to secure the support of various groups of people that made the revolution successful. Once the Abbasids were in power, however, the reality of their caliphate fell far short of expectation. The revolution did not mean a return to the era of the Rightly Guided Caliphs where piety, and not politics, dictated the decisions of the caliph. If anything, the Abbasid caliphs continued the same authoritarian traditions that they had denounced the Umayyads for. The caliphate remained a hereditary title in the possession of a Qurayshi family, and those who supported 'Ali's family as caliphs were left with unfulfilled promises.

The Abbasid caliph Harun al-Rashid was known for his immense wealth and diplomatic relations with distant states. In 802, he sent an embassy to Charlemagne in France that included an elephant and a water clock.

The one area where the Abbasids made real progress was the role of non-Arabs in society. Although the caliphate itself remained in Arab hands, administration was increasingly Persianized. For hundreds of years before Islam, the Persians had developed a complex but efficient bureaucratic system. Now that non-Arabs were no longer systematically discriminated against, this experience would be put to use in the administration of the Empire. Recognizing the usefulness of the Persians caused the Abbasids to move the capital of the Muslim world closer to the Persian heartland. The second Abbasid caliph, Al-Mansur, established a new city to serve as his capital in the fertile plain between the Tigris and Euphrates Rivers in 765 near the old Persian capital of Ctesiphon. Within twenty years, Baghdad became the largest city in the world, with over one million residents. The seat of the Muslim empire would become a metropolitan center where government, culture, science and art would all intersect.

A true understanding of the accomplishments of the Abbasid age does not come with discussions of military exploits and distant conquests, as it did with the Umayyads. In fact, outward expansion essentially halted when the Abbasids came to power. Seasonal raids across the border with the Byzantines remained, but the campaigns were generally indecisive. In the West, the Battle of Tours in 732 in Umayyad times meant the end of Muslim expansion into Europe, and consolidation of gains in al-Andalus was the main focus of the Umayyad refugees who controlled it. In the East, only incremental gains were made in creating inroads into Central Asia. The Turks who roamed the Central Asian plains would not come into Islamic civilization through conquest, but through migration into the heartland of Islam in the 800s and 900s. The era of Muslim military conquest was over for the time being. Instead, the era of Muslim intellectual conquest was about to begin.

5

INTELLECTUAL GOLDEN AGES

The ninth through thirteenth centuries in the Muslim world mark an era of scientific, religious, philosophical and cultural development the scale and depth of which had never been seen in world history before or since. After its meteoric rise from the barren deserts of Arabia, Islamic civilization now encompassed many diverse cultures, religions and intellectual traditions from Spain to India. In this realm, the previous accomplishments of distant civilizations could be brought together, compared and built upon to create a new golden age of scientific discoveries. Nowhere else in the world possessed the same capability to bring together so many diverse people, supplemented by homegrown intellectual giants. The result was an era which not only served as a bridge between the knowledge of the ancients and Renaissance Europe, but also laid the foundation for today's modern scientific world.

THE HOUSE OF WISDOM

The Abbasids, like countless political parties in history, rose to prominence on the back of promises of a positive and idealistic

---

The world's oldest university, the University of Karaouin, was established by a Muslim woman in Fez, Morocco in 859.

---

future. Their assurances of a more equitable society and a return to pious leadership helped propel them to prominence as the Umayyads disintegrated. By the early 800s, they had their empire, which stretched from the Atlantic to the Indus. They had their capital, a world city of over a million people in Baghdad, and they had the diverse cultures of the Greeks, Copts, Persians, and Indians from which to adopt the best aspects of previous civilizations. It was high time for the inauguration of the idealistic society they promised. In the mind of the seventh Abbasid caliph, al-Ma'mun (r. 813–833), that future idealistic society could only be achieved through science and rationalism. In order to achieve this, the various threads of scientific knowledge that existed throughout the empire had to be brought together in a central location. He believed that if the best scholars from the Muslim world could be brought together to learn from each other, limitless possibilities would open up.

In the tenth century, the Catholic Pope Sylvester II was one of the first Europeans to promote the study of math that was developed by Muslims after he spent time studying in Muslim Spain and North Africa.

With this in mind, he established an educational institute in Baghdad known as the House of Wisdom (Arabic: *Bayt al-Hikmah*). Its scope was such that it defies definition by modern understandings of educational establishments. It was at once a university, library, translation institute and research lab, all on one campus. Libraries and small schools had existed since Umayyad times, but the emphasis placed on the acquisition of knowledge by the Abbasids far surpassed that of their predecessors. It was said that if a scholar would translate any book from its original language into Arabic, he would be given that book's weight in gold. The most renowned scholars, Muslim and non-Muslim, from across the world flocked to Baghdad to be a part of al-Ma'mun's project. For the first time in history, the best of Persia, Egypt, India, and former Byzantine lands could be brought together to advance science in ways that would benefit the entire world.

Al-Ma'mun was hardly the only leader in history to have placed special emphasis on science. What makes the House of Wisdom and the Muslim Golden Age unique is the context in which it all took place. First, the expansive Muslim empire knocked down walls that had previously separated different groups. Before Islam, there would be no reason for a scholar in Alexandria to travel to Ctesiphon to study and teach. Even if he did travel, language barriers would prevent him from being of much use to the Persians. That is the second unique aspect of the early Abbasid era: Arabic became a lingua franca that could unite people from diverse backgrounds. Regardless of if someone's mother tongue was Berber or Syriac or Persian, if he was a Muslim, at least a rudimentary knowledge of Arabic was necessary in order to pray and read the Quran as the Prophet Muhammad had taught. Arabic thus served not just as a liturgical language, but also one that scientists could use to communicate and research. Thirdly, Islam itself orders the acquisition of knowledge, making scientific research an act of worship. Numerous verses in the Quran and sayings of the Prophet emphasize the role that scholarship has in the life of a pious Muslim. The Prophet was reported to have said that God makes the path to Heaven easier for whoever treads the path in search of knowledge. For Muslim scientists just a few hundred years removed from the life of the Prophet, seeking God's pleasure seems to have been the main reason for their research and studies. Scientific literature from the Golden Age commonly begins with Quranic verses that encourage seekers of knowledge and call on Muslims to reflect on the world around them. These three motivating factors for scientific endeavors were unique to the Muslim world, and could not have existed without the rise of Islam as a geopolitical force in the centuries after the life of the Prophet.

MATHEMATICS

Muslim contributions to mathematics in the Golden Age can only be described as monumental. Mathematics itself is of course the basis for almost all other sciences including physics, chemistry, astronomy and geography. For Muslim scientists of the Golden Age, however, it was also a sacred science. They hoped that through the understanding of advanced mathematics they could discover the underlying numerical principles that dictate the natural rules of the world. Today, anyone who has taken a basic physics class understands that formulas dictate the movement of objects through space. In the Golden Ages, that formula was a mystery, and through theory and experimentation, scientists hoped to find these seemingly magical algorithms. Through that understanding, a greater appreciation and love for God's power and relationship with His creation could be achieved, making mathematical study a religious journey as well.

One of the first great Muslim mathematicians was Muhammad ibn Musa al-Khwarizmi, a Persian who lived from 780 to 850. He was one of the first to work at the House of Wisdom, and thus laid the groundwork for future advances in mathematics. Among his greatest contributions was the adoption of the Indian numeral system and its dissemination. Previously, the de facto system was based on the ubiquitous Roman numerals, which had their limitations. Complex math problems involving non-integer numbers were near impossible with the Roman system, but the Indian system (1, 2, 3, 4…) allowed large and negative numbers to be more easily expressed, easing complex problems. Al-Khwarizmi not only borrowed the system from the ancient Indians, but also added on to it an important missing link: the zero. Although he was unable to mathematically prove zero (since anything divided by zero is undefined), al-Khwarizmi implemented it in his further studies, revolutionizing some subjects and inventing others.

Perhaps al-Khwarizmi's greatest contribution was the development of algebra. In his monumental work *The Compendious Book on Calculation by Completion and Balancing*, he explains how algebraic equations can be used to solve everyday problems, ranging from dividing up inheritance to geography. Here al-Khwarizmi was a trailblazer. While the ancient Greeks were masters of geometry, they failed to separate theoretical algebra from it, and thus found limitations to the science. Al-Khwarizmi's book established algebra as a unique subject within mathematics with its own practical applications. In fact, the word algebra itself derives from al-Khwarizmi's title for his book. It comes from *al-jabr*, meaning "completion", referring to the balancing of both sides of an algebraic equation to find a solution.

Another of the great Persian mathematicians was Omar Khayyam, who lived from 1048 to 1131. Although he is mostly known in the West for his poetry on love and mysticism, he was also an accomplished mathematician, helping to push the boundaries of the subject in ways his predecessors could not. He managed to find a method for solving cubic equations—algebraic expressions in which the variable is raised to a power of three. Pushing further into theoretical algebra, he was also one of the earliest, if not the first, to formulate the binomial theorem, which helps solve algebraic expressions by expanding them into sums. These discoveries may seem overly theoretical and only useful for torturing secondary school math students, but they have important applications. Through advanced algebra, subjects such as trigonometry and calculus could be developed. Muslims further developed trigonometry itself, particularly the tenth-century scientist al-Battani, for a very practical reason. Through trigonometric functions and a basic understanding of the stars, people could calculate their exact position on earth, which was of vital importance for Muslims, who must pray in the direction of Mecca. Handbooks produced in the Golden Age listed hundreds of cities, their coordinates and the direction from there to Mecca. For this reason, many mosques built over a thousand years ago are now being found to point directly at Mecca, even from thousands of kilometers away. The basic trigonometric properties put forth by Muslim mathematicians even serve as the basis for how GPS systems work today.

ASTRONOMY

A natural outgrowth from the Muslim development of advanced mathematics was work in the astronomical field. Formulas and methods developed by Muslim mathematicians laid the foundation for the study of the stars, while Islamic belief provided the motivation. Numerous verses in the Quran allude to the heavenly bodies and their movement. Regarding the sun and the moon, the Quran states they "move by precise calculation". Furthermore, it states that through the stars, mankind can "be guided by them through the darkness of the land and sea". For an empire of faith that stretched from the Atlantic Ocean to India, allusions in the Quran to the mathematical nature of the heavens were too much to ignore.

With the Quran as a motivating factor, Muslim astronomers were the first to truly develop this science. In ancient times, astronomy and astrology were one and the same, leading to erroneous scientific beliefs about the impact of the stars on the daily lives of humans. Muslims were the first to separate the science of astronomy from the guesswork and mythology of astrology. With the patronage of al-Ma'mun and the House of Wisdom, astronomers were collected to study the ancient theories of Ptolemy, whose work was seen as final word on astronomy until Muslim times. The key aspect of Ptolemy's ideas was the geocentricity of the universe, that the earth is motionless and everything revolves around it. This motionless theory of the earth started to come into question when Muslim astronomers realized that the calculations Ptolemy put forth for the movement of planets and stars were flawed and needed correction. While many simply created more accurate formulas, some began to question Ptolemy altogether.

In the eleventh century, al-Biruni proposed that Ptolemy never fully proved that the earth does not move in a scientific way, and that it may in fact spin on its axis. According to him, this would explain why Ptolemy's calculations were off, since he did not take into account the earth's motion. While the rotation of the earth was

never fully accepted by Muslim astronomers due to lack of definitive evidence, it was certainly debated among the scholars of the
Muslim world. These debates found their way into Europe, specifically through Latin translations of the works of al-Majriti, an Andalusian scholar who focused on revising and perfecting astronomical
tables and calculations. Even after his death, the learned classes
from all over Europe would travel to the Muslim state in Iberia to
study the works of al-Majriti and others. Eventually, as the Muslim
ideas on astronomy disseminated throughout the continent, scientists such as Copernicus and Galileo would build upon them to
come up with the theories that we accept as fact today. Unlike European astronomers, however, Muslims would not be harassed by the
religious establishment for their views. Scientific endeavors were
seen, after all, as a form of worship.

Like algebra, astronomy would have its practical applications.
One of the most important was the development of the astrolabe.
An instrument first invented by the ancient Greeks, its purpose
was to determine one's latitude by using the stars. It combined the
capabilities of the astrolabe with the more precise astronomical
calculations of Muslim scientists, and became a staple of navigation, particularly by ship. By holding up an astrolabe at the night
sky to calculate the position of certain constellations, a navigator
could determine his precise location, and compare that with accessible handbooks that listed the latitudes of known locations
throughout the world to help set course to a destination. Travelling to Mecca for the pilgrimage thus became much easier for
Muslims travelling long distances. For a civilization that stretched
from Spain to India, technology such as this, which made travel
easier, was indispensable. The astrolabe revolutionized sailing and
was in use until the 1700s as the standard for navigation.

GEOGRAPHY

Just as astronomy grew out of mathematics, geography grew out of astronomy. Few empires in history spanned an area the size of the Muslim world in the Golden Age. With a generally unified political system extending across such a wide area, long-distance travel became safe and relatively common. It is no wonder, then, that Muslims would emerge as some of the leading geographers of the Middle Ages.

The old myth that Christopher Columbus discovered that the earth is round is just that—a myth. It had in fact been accepted since ancient times that the earth was not flat. Sailors were particularly aware, since they could see the lower part of a boat descend under the horizon before its masts as it sailed away. The ancient Greeks even attempted to calculate the size of the earth, although they grossly underestimated the size of the Atlantic Ocean, leading to a much smaller number than the earth's actual size. Geographers working in the Abbasid caliphate came to much more accurate conclusions. Using trigonometry and spherical geometry they calculated that the earth is 12,728 kilometers in diameter—they were off by a mere 37 kilometers. Furthermore they calculated the earth's circumference to be 39,968 kilometers, when in actuality it is 40,074 kilometers. Without modern satellites and telescopes, these calculations can only be described as astounding.

During the 1300s, Ibn Battuta, a scholar of Islamic law from Morocco, traveled over 170,000 kilometers. His journeys included West Africa, India, China and Southeast Asia.

Islamic geography was not limited solely to calculations of the earth's size. Great effort was also put into mapping the world. Ancient Greek maps (particularly Ptolemy's) were expanded upon and improved. One of the best examples is the atlas made by Muhammad al-Idrisi, who lived in twelfth-century Sicily. Although Sicily had previously been part of the Muslim world until its conquest by the Normans in the late eleventh century, the reigning king in al-Idrisi's time, Roger II, was a tolerant and well-informed sovereign. Under his patronage, al-Idrisi produced a world map unrivaled in its accuracy and detail in the Middle Ages. For hundreds of years afterwards, it was the benchmark by which other maps were judged. It was not only a drawing of the physical geography of the known world, but it also included descriptions of the cultures, politics, and societies of the various regions to which explorers had travelled.

Just as fascinating to Muslim geographers as the known world was what was unknown. Western mythology holds up Christopher Columbus as the great explorer who was the first to brave the vast Atlantic Ocean to discover the New World in 1492. Besides narratives of his "discovery" discounting the fact that natives had been living there for centuries, and that there is very strong evidence that Vikings ventured to what is now Canada in the tenth century, there is mounting evidence of Muslim trans-Atlantic voyages hundreds of years before Columbus. In the mid-tenth century, the great geographer and historian al-Mas'udi wrote of a voyage from Muslim Iberia in 889 that sailed west from the port of Delba—the same port from which Columbus would sail—for months until it happened upon a very large, previously unknown landmass. His account states that they traded with the locals and then returned home. Al-Mas'udi's world map even includes an "unknown land" across the Atlantic Ocean because of this account. Another account is recorded by al-Idrisi, who wrote that a group of Muslim sailors ventured for thirty-one days across the Atlantic Ocean and landed on an unknown island. They were taken captive by the local natives, but eventually freed when one of the natives who spoke Arabic was able to mediate between the two groups and arrange for their release. A final report of a trans-Atlantic voyage comes from Mali, the Muslim kingdom in West Africa that peaked in the fourteenth century. As told to Ibn Battuta, the great Muslim traveler, 200 ships sailed west from the coast of Africa to discover the unknown. When only one returned, it reported they had found land across the ocean but had to turn back because of a storm. The king of Mali, Mansa Abu Bakr, reportedly outfitted 2000 ships this time, sailed with them into the Atlantic Ocean and was never heard from again. These stories of Muslim voyages across the ocean are certainly not definitive proof of trans-Atlantic contact before Columbus. But the fact that they are recorded by geographers known for their insistence on accuracy, coupled with allusions to Muslim communities in the Americas found in the journals of the first generation of European explorers of the New World, point to possibilities which could entirely rewrite the accepted history of the Age of Discovery.

MEDICINE

Common misperceptions about the history of medicine include the belief that it was mostly guesswork until the past few hundred years. Mental images of charlatan medical "experts" selling their phony cure-alls come to mind when thinking about medicine before the twentieth century. In actuality, however, there exists a long medical tradition in the Muslim world based on earlier

Greek knowledge that emphasized empirical study and clinical professionalism. While this is lost in the modern popular imagination, there still exist writings from some of the greatest medical minds the world has ever known who lived and practiced in the Muslim Golden Age. Their work points to an era of medical enlightenment and advancement that forms the basis of modern medicine.

In the tenth century, Baghdad instituted a licensing exam that all doctors had to take before practicing as physicians.

Muslim advances in medicine picked up where the ancient Greek physician, Galen, left off. Galen was the giant of this field in ancient times. This second century CE physician and philosopher wrote extensively on medicine, and supported the theory that the body is composed of four humors: blood, black bile, yellow bile, and phlegm. According to him, diseases were caused by an imbalance of these fluids in the body. Although some of his ideas were revolutionary in his time, others were seriously flawed. Despite this, he was uncritically accepted by physicians for hundreds of years after his death.

The first to critically challenge the ideas of Galen was Muhammad ibn Zakariya al-Razi, who lived in the ninth century. Based in Baghdad, he was a strong proponent of a rational, instead of theoretical understanding of the human body. In his bluntly titled *Doubts About Galen*, he concluded that physical ailments could not simply be attributed to an imbalance among the humors or to punishment from God as Middle Age Europeans believed, but to certain external and internal factors that must be resolved in order to treat the problem. Along these lines, he developed specific and effective cures for common problems such as coughs, headaches, and constipation. But he was not limited to simply treating the symptoms or physical causes of ailments. His giant medical encyclopedia, *The Virtuous Life*, extolls the importance of dedication to the field of medicine and constant improvement and learning. Furthermore, he believed that medical practice is a sacred endeavor, and that doctors are entrusted by God to do good to anyone who requires it, even their enemies or those who cannot afford medical attention. He was thus known for treating poor patients free of charge in Baghdad's famous hospitals. His works were widely disseminated, and helped guide future generations of physicians in the Muslim world and Europe for centuries.

The next great Muslim physician, and perhaps the most well-known, was Ibn Sina, known as Avicenna in Medieval Europe. Despite constantly moving from city to city in the turbulent political environment of Persia in the early 1000s, he managed to have one of the most accomplished careers of any polymath of the Muslim Golden Age. He applied the rational approach to science that Muslims were taking in other fields to medicine, giving him insight that others, including al-Razi, lacked. He formulated a theory that everything in the body can be understood through a causal chain of events. While this may seem like common sense in today's scientifically advanced world, it was a new idea in the early eleventh century; one that Ibn Sina was keen to prove. Based on years of clinical observation and scientific study, he concluded that diseases can be spread through air, water or soil. Furthermore, each disease had unique characteristics and thus must be treated in a unique way. He was one of the first to promote experimental medicine, and in his monumental work, *The Canon of Medicine*, he insisted that drugs be tested under controlled conditions and not be trusted simply based on theory. Drugs that were not universally effective, or could not be proven to actually treat a disease meant nothing to him, as he believed medicine was a science of observation and rationalism, not mysticism and luck. His *Canon* became the standard textbook for anyone desiring to learn about medicine in the Muslim world and beyond. European medical schools relied on Latin translations of it into the seventeenth century, and, in the Yuan Dynasty (thirteenth- and fourteenth-century), it was translated into Chinese by the sizeable Muslim community in China. It is easy to understand why the *Canon* enjoyed such widespread popularity and reverence. Ibn Sina's greatest work was not simply a handbook of common ailments and cures. It was a complete medical encyclopedia. Descriptions can be found in it of anesthesia, breast cancer, rabies, toxins, ulcers, kidney disease, and tuberculosis. Beyond this, Ibn Sina wrote about the connection between mental and physical health, and concluded that negative thoughts can cause illness just as much as other factors such as toxins, injury or diet. Today the possibility of a connection between mind and body is attributed to the first generation of psychologists like Freud and Jung. In reality, it was a possibility that seemed very real to Ibn Sina and other physicians and philosophers of his time.

In 872, the ruler of Egypt, Ahmad ibn Tulun, spent 60,000 gold dinars establishing a hospital in Fustat. It provided free healthcare to the public and included a ward for mental illness patients.

The greatest medical minds of all time would not have been able to accomplish great feats without the support of great institutions. The Muslim world of the Golden Ages, with its vast financial resources and strong political institutions, established some of the first hospitals in history. The impetus to build hospitals came from the need to care for the health of poorer citizens. The wealthy were able to hire private physicians and pay for home treatment, but the poor had no such luxury. To provide for them, caliphs and emirs established large institutions in the great cities of the Muslim world aimed at providing affordable or free healthcare to anyone who would need it. In the early ninth century, the first hospitals began to appear in Baghdad. As the hospitals grew over time, they began to resemble modern hospitals in size and scope. Hospitals had dozens of doctors and nurses, including specialists and surgeons. They contained outpatient centers, psychiatric wards, surgery centers and maternity wards. Perhaps the biggest difference was that the hospitals of that era were free to those who could not afford it; a far cry from the revenue-fueled hospitals of today. To the patrons of these hospitals, the Prophetic example of compassion was clear. In their eyes, a society based on Islam was expected to care for all its citizens, regardless of wealth, race or even religion. After first being established in Baghdad, these enlightened institutions of healing spread to the rest of the Muslim world's major cities throughout the tenth to fourteenth centuries. Hospitals could be found in Cairo, Damascus, Baghdad, Mecca, Medina, and even distant Granada in Iberia. The Ottomans would later carry on this tradition of public hospitals, and it was during their long reign that Europe would begin to catch up, and even surpass, the Muslim world.

The Renaissance saw a move to translate hundreds of Arabic texts into Latin in the great cultural and scientific centers such as

Padua and Bologna. Europeans were able to further advance the knowledge of giants such as al-Razi and Ibn Sina, who advanced the knowledge of Galen and Hippocrates. Today's medical knowledge and institutions come largely from the West, but are based on the earlier Muslim medical tradition, which in turn was based on ancient Greece. The clash of civilizations narrative that is promoted by extremists on both sides of modern conflicts neglects examples of cross-cultural intellectual traditions such as this.

In the 1200s, Ibn al-Nafis wrote that blood circulates from the heart to the lungs where it absorbs oxygen and then back to the heart and the rest of the body.

PHYSICS

Mathematics only took Muslim scientists so far. If they truly wanted to understand the principles through which God controls the universe, the ideas formulated by mathematicians had to be applied to the real world. That is where the talented crop of Muslim physicists came in; like in other fields, Muslim physicists built on earlier advance by ancient civilizations, whose works were translated into Arabic. Drawing on various intellectual traditions as well as the wide range of sciences that the Muslim world was at the leading edge of, the physicists of the Golden Age developed some of the core concepts of the subject. Their work helped lay the foundation that giants such as Newton and Einstein built upon.

One of the primary scientists who contributed to this continuous intellectual tradition was Ibn al-Haytham, who lived from 965 to 1040. He was originally from Iraq, and early in his life he worked as a civil official in the Abbasid government, but soon abandoned the post to join a promising intellectual center in Cairo, the capital of the rival Fatimid Empire. After running afoul of the Fatimid ruler, he was put under house arrest in Cairo, which proved to be a blessing for him, and the field of physics itself. While contained within his home, Ibn al-Haytham was able to focus his efforts and studies on light. Since ancient times the study of light and its properties had perplexed even the brightest minds. One of the leading ideas about light in Ibn al-Haytham's time was promoted by Ptolemy, who argued that light is a ray that is emitted from the eye, bounces off objects, and comes back into the eye, allowing someone to see. The ancient Greek tradition of understanding the world entirely through philosophy ran contrary to the beliefs of Ibn al-Haytham, who advocated that scientific theory be formulated through empirical study and experimentation. Thus, he ran hundreds of experiments on the nature of light. By relying less on philosophy and more on science, he concluded that Ptolemy's theory of light being emitted by the eye was simply impossible. Rather, he theorized that light bounces off every point on an object into the eye, where the numerous rays of light are turned into information that the brain can process. At the same time that Ibn Sina was dissecting eyes in Persia to understand how light travels through them, Ibn al-Haytham was conducting similar experiments in Egypt.

After years of hard work, research and experimentation, Ibn al-Haytham wrote a book that was groundbreaking at the time. In his *Book of Optics*, Ibn al-Haytham argued that light was composed of rays, which travelled in straight lines. He furthered this idea by building the Camera Obscura, a device which consists of a light-proof box, through which a tiny hole (an aperture) is punctured. On the wall inside the box opposite the hole, an image depicting whatever the hole is pointing at is projected. He argued that this is only possible if straight rays of light were coming from objects outside the box, were focused by the aperture, and landed on the opposite wall. Ibn al-Haytham lacked the technology necessary to advance his Camera Obscura a step further into the modern cameras that can capture images today. But without his pioneering study in optics, cameras would not be possible 1000 years later. He also managed to bring together the fields of optics and astronomy in his calculations on the depth of the earth's atmosphere. Using principles he derived regarding the properties of refracted light, he concluded that at sunset, the color of the sky changes based on the angle at which the sun's rays hit the atmosphere. Based on the colors and the sun's position in relation to the earth at numerous times, he came up with a calculation for the depth of the atmosphere that was not off by much. It was not until spacecraft from the United States and the Soviet Union blasted off into the skies that they were able to verify his calculations.

Ibn al-Haytham's scientific achievements can fill volumes on their own, and indeed they did. He reportedly wrote over 200 books, but no more than a few dozen survive today. He pioneered work in magnifying lenses, the laws of motion, analytical geometry, calculus, astronomy, and even experimental psychology. When taking all of his accomplishments together, one can truly appreciate the real legacy of Ibn al-Haytham: the scientific method. Today, this method is the technique through which all scientists acquire scientific knowledge. Ibn al-Haytham's absolute reliance on observation and experimentation—which we now call the scientific method—separated the sciences from the philosophy of the ancient Greeks. The modern world's understanding of the entire field of science is based on the methods initiated by this intellectual giant. In explaining why he dove so deep into scientific study, Ibn al-Haytham concluded, "I constantly sought knowledge and truth, and it became my belief that for gaining access to the effulgence and closeness to God, there is no better way than that of searching for truth and knowledge."

After Ibn al-Haytham's death, Muslim scientists continued to build on his discoveries and find practical uses for them. New inventions and improvements on old devices were constantly popping up, from improved water clocks to chemistry laboratory equipment. Crankshafts, water pumps, eyeglasses, compasses, gliders, drinking glasses and even water-powered robots all appeared in the Muslim world by the thirteenth century. The list goes on. What is important to note is that through the advanced study of the sciences, a technological revolution occurred in the Muslim world. When the light began to dim on Muslim scientific creativity—as the Crusaders and the Mongols wreaked havoc on the Muslim heartland in the twelfth and thirteenth centuries—Christian Europe picked it up. There, another scientific revolution was spurred from the works of Copernicus, Galileo and Newton, all of whom where familiar with earlier Islamic scientific literature and were almost certainly influenced by it.

In the twelfth century, a Muslim inventor, al-Jazari, designed and built numerous automatic machines. Among them were automatic hand-washing systems, clocks and even musical robots powered by water.

6

THE ISLAMIC SCIENCES

Concurrent with the development of the physical and mathematical sciences was the flourishing of the Islamic sciences in the centuries after the Prophet. Various disciplines and sub-disciplines developed in an attempt to interpret and understand the message of the Quran and the Prophet's example.

A basic framework for the Islamic sciences can be seen in a *hadith* attributed to the Prophet and recorded in later *hadith* collections, notably that of al-Bukhari. It states that a mysterious man once approached the Prophet and asked him to define three terms: *Islam*, *Iman*, and *Ihsan*. The Prophet answered that Islam was to believe in God and His Messenger, to pray five times daily, to pay alms, to fast in the month of Ramadan, and to perform the *hajj* if able to do so. He defined *Iman* as belief in God, His Angels, revealed Holy Books, His Messengers, the Day of Judgment, and in predestination. *Ihsan* was explained to be worshipping God as if you could see Him, and if you could not, then to know that He can see you.

Using this basic framework, scholars of the Islamic sciences could divide the field into three broad categories that deal with Islamic action, Islamic belief, and Islamic spirituality respectively.

FIQH

Fiqh is commonly defined generally as "Islamic law". This definition is somewhat lacking, as the modern Western concept of law is ill suited to fit what *fiqh* entails. Early Muslims understood *fiqh* to encompass all aspects of Muslim action, from individual worship to social interactions, to government policy. It is thus better to define *fiqh* more broadly as Islamic jurisprudence.

The challenge for the early scholars of *fiqh* was to know how to apply the example of the Prophet to a dynamic and cosmopolitan world. As the Muslim world grew to encompass lands as distant and as diverse as Iberia, Iraq, and India, jurists developed a variety of methods aimed at applying the Prophet's teachings to situations he may never had experienced.

Nowhere is the creativity and dynamism of *fiqh* more apparent than in the career of the first great jurist, Abu Hanifa (d. 767). A Persian born and raised in Iraq, he found himself squarely in the middle of a society that was a world apart from the Medina of the Prophet a century earlier. Iraq was a meeting point of Arab and non-Arab, Muslim and non-Muslim, and desert nomads and city dwellers. Thus the challenge for Abu Hanifa and his Kufan colleagues (notably Abu Yusuf and Muhammad al-Shaybani) was how to negotiate implementing Islamic legal imperatives in a land with diverse ethnicities and lifestyles. Furthermore, other questions—such as what is to be done when the Quran, the ultimate guidebook of Islam, does not discuss a particular issue, or how to reconcile seeming contradictions between various *hadith* reports—also played into the challenge early jurists faced.

One example confronting Abu Hanifa (and other early jurists) regarding the role of the Quran and the example of the Prophet (the Sunnah) in Muslim life arose from a *hadith* report, in which the Prophet sent one of his Companions, Muʻadh ibn Jabal, to govern the region of Yemen. When asked by the Prophet how he would react when required to make a ruling on a situation, Muʻadh replied that would rely on the Quran, and if he could not find an answer there, he would rely on the example of the Prophet, and if the Prophet had never spoken on the issue, he would rely on his own reasoning to find a suitable solution. This *hadith* provided a basic framework from which jurists could create an epistemological hierarchy for *fiqh* known as *usul al-fiqh* (lit. "the sources of jurisprudence").

The Quran was the first and foremost source of guidance for Muslim action. As the Word of God, it obviously could not be trumped by anything else. However, the Quran is not simply a law book. The verses in the Quran that directly command Muslims to perform specific acts are relatively few. And even those verses are commonly vague regarding the specifics of *how* Muslims should perform certain actions. For example, the Quran commands Muslims to pray, but it does not specify exactly how to perform the prayer, nor does it specify at exactly what times prayers should be performed. That is where the *Sunnah* would come in. Muslim jurists understood the *Sunnah* as an explanation of the Quran itself. So when the Quran was silent on the manner in which Muslims should pray, jurists would look to the Prophet's prayer, as passed down first through his Companions and then through the generation after them, as the definitive answer on how Muslims should pray. In this way, the *Sunnah* and the example of the Companions occupied the second and third rungs on the ladder of *usul*.

However, issues remained, particularly in places like Abu Hanifa's Iraq, on which the Quran, Sunnah, and example of the Companions were all silent. It was here that the early jurists advocated a form of analogical reasoning known as *qiyas*. The logic behind it was quite simple: if a new issue arises with no precedent in the first three sources, the jurists must look for a similar issue that *is* addressed in either the Quran, the Sunnah, or the example of the Companions, and base their ruling on an analogy that can be drawn between the two. To take a simple modern example, jurists may decide to investigate whether driving cars is permissible in Islamic *fiqh*. Obviously, cars did not exist in the seventh century and the Quran, the Prophet, and the Companions would thus all be silent on the permissibility of driving. But since the primary purpose of a car is transportation, and it is well known that other forms of transportation such as horses and camels were widely used by the Prophet and the Companions, jurists can analogize that modern cars, too, are permissible.

While the example of the permissibility of a car is a fairly simple and straightforward one, the realm of *qiyas* developed into something very broad and deep. Scholars differed on issues such as what types of analogy were appropriate, whether all rulings from the Quran and *Sunnah* were appropriate to use as the basis of an analogy, and how similar the two cases should be to make analogy possible. Underlying questions such as these was the role that reason should play in *fiqh*. Abu Hanifa, living in cosmopolitan Iraq, felt it necessary to allow reason a major role in determining how *fiqh* would operate on a practical level. To him and his group of students, adhering to a literalistic approach to the Quran and *Sunnah* would render Islam almost impossible to apply in a constantly changing society starkly different from that of the Prophet's Medina.

However, Abu Hanifa's contemporary Malik ibn Anas (d. 795) took a different approach. Born and raised in Medina itself, Malik believed that his city had not radically changed in the century since the Prophet's time. His neighbors and colleagues in the city were the children and grandchildren of the Companions, and had learned their approach to the religion from those Companions who were so close to the Prophet himself. Thus, he argued, the example of the people of Medina at his time could also serve as a source of jurisprudence. He reasoned that if all of the people of Medina agreed on a particular action or way of doing something, then that must come directly from the Companions, who learned it from the Prophet, making it almost as strong as the *Sunnah* itself. To Abu Hanifa and his Iraqi students, local custom was a very fickle institution and thus invalid for inclusion in the realm of *usul al-fiqh*. One of Abu Hanifa's primary students, Muhammad al-Shaybani, went to Medina to study with Malik, and concluded that he preferred the Iraqi system; he even wrote a treatise titled *A Response to the People of Medina*, in which he attacked what he saw as inconsistencies in Malik's approach and the inability to base a jurisprudential methodology on local custom. It is important to note, however, that while strong differences of opinion regarding *fiqh* arose fairly early on, these developing schools did not view each other as heretics or even necessarily as misguided, since their differences concerned relatively minute issues and not base creedal ones, as will be seen below.

The third approach to develop came from Muhammad al-Shafi'i (d. 820), a Gazan who went to Medina at a young age to study with Malik himself. Unlike the earlier two jurists, al-Shafi'i did quite a bit of travelling, living in Yemen, Iraq, and Egypt after his stay in Medina. While in Iraq he managed to study under al-

Shaybani, thereby becoming a student of both the major approaches to *fiqh* of his day. His own methodology, however, differed from the earlier two, in that he was less likely to use reason to the extent that the people of Iraq and Medina were. His approach to the *hadith* exhibits these differences with the earlier schools. For example, Abu Hanifa prioritized extremely widespread and well-*known hadith* (known as *mutawatir*) above all others, and built maxims based on them that could be used to interpret other, non-*mutawatir* reports. This meant a small group of core maxims formed the basis of his *fiqh* approach, allowing reason a greater role in the juristic process outside those maxims. Al-Shafi'i, on the other hand, did not believe that single-transmitter reports (*ahad*) were necessarily epistemologically inferior to *mutawatir* ones. Thus, when faced with conflicting *hadith* reports, al-Shafi'i advocated a system of abrogation, arguing that *hadith* from earlier in the Prophet's life could be ignored in *fiqh* if it was contradicted by another from later in his life. In this way, Shafi'i's approach developed into a system that provided for the use of reason in *fiqh*, but not to the extent that his earlier counterparts had advocated.

The last of the four great jurists was Ahmad ibn Hanbal (d. 855), who was himself a student of al-Shafi'i. Of the four, his approach is by far the most literalist and most resistant to reason. While he still made room for *qiyas* in his methodology like the other three, he believed it should be limited as much as possible, and that a literal approach to the *hadith* was optimal.

The methodologies of Abu Hanifa, Malik, al-Shafi'i, and ibn Hanbal formalized into four distinct schools of jurisprudence (*madhahib*, sing. *madhab*): the Hanafi, Maliki, Shafi'i, and Hanbali schools. Over time these four came to be recognized as the four valid schools of *fiqh* in Sunni Islam. Together they form a spectrum, with the Hanafis on one end and the Hanbalis on the other, regarding the role of reason in the interpretation of the Quran and *Sunnah*. The Hanafi school, probably the most flexible due to its reliance on reason, soon became the dominant school in the Muslim world. Through association with major empires such as the Abbasids, Seljuks, Ottomans, and Mughals, and through its ability to adapt easily to diverse environments through its core legal maxims, the Hanafi school took precedence in Central Asia, Turkey, the Balkans, the Indian subcontinent, and parts of Iraq, Syria, and Egypt. The Maliki school quickly disseminated westward, even during the life of Malik himself, to become the dominant school in North and West Africa, and the Iberian Peninsula. The Shafi'is became popular in Egypt, Persia, the Levant and Yemen, and along most of the Indian Ocean coast, as far away as Indonesia and Zanzibar. The Hanbali school remained mostly confined to the Arabian Peninsula, with pockets of scholarly activity in Iberia and the Levant.

It should be noted that the schools of law did not begin and end with their eponymous founders. While Abu Hanifa, Malik, Shafi'i, and Ahmad laid the foundation with regards to the legal theory each school would employ, their followers over the next few hundred years would use that framework to compile exhaustive works of *fiqh* providing rulings for everything from worship and business transactions to government structure and policy. Whenever new issues would arise in the Muslim world that had not been encountered before, such as the arrival of coffee and tobacco in the fifteenth and sixteenth centuries, scholars of *fiqh* would employ the legal theory of the four schools to arrive at rulings for these new situations. It's important, therefore, not to think of the schools of law as static, unchanging doctrines, but as adaptable methodologies that remain dynamic today.

ʿAQIDAH

The realm of Islamic theology was a much more contentious place than that of *fiqh*. Early scholars generally agreed that divergences on legal issues were relatively minor procedural matters, but that if one's belief system deviated from the example set forth by the Prophet, one's entire salvation in the next life could be in jeopardy. Thus, while differences of opinion in legal matters could easily be tolerated as part of the broad field of *fiqh*, differences in belief among Muslims could threaten the existence of Islam as a unified religion.

The first scholars of Islamic theology to address a major issue of this kind were the aforementioned Kharijites (see Chapter 3), in the second half of the seventh century. In their rebellion against ʿAli after his arbitration with Muʿawiya, they had to justify their decision to assassinate their former leader. They did so by arguing that ʿAli had sinned by deferring to a third party, and that major sins necessarily invalidated one's belief in God. In their eyes, this made ʿAli and anyone who agreed with him an apostate worthy of execution. This small band of extremists thus embarked on a campaign of murder and intimidation, hunting down Muslims who disagreed with their approach to theology.

Their problem was that the Kharijite approach fundamentally diverged from the view of most Muslims at that time. They remained a small group, while the majority of scholars of Islamic theology argued that such a blurring of the lines between action and faith had no precedent in Islamic thought. The same Abu Hanifa who founded a school of jurisprudence wrote a short treatise on theology, in which he stated, "we do not charge any believer with unbelief for any sin he commits, even if it is an enormity". He based this on the fact that there was no record of the

Prophet or his Companions having advocated such an approach. Early scholars thus opted to continue in the existing tradition of theology rather than upend the system and adopt Kharijism. While the physical threat the Kharijites posed remained for a few decades after they assassinated 'Ali in 661, their approach never gained a foothold in mainstream Islamic thought.

But just as the Kharijite threat diminished, a new approach arose that sought to re-interpret the theological tradition. Its advocates were known as the Mu'tazila and they proposed an approach to theology that relied heavily on human reason, in an attempt to understand and discuss the nature of God and the unseen. Like other Muslims, they believed in the Quran, the text of which is fairly straightforward regarding God and His attributes. However, whereas previously Muslims had not devoted much time to discussing the nuances of God's attributes as mentioned in the Quran, the Mu'tazila sought to subject those attributes to human reason.

For example, the Quran states that God has a hand. The Mu'tazila argued that such verses must be taken metaphorically, as "hands" are a human attribute and it is entirely unbefitting to apply human attributes to the Divine. The Mu'tazila raised similar contentions regarding God's seeing, hearing, and notably, His speech. They argued that the Quran could not literally be the Word of God, since that would make it co-eternal with Him and only He could be eternal. They viewed Him as so entirely transcendent of humanity that humans are incapable of applying any characteristics to Him, even ones that are specifically mentioned in the Quran. This proved to be a controversial approach, as their well-meaning attempt to portray God as entirely transcendent depended heavily on viewing certain verses of the Quran as metaphorical, a methodology that others considered arbitrary, its natural conclusion possibly resulting in the entire Quran itself becoming devoid of any real meaning.

The Muʿtazila also ruffled feathers (and further demonstrated their reliance on reason) over their beliefs regarding God's divine justice. They reasoned that since God is fair in His judgment over His creation, even He is incapable of forgiving any sinners, since that would necessarily be unfair to sinners who are not forgiven. In their estimation, God was *incapable* of exercising such forgiveness. Naturally, such a position proved to be very controversial, with traditionalist detractors arguing that it was inconsistent with the Islamic imperative to believe in an omnipotent God, and that early Muslims had never made such claims.

Unlike the Kharijites, the Muʿtazila did manage to count some scholars among their ranks and went on to be a formidable intellectual force. However, their most prominent supporter was the caliph al-Maʾmun, who adopted Muʿtazili ideology as state doctrine and embarked on an inquisition to impose it on all religious scholars within the Abbasid Empire. He was most vehemently opposed by Ahmad ibn Hanbal, who resisted attempts to subject Islamic theology to the speculations of the Muʿtazila. To him and his followers, God's attributes were as He said they were in the Quran. Any attempt to subject the understanding of those attributes to human reasoning was futile. Ibn Hanbal was eventually imprisoned by the Abbasids, but through his defiance he became a symbol of resistance to both Muʿtazili theology and government overreach into theological affairs.

While ibn Hanbal's school (often called *Athari*, meaning literalist) ensured the survival of traditionalist approaches towards Islamic theology in the face of Muʿtazilism, the greatest opponents of the Muʿtazili project came from the Ashʿari and Maturidi schools. Abu al-Ḥasan al-Ashʿari (d. 936) and Abu Mansur al-Maturidi (d. 944) provided an alternative to both the Muʿtazili overemphasis on reason and the Hanbali rejection of it. Their schools advocated use of the same type of logical devices as the Muʿtazila employed, but simply to explain the Quran's statements about God and theology, rather than to re-interpret what the Quran said. In short, the Ashʿaris and Maturidis believed that reason had to correspond with revelation, while the Muʿtazila believed that revelation had to correspond with their reason.

As the tenth and eleventh centuries wore on, Muʿtazili ideology diminished in importance. Al-Maʾmun's inquisition did nothing to promote the ideology and was eventually ended by later Abbasid caliphs, and the Muʿtazila themselves split into numerous competing factions, thereby lacking a unified theological approach to advocate. Meanwhile, works by scholars such as the Ashʿari theologian al-Ghazali (d. 1111) and the Maturidi theologian al-Nasafi (d. 1142) offered strong refutations of the Muʿtazili approach that helped diminish its appeal. Despite minor differences among the three schools, often amounting to semantics, the Athari, Ashʿari, and Maturidi schools came to be recognized as the three schools of Sunni Islamic theology. The full name of Sunnism, *Ahl al-Sunnah wal-Jamaʿah*, indicates their emphasis on the traditional approach towards theology, based on the Prophet's teachings (*Sunnah*), and the consensus of the bulk of the Muslim world (*al-Jamaʿah*) on those theological points. These three schools have managed to maintain their canonical status up to the modern day.

SUFISM

The third major category of the Islamic sciences encompasses the science of spirituality, and is oftentimes referred to as *tasawwuf* or *tazkiyah*. As an esoteric science based around an individual's personal relationship with God, it is slightly harder to trace historically than the fields of *fiqh* and *'aqidah*, which deal with very outward manifestations of religion.

Like *fiqh* and *'aqidah*, the science of Sufism developed around major scholars of the early centuries, who sought to base their practice of it on the example of the Prophet and the proscriptions of the Quran. One of the earliest major figures was al-Hasan al-Basri (d. 728), an ascetic from the Iraqi city of Basra who was famous for his renunciation of the world and reliance on God. His contemporary, Rab'ia al-'Adawwiya (d. 801), was another proto-Sufi, whose spirituality became renowned throughout the Muslim world. Her aphorism regarding the role of an individual's love for God—"Oh my Lord, if I worship You, from fear of hell, burn me in hell. If I worship You from hope of Paradise, bar me from its gates. But if I worship You for Yourself alone, grant me then the beauty of Your Face"—became particularly popular as a means of summarizing the spiritual path's emphasis on love of and reliance on God.

As happened with early *fiqh*, the unofficial strands of early Sufi thought eventually crystallized into concrete paths and schools of thought. Various *tariqas* (paths) developed throughout the twelfth to fifteenth centuries around the personalities of certain Sufi leaders such as 'Abd al-Qadir al-Jilani (d. 1166), Mo'inuddin Chisti (d. 1236), Ibn 'Arabi (d. 1240), and Abu al-Hasan al-Shadhili (d. 1258). The paths advocated various methods aimed at purification of the soul, with emphasis falling on traits such as extreme generosity, selflessness, remembrance of God, and humility. Membership in a *tariqa* entailed following the *shaikh* of the path as a teacher who could help *murids* (lit. aspirants) build a closer relationship with God. When a *shaikh* would die, one of his *murīds* would take charge of the *ṭarīqa*, leading the next generation of students. Each *tariqa* thus established a chain of *shaikhs* going back through their eponymous founder to the Prophet himself, through which they claimed legitimacy. This paralleled how schools of *fiqh* and *ʿaqidah* recognized the legitimacy of scholars throughout the centuries based on teacher-student relationships.

The history of Sufism was not without controversy, however. Early Sufis debated whether experiential knowledge of God through spiritual methods meant that one no longer had to follow the letter of the law with regards to *fiqh* and *ʿaqidah*. Perhaps the most notable example of this debate occurred in the early tenth century, when the Sufi mystic al-Hallaj (d. 922) publicly made claims that were interpreted by many to be blasphemous statements regarding God. Despite his insistence that such statements were made only because of his supposed attainment of a high spiritual state, he was condemned to death by the Abbasid government. Interestingly, Hallaj was likely denounced by Junayd al-Baghdadi (d. 910), a prominent contemporary Sufi who advocated a more "sober" approach to the spiritual sciences. As the decades and centuries wore on, Sunni Islam accepted as orthodox Junayd's approach to Sufism, which sought a more balanced relationship among the three fields of the Islamic sciences. Today, most modern Sufi *tariqas* trace their lineage through Junayd.

SHIʿISM

While most of the Muslim world accepted the approaches to *fiqh* and *hadith* taken by its leading scholars, a minority rejected them altogether. Their departure from the mainstream Muslim community was originally political, but over time a religious dimension evolved. The group that believed 'Ali and his descendants had the most right to the caliphate began to develop divergent thoughts on Islamic law and *hadith* that stemmed from the political differences of the early caliphate. This group called themselves *Shi'at 'Ali*, meaning The Party of 'Ali, but is colloquially called the Shi'a.

For the Shi'a, it all stemmed from the election of Abu Bakr as caliph on the day the Prophet died. In the meeting where 'Umar historically nominated Abu Bakr and gave an oath of allegiance to him, 'Ali was absent. While 'Ali himself accepted Abu Bakr's caliphate, later generations of Shi'a began to question its legitimacy. In their eyes, the cousin and son-in-law of the Prophet should have been at that meeting and should have been elected as the first caliph. This led to a belief that Abu Bakr, 'Umar, and all who supported them (excluding 'Ali, of course) were usurpers, who denied the family of the Prophet their rightful role as leaders of the Muslim *Umma*. To the Shi'a, the entire concept of the caliphate was void. Instead, they advocated that the Muslim world should be ruled by a descendant of Muhammad through his daughter Fatimah, who was married to 'Ali. These leaders were dubbed imams. Instead of a caliphate, the Shi'a promoted an imamate in which only descendants of 'Ali had the right to rule. The Shi'a considered 'Ali as the first imam, while his sons Hasan and Husayn were the second and third, respectively.

Even with their belief in an imamate instead of a caliphate, the Shi'a were not yet a separate sect of Islam. The imamate was simply a political concept which did not automatically have any religious implications. In fact, Umayyad and Abbasid caliphs were commonly referred to as imams as well. In order for the Shi'a to be considered a religious group instead of just a political one, their arguments about the first caliphs had to go a step further. That step was the idea that if Abu Bakr and his supporters were usurpers, then any *hadith* narrated by them could not be trusted. This argument carried huge religious implications. People who supported Abu Bakr's caliphate narrated the vast majority of the *hadith* that was accepted by Muslim scholars. The Prophet's wife Aisha and his neighbor Abu Hurairah together accounted for hundreds of the *hadith* listed in *Sahih al-Bukhari*. To the Shi'a these *hadith* could not be trusted because of their political support for Abu Bakr, 'Umar and 'Uthman. To fill the void created by the rejection of thousands of *hadith*, the Shi'a elevated the sayings of the imams to a level just below, or in some cases equal, to the Prophet's sayings. To the rest of the Muslim world, this was blasphemy. But to the Shi'a, the imams, due to their special lineage, were infallible interpreters of religion, given special knowledge directly from God. Much of this ideology seems to have been influenced by the Mu'tazili philosophy. Whereas in orthodox approaches to Islam, the idea of humans with a special semi-divine status was unheard of, the neo-Platonic ideas of some of the major philosophers of the early Abbasid age could help the Shi'a legitimize the imamate from a theological perspective.

The main branch of Shi'ism is known as the *Ithna'ashariyyah*—the Twelvers—due to their belief that there were twelve imams after Muhammad. According to them, the line of imams ended with Imam Muhammad al-Mahdi, who went into hiding when he was just five years old in 874. Thus began the period known as the "Minor Occultation", during which special representatives were able to remain in communication with him and receive guidance for the Shi'a community. In 941, however, it was announced that al-Mahdi had gone into the "Greater Occultation", and further communication with the hidden imam became impossible. The

Shi'a believe that the hidden imam will only return at the end of time to inaugurate a utopian era under his leadership. Until he returns, however, Twelvers insist that guidance can be found in the Quran, the *hadith* compilations that they accept as authentic, and the actions and beliefs of the twelve imams. The Twelvers were not the only Shi'a group to have developed in the turbulent early Abbasid age. Another group believed in only seven imams, and thus came to be known as the *Sab'iyyah*—Seveners. The Seveners were much more successful politically than their Twelver cousins, and the tenth century saw the rise of major Sevener Shi'a states in eastern Arabia and Egypt. The smallest of the Shi'a groups believe in only five imams, and are generally known as the Zaydis, due to their acceptance of Hussein's grandson, Zayd, as the final imam. The Zaydis share much in common with mainstream Islam, and are generally much more moderate in their views on the early caliphate than the Seveners and Twelvers.

Shi'a ideas never caught on in the way their proponents had hoped. Despite intense vigor in preaching and appeals to Muslim emotion by invoking the conflicts of 'Ali and Husayn, the majority of the Muslim world did not accept the theological and juristic deviations of Shi'ism. In fact, for much of the mainstream, majority Muslim body, Shi'a ideology posed a grave danger to Islam itself. After all, since the beginning the Islamic movement had considered itself unique. The Quran described in detail how previous nations who were sent prophets had changed the message and corrupted it to suit their needs, citing Jews and Christians as prime examples. According to Islamic belief, Muhammad had been sent as the final prophet with a pure message that could not be changed or distorted, as previous messages had. When this internal intellectual force began to threaten the sanctity of the

Islamic movement, the reaction was largely negative. Besides political persecution by the Abbasid government, mainstream theologians rushed to refute Shi'a ideology, and dubbed themselves *Ahl us-Sunnah wal-Jama'ah* (literally: the people who follow the example of the Prophet and the consensus of the community), shortened to Sunni. The most influential of these theologians is Abu Hamid al-Ghazali, the same al-Ghazali who spent much time refuting the Mu'tazili arguments of the philosophers. With the combination of intellectual arguments and political-military defeat of Shi'a states in the twelfth century, Shi'ism waned in popularity from the 1100s. It was not until the rise of the Safavid Empire in the early 1500s that Shi'ism would again become a major force in the Muslim world.

7

UPHEAVAL

After the first 300 years of Islamic history, Muslims certainly could have believed that the ultimate triumph of Islam in the world was near. During that time, Islam spread rapidly throughout the Middle East, North Africa and Persia, with Muslim armies knocking on the door of France and India. When the military expansion stopped, the intellectual expansion began and the sciences were pushed into new frontiers never before seen. Even economically the Muslims led the world, as Baghdad became the center of political and economic power, with banks that had branches as far away as China. Clearly it would seem that Islam was destined to spread to every corner of the earth through armies, books and coins.

Yet that destiny was not to be. The year 900 marks the beginning of a turbulent few hundred years for the Muslim world that would not truly end until the golden age of the Ottoman Empire in the 1500s. From the tenth to the thirteenth centuries, the Muslim world was under almost constant attack. The Shi'a, European Crusaders and Mongol hordes combined to reign terror upon the Islamic heartland, leading some to believe in the 1200s that the end of time was near, not because of the triumph of Islam, but because of its destruction.

ISMA'ILISM

Since its development, Shi'ism has based itself around the idea of an alternative to the mainstream Sunni caliphate. Leadership of the Muslim world belonged to the imams who had a special connection to God, they argued, not to any layperson who happens to belong to the Umayyad or Abbasid dynasties. When Shi'ism itself was divided into numerous sects, differing ideas about how to bring about the Imamate developed. The Twelvers, the largest group, seem to have preferred political inaction. In their view, since the Twelfth Imam went missing, no legitimate Muslim government could exist without him. For them, it was a patient waiting game until he returned to inaugurate a utopian civilization at the end of time.

For the Seveners, however, such complacency would not do. They believed the Seventh Imam, Isma'il, had gone into hiding to avoid being caught by Abbasid authorities sometime in the mid-700s. Unlike the Twelvers, who believed no more imams would come until the return of the last one, the Seveners believed Isma'il's descendants continued to live in hiding among the mainstream Muslim population. Thus they are more commonly referred to as Isma'ilis. The truth about Isma'il's life and even whether or not he ever existed is lost somewhere in the realm of history and mythology. What is clear is that soon after his disappearance (or death), missionaries began to travel throughout the Middle East and North Africa trying to build support for the Isma'ili Imamate. The Abbasids, who had come to power themselves through secret support networks, did everything they could to eradicate the threat the Isma'ilis posed. This only served to push the Isma'ili movement further underground and away from Abbasid reach. The Isma'ili missionaries spread throughout the major cities of the Muslim world, and seem to have gathered support not based on their revolutionary ideas, but on any discontent people may have had with Abbasid authority. They were especially popular among the lower classes, non-Arabs who resented Arab rule, and the traditional Bedouins who had always hated central authority.

After decades of missionary work, the Isma'ilis were ready to strike the first major blow against Sunni power right around the year 900. The Isma'ili missionaries had managed to rouse up the Bedouin tribes of the eastern Arabian Peninsula to become a real threat to the Abbasids. Known as the *Qaramita* (the Qarmatians), this group of Isma'ilis struck unexpectedly into Syria in 903, when they captured Damascus and defeated an Abbasid army sent to conquer them. Their control of Syria was short-lived however, and they were forced back into the Arabian Desert just two years later. From 905, onwards, the Qarmatians took to a new approach to bringing about an Isma'ili revolution. Instead of seeking to conquer land and establish a new government, they resorted to terrorizing the Abbasids from their base in Bahrain in order to achieve their political goals. In 906, they massacred 20,000 people travelling to Mecca for the pilgrimage. In the mid-920s, the Iraqi cities of Basra and Kufa were sacked by the Qarmatians, and even Baghdad itself came close to being captured by Bedouin raiders. Their sacrilegious attacks reached a peak in 928 when the Qarmatians attacked Mecca, massacred its population, and stole the Black Stone from the Ka'ba moving it to Bahrain, where it would remain until 952.

Religiously, the Qarmatians were extremists who incorporated fanatical apocalyptic ideas as well as pre-Islamic religious beliefs into their worldview. Visitors to Bahrain relate that in the Qarmatian domain, one could not find mosques or even people praying. The Qarmatians rejected Mecca as a holy site and the pilgrimage as anti-Islamic, thus leading to their attacks on pilgrims and the city of Mecca. It is no surprise that traditionally Islamic orthodoxy has not even considered the Qarmatians as Muslim. The differences in belief and action between the Qarmatians and mainstream Islam is great, to say the least. But despite their reign of terror, the Qarmatians never became a real threat to the established order. Their methods were too extreme to be accepted by the Muslim world and their beliefs too unorthodox. The real threat to Sunni Islam instead came from the Maghreb, where another Isma'ili movement rose on the backs of the Berbers to become a regional power.

THE FATIMIDS

Isma'ili missionaries were relatively successful in North Africa, where they could exploit traditional tensions between the Berbers of the Sahara and the Arabs of the coastal cities to their advantage. Throughout the late 800s, Isma'ili missionaries built up support among the Sanhaja Berbers, leading to the violent overthrow of the ruling Sunni dynasties of North Africa, the Rustamids and the Aghlabids, by 908. In 909, this group of Isma'ilis declared the reappearance of an imam descended from Isma'il. He was 'Ubayd Allah, but he took the honorific title al-Mahdi, meaning the guided one, or savior. 'Ubayd Allah's origins are obscure. He claimed descent from Isma'il, and thus also from 'Ali and his wife Fatima, leading to the name of the dynasty he inaugurated: the Fatimids.

The Fatimids would not be content with being a thorn in the side of the Sunni world like the Qarmatians. They believed it was their duty to entirely take it over and establish Isma'ili rule through

'Ubayd Allah. He was thus declared caliph in 909, directly challenging the Abbasids for authority over the Muslim world. Although the Fatimids were not the first ones to declare their opposition to the Abbasids, they soon became the most dangerous. From their base in modern Tunisia, they fanned out quickly, conquering Sicily, moving eastward towards Egypt, and bringing western North Africa under their control by the 920s. After the death of 'Ubayd Allah in 934, the Fatimids slowed their military expansion. Numerous rebellions arose led by Muslims discontent with the unorthodox Isma'ilis and their views for a Sunni-free world. Even the *Kharijis* of North Africa rebelled against Fatimid authority. The rebellions failed to bring an end to the Fatimids, although they slowed the Isma'ili advance through the rest of the Muslim world for a few decades. But Sunni disunity proved to be too big of a handicap to permanently stop the growth of the Fatimid realm.

In 929, the Umayyad ruler of Iberia declared the establishment of a new caliphate based in Cordoba to combat the Fatimids in North Africa. In the 900s, there were thus three dynasties claiming the caliphate: the Abbasids, the Fatimids, and the Umayyads.

By the mid-tenth century, the Abbasid caliphate became essentially powerless. Throughout the ninth and tenth centuries, political decentralization coupled with the rise of hereditary governorships led by slave soldiers brought in from Turkic lands, led to the decline of the caliph's power. In 945, the Persian dynasty conquered Iraq and ruled in the caliph's name. Egypt, once an economic and agricultural center of the caliphate, was under an independent Turkish dynasty known as the Ikhshidids that was constantly quarrelling with an Arab state based in northern Syria. To say the Muslim world between Egypt and Persia was disunited is an understatement. Constant warfare among Muslims and a renewed Byzantine threat from the north gave the Fatimids an opportunity to invade Egypt in 969. The Fatimids led an army of around 100,000 soldiers against the Ikhshidids of Egypt, who were quickly defeated. Sunni governance in Egypt collapsed in the face of the marauding Fatimid armies. The victorious Fatimids established a new city, *al-Qahira* (Cairo), along the banks of the Nile as their capital. No longer a desert nuisance, the Fatimids were now the most powerful state in the Muslim world. With chaos reigning in Syria, Iraq, and Persia, it seemed conceivable that the Fatimids would continue their eastward march into Baghdad, overthrow the caliphate, and establish themselves as rulers of the entire Muslim world. This was not to be, however, as the Fatimids soon had to deal with Byzantine threats to Syria and, ironically, attack from their coreligionists, the Qarmatians of Bahrain, who considered the Fatimids not extreme enough in their Isma'ili beliefs. The capital of the caliphate thus escaped conquest by the unorthodox Fatimids and the Sunni world had time to recover and build strong political and military institutions under the Seljuk Turks in the eleventh century.

The Fatimids thus had to make do with North Africa, Egypt, the holy cities of Mecca and Medina, and parts of Syria and Palestine. Their revolutionary zeal continued, with their desire to turn their domain into a purely Isma'ili Shi'a land. Al-Azhar University was established in Cairo in 970 in an effort to spread Isma'ili beliefs among the mainly Sunni population of Egypt. Sunni Muslims, Christians, and Jews underwent periods of intense persecution as well as periods of relative freedom under the Fatimids, based on the whims of whichever caliph was in charge. One of the most interesting attempts to bring Isma'ilism to the masses was from 996 to 1021 during the reign of the Fatimid caliph al-Hakim, infamously known as "The Mad Caliph". Like all Fatimid rulers, he was hailed as a divinely chosen and holy leader by Isma'ilis, but by almost all others, he was hated as a tyrant, ruling based on whims and desire. Christians and Jews suffered as he ordered the destruction of churches and synagogues throughout his domain, including the Church of the Holy Sepulchre in Jerusalem, where Christians believe Jesus was buried and resurrected. Assurances for the safety of the church made by 'Umar in 637 were ignored and the site was entirely demolished in 1009. Christians were not the only ones oppressed by al-Hakim. Muslims were banned from performing communal prayers according to the norms of Sunni Islam, and the Fatimid caliph's name was inserted into Friday prayers, giving them an Isma'ili leaning. Sunnis were banned from entering the holy city of Jerusalem, along with Christians and Jews. Al-Hakim's irrationally oppressive laws were not restricted to religion. On a whim, all the dogs of a village near his palace in Cairo were killed because their barking annoyed the caliph. He decreed all business must be conducted at night. Chess was banned, presumably because he was not good at it, and the consumption of *mulukhiya* (Corchorus leaves)—a staple Egyptian food—was outlawed. He even placed the great Muslim physicist Ibn al-Haytham under house arrest because he failed to build a dam across the Nile. To the relief of many of his subjects, the reign of The Mad Caliph ended one night in 1021, when he ventured out into the desert alone, and mysteriously disappeared.

Al-Hakim's time in power was unique for its brutality and oppression. Society under the Fatimids cannot be easily generalized as either tolerant or oppressive. The Fatimids suffered from a lack of concrete legal guidelines that dictated governance, society and relations with non-Muslims. In contrast to the Abbasids and other Sunni dynasties, which were (at least officially) bound by Islamic laws, the Fatimid caliphs, as semi-divine beings, were allowed to exercise a much more personal form of authority. Thus each new caliph could radically change the character and direction of the empire, sometimes with disastrous results. Without a strong legal and intellectual basis, the Fatimids and their faith never became particularly attractive to their subjects, and Ismailism was relegated to the political elite as the population of Egypt, Syria and North Africa remained staunchly Sunni Muslim. Without widespread support, and hampered by radical changes in policy during each succession, the Fatimids slowly declined in power through the eleventh and twelfth centuries. They were finally eliminated by Salah al-Din during the Crusades, another conflict which wreaked havoc on the Muslim world.

THE CRUSADES

Perhaps no other conflict in Western and Islamic history has been as emotionally charged as the Crusades. The entire conflict itself was based around the city of Jerusalem, holy to Jews, Christians and Muslims alike. For Christians, it is the city where Jesus preached, was crucified and resurrected. For Muslims, its holiness stems from the belief that Muhammad miraculously travelled from Mecca to Jerusalem in one night and then from Jerusalem to Heaven to speak to God. During the Crusades, the memories of these events were evoked thousands of times by kings, sultans, generals, priests and imams to rally the faithful on both sides to stake their claim to the holy city. Starting in 1095, 200 years of conflict commenced that would fundamentally reshape Christian Europe as well as the Muslim world for good.

The impetus for the Crusades began far from Jerusalem in Central Asia. Here, the Turks had lived for thousands of years as a tribal, nomadic people who were feared for their battle toughness. The Abbasids put the Turkic expertise in warfare to good use by recruiting generals from Central Asia to serve in their militaries as early as the ninth century. Mass migrations of Turks soon followed as tribes moved out of Central Asia and into the Islamic world. As they migrated, the Turkic tribes adopted Islam and began to set up their own states in the political chaos of the tenth century. The greatest of these was the Great Seljuk Empire, established in 1037. The Seljuks built a stable state that stretched from Syria to Central Asia. The era of Abbasid power was by this point nothing more than a memory, but the Seljuks assumed a role as protectors of the caliphs, who remained entrenched in their palaces in Baghdad. As staunchly Sunni Muslims, the Seljuks even managed to provide a counterweight to the heretical Fatimids and helped prevent Fatimid expansion in the eleventh century.

The Seljuks established the Nizamiyyah School in Baghdad in the late eleventh century. It was the largest university of the Middle Ages and charged no tuition.

In 1071, the Seljuks won an important battle against the Byzantine Empire in eastern Anatolia. The Battle of Manzikert effectively ended the ability of the Byzantines to hold onto Anatolia as a complete unit. In the years following the battle, the Seljuks gradually expanded westward throughout the peninsula, until they began to appear on the shores opposite Constantinople, threatening to expand Turkic Muslim power into the imperial city and beyond. In 1095, the Byzantine Emperor Alexios realized the Byzantine could not battle the Turks alone. Despite a rivalry between the Eastern and Western halves of Christianity that spanned centuries, Alexios wagered that Christian unity was the only thing that could prevent the fall of the Byzantine Empire. He sent an urgent appeal to Pope Urban II in Rome for assistance, perhaps hoping for an expeditionary force that could help him turn the tide and regain the lands lost since Manzikert. Urban took the opportunity to rally a pan-European Christian army in the name of Christ that numbered in the tens of thousands. But he had no intention of helping Alexios, or even fighting the Turks. Urban's Crusade set its sights on Jerusalem. Decrying the fact that Jerusalem had been in Muslim hands since 'Umar's caliphate, Urban called on all Christians to support an expedition to conquer the city and establish a Latin Christian kingdom in Palestine, under the authority of the Papacy.

Urban's army was slow to mobilize. It was not until 1096 and 1097 that armies led by nobles and knights began marching towards Eastern Europe from modern-day France, Germany and Italy. Along the way, European Jews were massacred in huge numbers due to the religious zeal stoked by the Church. The First Crusade was so fearsome that when it arrived at the walls of Constantinople, Emperor Alexios refused to allow them entry into the city, for fear that they would plunder it as they did with dozens of cities and towns along the way. The 30,000-strong army crossed the Bosphorus and began a long march through Anatolia that the newly-established Turks were unable to resist. In late 1097, the

Crusaders reached Antioch, a well-defended, major city that today lies near the border of Turkey and Syria. This was to be the first test of the Crusades. If the Christians were successful here, they could expect to continue their march towards Jerusalem. If they failed, it could be harder to recruit future armies to venture far into the Muslim world to conquer Jerusalem.

The Siege of Antioch reveals much about the political situation of the Middle East late in the eleventh century. The city was incredibly well-defended, and posed a considerable challenge to the invaders. But politically, the city was an island. The Great Seljuk Empire had disintegrated in the years leading up to the Crusades. No longer was it one united political entity. Instead, petty Turkic emirs administered individual cities, and seemed to be constantly quarrelling. The major cities of Syria: Damascus, Aleppo, Antioch and Mosul were all disunited, and their emirs had all been in perpetual war throughout the 1090s. When the ruler of Antioch, Yaghi-Siyan, asked for help from his Turkic brethren against the Crusaders that surrounded his city, he received no response. The other emirs were probably happy to see their rival being attacked, as his demise would mean their increased power and influence. As such, Antioch received no help from the surrounding Muslim cities. Furthermore, an armor maker that was in charge of the defense of a section of the city's walls ended up allowing the Crusaders entry into the city because of a personal feud he had with the emir.

Once the Crusaders captured the city, its population was put to the sword. The massacre of Antioch and other cities along the way to Jerusalem (along with at least one incident of cannibalism) instilled terror in the surrounding areas. Muslim emirs were keen to avoid conflict with the Crusaders, and once they realized the target was Jerusalem, many decided to support the Crusaders with food, arms and safe passage rather than to fight them. By the summer of 1099, the Crusaders finally reached the walls of Jerusalem.

Jerusalem was in no position to defend itself. In the years before, it had gone back and forth between Fatimid and Seljuk control, and its defenses were in shambles. Furthermore, the Fatimids were slow to recognize the threat the Crusaders posed to Jerusalem, and there was nothing more than a token garrison in the city, certainly not enough to withstand a siege against tens of thousands. The Fatimids mobilized an army in Egypt to go defend the city. But by the time they reached Palestine, it was too late. On 15 July 1099, after a siege lasting only a week, the Crusaders managed to push into the city and take it from the Muslims. For the first time since 'Umar entered the city 462 years before, Jerusalem came under Christian control.

"In the Temple and porch of Solomon [the al-Aqsa Mosque] men rode in blood up to their knees and bridle reins."

– Raymond D'Aguilers, a Crusader, referring to the Conquest of Jerusalem in 1099

For the Islamic world, the conquest of Jerusalem was a disaster. Its entire civilian population, over 70,000 people, was massacred. In the al-Aqsa Mosque, where Muslims believe Muhammad led all previous prophets in prayer, the blood of Muslim civilians was up to the shins of the conquerors. Mosques and synagogues throughout the city were destroyed. Even Christians suffered as the Crusaders sought to impose their own Catholic version of Christianity instead of the traditional Greek, Georgian, Armenian, and other churches that had operated in the city. The news of the loss of Islam's third-holiest city was a shock to Muslims around the world. Expressions of anger and vengeance raged in Cairo and Baghdad. Yet the expected unified Muslim front in the face of Crusader atrocities never came. The Fatimids were defeated in battle on the coast of Palestine and, after that, they did not make much of an effort to liberate the city. Court intrigue and ineffective leaders rendered the Fatimids entirely incapable of dealing with the Crusaders. Meanwhile, the Abbasid caliphate was still powerless and the Turkic emirs in Syria, Iraq, and Persia remained in a state of constant civil war. With the Muslim world preoccupied, the Crusaders consolidated their position along the coast of Palestine and Syria. More cities (including the ones that had earlier aided the Crusaders in their march to Jerusalem) were conquered, and within a few years, four Crusader kingdoms ruled the Mediterranean coast.

In the new Middle East of the early 1100s, East and West began to mix in the Holy Land for the first time since the arrival of Islam. The Frankish knights who conquered the region began to establish European-style feudal societies, like the ones in Medieval Europe. While the Crusader armies had depopulated the city, the surrounding villages were mostly left unharmed and were simply made property of European knights. The Crusades did not usher in new demographics to the Muslim world. No mass migration of European peasants came into the Holy Land. Rather, the existing Arab Muslim demographic was incorporated into a European-style feudal society. This became one of the entry-points for Muslim knowledge in Europe, as more enlightened Crusaders took home knowledge of the sciences and philosophy that they were exposed to in the Levant.

Economically, the Crusades marked the beginning of new ties between the East and West. The most enterprising sailors of Medieval Europe were the Italian city-states. As the first Crusaders marched down the shore of Syria in the late 1090s towards Jerusalem, Italian merchant ships shadowed them in the Mediterranean. Once the Crusader kingdoms were established and consolidated, Italian states such as Genoa and Venice regularly sent fleets of merchants to the Holy Land. Trade in goods that were once distant and unreachable now became commonplace. The result was a huge influx of wealth into the Italian peninsula and the hands of the leading trading families of the major city-states. That wealth, coupled with knowledge gained from translations of Muslim scholarly works, would later help fuel the Renaissance starting in the fourteenth century. Furthermore, the wealth and power gained by the city-states made them formidable opponents to the Ottoman Empire in the fifteenth and sixteenth centuries.

Politically and militarily, not much progress was made against the Crusaders in the decades after their capture of Jerusalem in 1099. The Muslim world was far too weak and fractured to mount much resistance. When the challenge to the Crusaders finally appeared in the mid-1100s, it was not from the traditional centers of power in Baghdad, Damascus or Cairo. Instead, it came from a Turkish emir, 'Imad al-Din Zengi, who ruled over the city of Mosul in northern Iraq. A resilient and somewhat harsh leader, he managed to unite Mosul and Aleppo into one state. With the combined power of two of the largest cities in the region, his army conquered the County of Edessa, the northernmost Crusader state in 1144. At the time, the conquest of Edessa did not mean much politically. It was by far the weakest Crusader state and its loss did not affect the other three much, but looking back, 1144 was when the tide began to turn against the Crusaders and in favor of the Muslims.

Zengi had hoped to forge a united Syria in the face of the Crusader threat by bringing Damascus under his control, but the former imperial city remained out of his grasp. Petty warfare among Turkish emirs was not over yet, and the emir of Damascus could not stand to give up his domain, even in the name of Muslim unity. When 'Imad al-Din Zengi died in 1146, his son Nur al-Din Zengi picked up the struggle to unify the Middle East. The younger Zengi managed to conquer most of the territory around Antioch in 1149, and in 1154, he overthrew the emir of Damascus with the help of the local population who had grown sick of Damascus's alliance with the Crusader states. With Syria unified under the Zengid dynasty, it would seem that the liberation of Jerusalem and the rest of the occupied land was on the horizon. But a bizarre and unexpected series of events brought Nur al-Din's attention to Egypt and the declining Fatimid Empire.

With Syria unified and stronger than it had been since the demise of the Great Seljuk Empire, the Crusaders had to look south if they wanted to expand their realm. That meant invading into the ancient and fertile land of Egypt. In 1163, the king of Jerusalem led an invasion of Fatimid Egypt under the pretext of Fatimid refusal to pay tribute. To counter this invasion, the Fatimid grand vizier, Shawar, who had been overthrown by rival court forces just before the invasion, appealed to Nur al-Din Zengi for military aid, lest the Crusaders manage to conquer Egypt. Despite misgivings about the expedition, Zengi sent an army to Egypt in the name of Muslim unity to fight the Crusaders and reinstate Shawar in 1164. After successfully defeating the Crusaders, Shawar was again made grand vizier, and it seemed an alliance between Shi'a Egypt and Sunni Syria would soon crush the Kingdom of Jerusalem between them. But as soon as Shawar regained power he changed sides, signing an alliance with the same Crusaders he had just fought against in an attempt to dislodge the Zengid army from Egypt. Zengi's army was forced to retreat to Syria and a combined Fatimid-Crusader force held Egypt. Just four years later, however, the Crusaders again invaded Egypt, hoping to annex the area once and for all. Once again, Nur al-Din was called upon in the name of Sunni-Shi'a unity to protect Egypt. And once again, the Zengid army arrived along the banks of the River Nile. This time, however, Zengi's army was not to be crossed by Shawar again. This military expedition defeated the Crusader army, and then Shawar, who was executed for his repeated treachery. The Fatimid Empire itself was not officially abolished, although it was brought under Zengid suzerainty, with Zengi's top general, Shirkuh, being appointed vizier in Shawar's place. After just two months as vizier, however, Shirkuh died of intestinal illness, and control of Egypt fell to his nephew, a young man with the given name Yusuf, but whom history knows as Salah al-Din (Saladin).

LIBERATION OF JERUSALEM

Salah al-Din seems to have been relatively disinterested in politics and warfare. Raised in Damascus, he studied traditional Islamic sciences under some of the greatest scholars of his era. He was staunchly Sunni, following the Shafi'i school of *fiqh* and the Ash'ari school of theology. It even seems he was more interested in a life of scholarship and religious studies than government, but his uncle's insistence that he accompany the Egyptian expedition altered the destiny of the young Salah al-Din. When he inherited his uncle's position as vizier of Egypt in 1169, his religious leanings greatly influenced his policies. The heterodox Fatimid Empire, which had been a thorn in Sunni Islam's side for centuries, was officially abolished on Salah al-Din's orders. The al-Azhar University, once a bastion of Isma'ili propaganda was converted into a traditional Sunni school, and it remains so today. The general population of Egypt, which had never fully embraced Shi'ism, welcomed Salah al-Din's reforms, and a closer relationship with Syria.

But one person who did not welcome the growing influence and power of Salah al-Din was Nur al-Din, his nominal master in Syria. Nur al-Din feared the growing influence of his governor of Egypt, and tension between the two was clearly very high. Many in Egypt and Syria believed war between Zengi and Salah al-Din was inevitable. However, the two never fought. Zengi died in 1174 from disease, and Salah al-Din was able to march into Syria unopposed and with broad public support. He was now his own sovereign, with Egypt and Syria—united for the first time since the Fatimid uprising—under his authority. The Crusader Kingdom of Jerusalem was now surrounded by a powerful, united Muslim state under a ruler who believed it was his religious duty to liberate the city of Jerusalem. Further compounding their problems, unity among the Crusaders was at an all-time low. Organizations such as the Knights Templar and the Knights Hospitaller regularly undermined the authority of the Kingdom of Jerusalem. In the 1170s and 1180s, the Muslim world was united while the Crusaders were quarrelling among themselves. It was the exact opposite of the situation in 1099.

Nonetheless, Salah al-Din was not eager to go to war; he signed peace treaties with the Kingdom of Jerusalem while he secured his domain from external and internal threats. His biggest problem was probably a secretive cult known as the Hashashin (their name was corrupted to Assassins in the West), an extremist group of Isma'ilis who believed the Fatimids had failed to bring a promised Shi'a revolution. Instead, they resorted to political assassinations and terrorism to bring the Sunni world to heel. Salah al-Din never managed to fully eliminate the Hashashin threat, but his conflict with them preoccupied him politically and led to at least two assassination attempts by Hashashin agents. Salah al-Din was forced to bring his focus back to the Crusaders in the mid-1180s, after repeated provocations by a hawkish knight, Reynald de Chatillon, who had broken numerous peace treaties, massacred a Muslim pilgrimage caravan, and even attempted to attack Mecca itself. The Kingdom of Jerusalem became involved in the conflict, leading to the final confrontation between the united Muslim forces of Salah al-Din and the Kingdom of Jerusalem.

At the Battle of Hattin in 1187, Salah al-Din's army completely routed the Crusader army of Jerusalem. Only a few knights were left in the holy city, which capitulated to Salah al-Din in October of that year. Eighty-eight years earlier, Crusaders had stormed into the city, massacring its population and subjecting its religious sites to Christian domination. Salah al-Din, keen to follow in the footsteps of the caliph 'Umar who had first conquered the city in 637, did not cleanse the Crusader occupation with another massacre. All the occupants of the city were given safe passage to Christian lands, and were allowed to take their belongings with them. Christian sites in the city were protected and pilgrimage to them allowed. Salah al-Din's noble behavior was not lost on the defeated Christians. Legends of his chivalry soon spread throughout Europe, and subsequent conflicts fought between Salah al-Din and Crusader kings, notably Richard the Lionheart, are filled with stories of mutual respect between Muslims and Christians.

Salah al-Din's domain evolved into the Ayyubid Dynasty after his death. His descendants continued to control Syria and Egypt for decades, even as more Crusader armies arrived at their shores to attempt to regain Jerusalem. The Crusades stretched on for over a hundred more years after the liberation of Jerusalem, but they never again became a major threat to the Muslim world or its control over the Holy Land. Instead, a new threat was brewing that would trump the Crusades in size and scope. Just twenty years after Salah al-Din's liberation of Jerusalem, a warlord known as Genghis Khan managed to unite the various Mongol tribes north of China into one state with a goal of constant military expansion. Although he was 5,000 kilometers away from the heart of the Muslim world, the expansion inaugurated by Genghis Khan would soon threaten the entire existence of Islam as a political force.

THE MONGOLS

Ironically, the Mongol invasion occurred when the Muslim world seemed primed for a comeback. The Fatimids were no more, and radical Shi'a revolutionaries only existed in small pockets throughout Persia and Syria. The Crusaders still held some coastal territory in Syria and Palestine, but were not a great threat to the sanctity of Muslim lands. The Byzantines still were incapable of recouping their losses from Manzikert, and were dealing with problems caused by Crusaders who seemed more intent on fighting fellow Christians in Constantinople than Muslims in Jerusalem.

Yet the stability of the early 1200s was short lived. Genghis Khan and the Mongols had gone from a tribal nuisance north of the Great Wall of China to a major world empire in a matter of a few years. Within ten years of coming to power, the nomadic Mongols managed to conquer and hold the entire northern half of China. Genghis Khan's attention then turned westward, where the Kara-Khitan Khanate of Central Asia stood in the way of Mongol domination of Asia. Central Asia's plains were similar to the landscape the Mongols hailed from, and the conquest of this vast region was quick and severe. By 1219, Genghis Khan ruled a land empire that stretched from Korea to the borders of the Muslim world in Persia.

The sudden explosion of the Mongols in the early 1200s is one of the most remarkable examples of military expansion in world history. The Mongols were nomadic horsemen who had not even mastered agriculture, but built a world empire that stretched from Central Europe to Korea to the borders of India. It was their nature as nomadic horsemen that made them capable of such conquests. The Mongols practically lived on horseback, and thus long distances and roadless terrain that deterred conventional armies were no barrier at all. In addition to their impressive speed, the Mongols employed a deliberate campaign aimed at instilling great terror in the hearts of their enemies, to the extent that they would voluntarily lay down arms rather than defend their homelands. When the Mongols arrived at an enemy city, the defending garrison was given three options. The first option was to avoid fighting, capitulate to the Mongols and join the Mongol army in their continued campaign of conquest. The second option was resistance: if the city resisted the Mongols and lost (as most cities did), its entire garrison would be put to the sword and the city looted. The third option involved mass resistance to the Mongols, by both the city's armed garrison and civilians. If that occurred, the Mongols promised to kill every single soul inside the city, a fate that numerous towns and cities across Asia faced. With such tactics, it is no surprise that the Mongols were able to snowball through Asia, creating the world's largest empire. Stories of Mongol atrocities preceded the hordes of warriors pouring out of Central Asia. From Iraq to China, those in the way of Mongol expansion commonly chose subservience to Mongol overlords rather than face the wrath of the Khan.

The Muslim state that touched the borders of the Mongol Empire was the Khwarezmian Empire. This empire picked up many of the pieces left by the demise of the Seljuk Empire, uniting most of Persia under the rule of Shah Muhammad (r. 1200–1220), a man with Turkic ancestry but raised in Persian court culture. During his reign, the Abbasid caliphs, who had been essentially powerless since the mid-tenth century, began to exert more direct authority. The caliph al-Nasir was the first Abbasid to lead an army out of Baghdad in centuries, as he consolidated most of Iraq and parts of Persia under his rule. Shah Muhammad was not ready to accept a caliphate with real sovereignty just as he was expanding his own power throughout the Muslim world. Naturally, this meant conflict between the caliph's young state and the Khwarezmian Empire of Muhammad. Perhaps it was because of this conflict, or perhaps it was Muhammad's over-reliance on overworked slave soldiers, but the Khwarezmians were not prepared when Genghis Khan and his fearsome warriors arrived on the Muslim frontier in 1219.

The Khwarezmians, however, decided to pick a fight with the Mongols. When merchants from the Mongol Empire entered the Khwarezmian domain, they were put to death as spies. Needless to say, Genghis Khan was less than pleased with this development, especially since he seems to have desired peaceful relations with the Muslim state. He swore vengeance, and the next year Mongol armies arrived in Muslim lands for the first time, beginning a period of destruction for Muslim civilization in Persia, Iraq and Syria. The Mongols combined their superior fighting ability with siege engines brought in from China to quickly conquer the major cities of eastern Persia. Bukhara, the city forever associated with the great *hadith* compilation of al-Bukhari, was completely destroyed. Ancient Balkh came to a similar fate, and its library of thousands of manuscripts was dumped into the Oxus River. The Mongol drive had no use for books or the academic achievements of Muslim civilization. They were nomadic warriors, and their only business was conquest and pillage. As they pushed into modern-day Iran and Afghanistan, some of the major urban centers were reduced to nothingness. Muslim historians of the era claim the Mongols massacred 1.7 million people in Nishapur and over 2 million people in Herat. These numbers may or may not be accurate, but what is clear is that the Mongols rained death and destruction wherever they went. Islamic civilization that had taken 600 years to build was being erased in a matter of weeks. The Khwarezmian Empire was essentially destroyed by 1222 after a short but destructive conflict. Genghis Khan chose not to continue into the heart of the Muslim world; he retired back to Mongolia where he died in 1225.

After the death of Genghis Khan, the Muslim world experienced a welcome reprieve from Mongol attacks. The new Khan, Genghis's son Ogedai, chose to focus on crossing the Ural Mountains and conquering Europe. The Mongols did this with incredible efficiency, as always, and, in 1237, led their armies across modern-day Russia and into Hungary and Germany. Christian monarchs across Europe were terrified at the prospect of these heathen Mongols decimating their land as they did to the Khwarezmian domain. Yet just as the Mongol incursion into Muslim lands ended abruptly, the Mongols abandoned their campaigns in Europe in 1241 when Ogedai died. At this point, Christian Europe was still very much enchanted with the idea of Crusading into the Holy Land and reconquering Jerusalem. The Ayyubids, however, still had the requisite power and ability to resist attempts on the Holy City. If Christian Europe wanted to re-establish itself in Palestine, it needed help. Luckily for them, an alliance with the Mongols became more of a possibility as Nestorian Christianity slowly crept into the upper echelons of the Mongol Empire, especially since many of Genghis's descendants had married Christian women. After repeated embassies sent by European monarchs requesting a Mongol invasion into Muslim lands, the Mongols finally mobilized an army with the aim of completely obliterating Islamic political power in 1255.

"Truly the Day of Judgment has been held in Baghdad ... The family of the Prophet and the household of learning have been taken captive, and whom, think you, after their loss, will cities contain?"

– Isma'il ibn Abil-Yusr, a contemporary poet

The leader of this Mongol army was Hulagu, a man whose stance against Islam was clearly influenced by his Christian and Buddhist advisors. The army was probably the largest the Mongols ever fielded, over 100,000 strong. Troops from Christian Armenia and the remaining Crusader states also joined in. The

Muslim world was ill-prepared for such an onslaught. The Khwarezmian Empire was dispersed and greatly weakened by the initial Mongol invasion thirty years before. The Abbasid caliphate barely controlled Iraq and was in constant struggle with the Hashashin sect for power. Meanwhile, the Ayyubid Dynasty of Salah al-Din's descendants was overthrown in 1250 by its own slave soldiers, known as Mamluks, who established the Mamluk Sultanate in Egypt. Once again, a disunited and weak Muslim world faced an invasion from a foreign land and, once again, disaster would ensue.

In 922, the Muslim traveler and jurist Ibn Fadlan wrote the earliest existing record of the Vikings.

The Mongols swept into Persia, where they made an overwhelming assault on the Hashashin. Their stronghold of Alamut, which had for so long eluded conquest by Sunnis, was destroyed by Hulagu in 1256. Before Sunnis could cheer the final downfall of the Hashashin, however, Hulagu set his sights on Baghdad, which had been the capital of the caliphate since 750. The caliph al-Musta'sim refused to surrender and accept Mongol authority. Never before in Islamic history had the caliphate itself fallen, or had the capital been taken. Even in the face of Fatimid and Crusader invasion, circumstances had always worked out in a way that the spiritual leadership of the Muslim world was spared. Perhaps this history had caused al-Musta'sim and others in Baghdad to hope that something similar would happen when the Mongols came in 1258. This time, however, no miraculous victory came.

No great alliance of Muslim states was forged to defend the caliphate, and no amount of individual bravery in the face of Mongol aggression could save the city. After a siege of just a week, Hulagu's army captured the capital of the caliphate on 10 February 1258.

The conquest of Baghdad was one of the most devastating events in Islamic history. The usual Mongol massacre soon followed the city's fall. Its entire Muslim population, with estimates ranging from 200,000 to 1 million, was killed. Only the city's Christian community was spared. The ancient House of Wisdom that was established by al-Ma'mun to push scientific learning to new frontiers was razed to the ground. Its books were dumped into the Tigris River, the ink from hundreds of years of scholarship turning the river black. Thousands of works on math, science, geography, history, theology and jurisprudence were lost forever. Such was this loss that today we only have a fraction of the works of the great scientists of the Golden Age such as Ibn al-Haytham, al-Biruni and Ibn Sina. What other discoveries they may have had that we are unaware of bled into the Tigris, never to be read again. As hundreds of years of knowledge was being destroyed, the caliph himself was taken by Hulagu, wrapped in one of his luxurious carpets, and trampled to death by Mongol horsemen. The Abbasid caliphate would have ceased to exist had another member of the Abbasid family not been installed in Cairo as caliph soon after the massacre. The Abbasid caliphate in Egypt lasted until 1517 under Mamluk authority, but the caliphs were nothing more than figureheads who never again held real power. The destruction of Baghdad was more than the conquest of a city. It was the end of a political, scientific and religious center that the Muslim world at that time never could have conceived of.

The Mongols of course had no intention of stopping at Bagh-dad. Hulagu continued his advance into Syria. Aleppo and Damascus were taken, much to the delight of Christians in the region, especially the Crusaders. A Christian mass was held in the Umayyad Mosque of Damascus, once the largest and grandest mosque in the world. It would seem that nothing was going to stop the Mongols from moving south into Egypt, destroying Islamic civilization there, and effectively erasing Islam from the world just as fast as it rose 600 years before. But that was not to be. The young Mamluk Sultanate halted the Mongol advance in 1260 in northern Palestine. Sultan Baybars led the Mamluks in a pitched battle where he used the Mongol's own cavalry tactics against them, leading to the first Mongol defeat since they arrived in Mus-lim lands. The victory meant Egypt, and perhaps Islam itself, was saved from Mongol atrocities. Follow-up invasions were also futile, especially since a Mongol khan in Russia, Berke, had converted to Islam and allied with the Mamluks against Hulagu. This Mongol civil war between the Muslim Berke and the Pagan Hulagu meant a temporary reprieve for the Muslim world. Furthermore, in the late 1200s, the entire Mongol Empire was divided into separate states and expansion was halted. Islamic civilization survived the Mongol assault, but only a shadow of the former glory of the Islamic world remained. Persia and Iraq were essentially destroyed politically. Syria was ravaged by warfare. The holy cities of Mecca and Medina had only narrowly avoided capture by pagans. For Muslims, it was one of the worst times in Islamic history. Some even lamented that the end of the world must be near.

As a result of the destruction of the thirteenth century, serious theological questions arose. Muslims of the era had trouble recon-ciling their belief that Islam is the perfect religion with the destruction that had befallen it. The caliphate, the special institution that was inaugurated by Abu Bakr after the death of the Prophet was no more. Millions of Muslim souls perished under the swords of the invaders, and, worst of all, the Mongols were overwhelmingly heathen pagans; they were not even People of the Book. For Islam to come to such a fate at the hands of the Mongols was problematic. Some began to wonder if there was something wrong with Islam.

Muslim theologians rose to combat this idea, led by Ibn Taymiyyah (1263–1328). He argued that there was never anything wrong with Islam. The problem, according to him, was that Muslims digressed from the correct practice of it, and that the Mongol disaster was a result of Muslims losing their way. Much like al-Ghazali 200 years before him, he sought to purge Islam from what he saw as innovations that ran contrary to the example of Muhammad. Although he was a Sufi, he denounced the excessive mystical philosophy of some Sufi branches, believing that they ultimately led to polytheism. At the same time, he rejected the legitimacy of Muslim leaders who did not uphold Islamic law and conduct themselves in an Islamic fashion. This brought him into inevitable conflict with both Mongol and Mamluk rulers, leading to numerous imprisonments and eventual death in the citadel of Damascus. His ideas helped spawn hope for many in the Muslim world that if they simply adhered to a pure and unaltered version of Islam, they could once again rise up to become world dominators. Islamic civilization would in fact experience a rebirth, but not in the traditional heartland of Islam between the Nile and Oxus Rivers. Instead, this rebirth began in the northwest frontier of the Muslim world, where the nomadic warrior society of the Turks clashed with the established and urban Byzantine Empire.

8

AL-ANDALUS

In the story of Islam and the Muslim people, attention is usually focused on the core region of the Muslim world, stretching from the Nile to the Oxus Rivers, including Egypt, Syria, the Arabian Peninsula, Iraq and Persia. However, it is also important to contextualize Islamic history in the region where Muslim civilization directly bordered the rest of the world. In the Iberian Peninsula, home today to Spain and Portugal, Islam interacted directly with Christian Europe. A complex and diverse society developed here that was both Muslim and Western European.

ESTABLISHMENT OF ISLAM IN SPAIN

After the rapid conquest of North Africa in the mid-seventh century by the Umayyads, Muslim conquest slowed for a time. The Atlantic Ocean and Mediterranean Sea seemed a natural border to the new Muslim empire, and the late 600s were dedicated to consolidating the conquered land and incorporating its people into the Muslim world. But the floodgates of conquest opened again in the 710s, when Muslim armies began to pour into the Iberian Peninsula, adding yet another distant land to the Muslim domain.

The reasons for the rapid conquest of the peninsula have long been debated. To the people who witnessed the campaign, on both sides, it was simply a manifestation of God's pleasure or displeasure. For the Muslims, the conquest was so fast and easy simply because God had willed that this land would enter into the Muslim empire. For the Christians, they explained their massive loss by claiming that God was upset with the immoral behavior of the Visigoths and thus He sent the Muslim invaders as punishment. There are of course more concrete factors to understand. Firstly, the unpopularity of Roderic and the Visigothic monarchy due to pre-existing political conflicts. Some aristocrats failed to support the king in the face of invasion from Africa and during the Battle of Guadalete, desertion by soldiers and nobles helped turn the tide. The fact that the Visigoths were unpopular is evidenced by the fact that after the climactic battle, few cities put up any resistance to the Muslim invaders. In fact, the main resistance was seen in the northern mountains and was not led by the Visigoths, but by political separatists fighting for independence before the Muslim invasion. The main cities of the Visigothic realm quickly capitulated to the Muslims who promised favorable surrender terms and local autonomy. The relative freedom granted by the Muslims to the general population must have contrasted sharply with an unpopular Visigothic regime.

After the quick conquest was over, the settlement of the land by Muslims began. Unlike the settlement pattern in parts of the Middle East, where armies settled in garrison towns organized by the Rashidun and Umayyad authorities, in al-Andalus, settlement was mostly unorganized and haphazard. The Muslims did not confine themselves to garrison towns, choosing instead to become property owners throughout the peninsula. The Berber immigrants tended to settle in the north and west, seeking pastoral environments similar to what they were used to in North Africa. The Arab tribes that came to al-Andalus were mostly from Yemen and had a long history of settled farming. As a result, they settled mainly in the fertile regions of the south and the country's main cities such as Cordoba, Valencia and Zaragoza. Both Arabs and Berbers regularly intermarried with the local population, eventually creating a new unique society that incorporated aspects of Arab, Berber and Hispanic culture.

UMAYYAD RULE

For the first few decades of Muslim rule, al-Andalus was little more than a distant and uneventful province of the vast Umayyad Caliphate. That changed in the 750s, when the Abbasids succeeded in overthrowing the Umayyad family. In Syria, most members of the Umayyad family were jailed or executed. One young Umayyad managed to escape the carnage, however. 'Abd al-Rahman, a twenty-year-old prince, escaped from Damascus in 750 just ahead of the Abbasid army, and began an epic journey across the Muslim world in search of help and support after the rest of his family had perished. His mother was a Berber, so he naturally sought aid in the Berber homeland in North Africa. Always just one step ahead of the pursuing Abbasid agents, he finally found support for the Umayyad family in al-Andalus in 755. Here, he established himself as the ruler of an Umayyad state, with Cordoba as its capital, politically separate from the Abbasids based in faraway Baghdad. His journey from Syria to this distant western land gave him the nickname al-Dakhil, the immigrant.

The Umayyad Emirate established by 'Abd al-Rahman al-Dakhil became a cultural melting pot during the centuries after his rule.

People from the rest of the Muslim world continued to immigrate to this distant land, carrying with them aspects of their home cultures. In addition to that, a large portion of the native Hispanic population converted to Islam in the late 800s and early 900s. By 950, about half of the peninsula's population was likely Muslim, and by the 1100s, Christians would make up only about 20 per cent of the population. Arab, Berber and Hispanic Muslims combined to create a unique Andalusian culture that brought together diverse backgrounds and traditions under the banner of Islam. Even Christians living in al-Andalus adopted Islamic culture and began adopting Arabic language, art and customs. This influence culture and language is still seen today in the Spanish language, which retains many loanwords from Arabic. Jews also benefitted greatly from Andalusian society. Throughout the rest of Europe, Jews were barely tolerated in the Middle Ages, and pogroms against them were a constant threat. In Muslim Spain, however, Jews were given the freedom to practice their religion as they pleased and became integral parts of society. Jewish philosophy reached its zenith in Muslim Spain, producing scholars such as Maimonides, who is known to this day as one of the greatest Jewish philosophers of all time.

The Great Mosque of Cordoba was built over a 200 year period in the Umayyad capital. It exhibits 856 columns, many of which originally came from older Roman ruins.

The peak of the Umayyad state in Spain occurred during the reign of 'Abd al-Rahman III, from 912 to 961. During his almost half-century in power, he declared himself as caliph of the Muslim world. Although he did not have any power outside of the Iberian Peninsula, his claim to the role his Umayyad ancestors held in the seventh and eighth centuries was meant to combat the growing power of the Fatimids in North Africa. The Abbasid caliphs of Baghdad were by now ineffectual prisoners in their own palaces under the command of various Turkic dynasties and the Shi'i Fatimids were a real threat to the continued existence of Sunni Islam as a political force.

'Abd al-Rahman III was a true patron of the arts and sciences, on the same level as the earlier Abbasid al-Ma'mun and the later Ottoman Suleiman the Magnificent. Over 600 libraries dotted Cordoba, the capital. Its largest library boasted a collection of over 400,000 books in a multitude of languages. Shops were numerous in the city, producing goods that were valued throughout Europe. Leather, silk, paper, wool and crystal were all produced in Cordoba and traded throughout Europe as well as the Muslim world. It was a world-class city that served as a bridge between undeveloped, generally illiterate Europe and the great cultured cities of the Muslim world. If a European wanted to be well-educated, they would travel to al-Andalus to be in the presence of its great scholars and libraries. Even a tenth-century leader of the Catholic Church, Pope Sylvester II, studied in al-Andalus in his youth, and was mesmerized by the scientific achievements of Muslim civilization. In later centuries, when the first universities opened up in Italy, France and England, much of their libraries were made up of Latin translations of the works in Cordoba's library. Muslim Spain was the main thoroughfare through which the accumulated knowledge of the Muslim world made its way into Europe, helping spark the Renaissance in the 1400s.

Cordoba's magnificence was not limited to its knowledge. 'Abd al-Rahman and earlier rulers of al-Andalus emphasized their power and wealth through elaborate and beautiful mosques and palaces, the best example being the Grand Mosque of Cordoba. Originally built by 'Abd al-Rahman al-Dakhil, it was expanded numerous times in the 800s and 900s, eventually becoming a vast building capable of holding thousands of worshippers. Its trademark forest of columns topped by two levels of arches made of alternating red and white stone made it an architectural marvel that was rivaled in Europe only by the Hagia Sophia in Constantinople. Unlike the paintings and statues that abound in Christian churches, calligraphy and geometric design were the main form of artistic impression throughout the building. Verses from the Quran written in the angular kufic script of Arabic calligraphy wrapped around the walls of the mosque, invoking the Islamic belief that the Quran was the highest form of literary expression and thus deserved to be in Islam's most beautiful mosques. Architectural achievements also occurred in the secular realm, when 'Abd al-Rahman III built a giant palace city outside of Cordoba. *Madinat al-Zahra*, the Beautiful City, was the Versailles of its time, captivating visitors from distant states who came on diplomatic missions to al-Andalus' capital. All this contributed to Cordoba's nickname throughout the rest of Europe: The Ornament of the World.

Unfortunately for the people of al-Andalus, however, the beauty and emphasis on knowledge in al-Andalus had some negative consequences. The early enthusiasm for warfare that was seen in the rapid conquest of the peninsula and invasions into Frankish territory subsided as citizens began to live more comfortable lifestyles. The Cordoban rulers had trouble rallying men from the cities and the countryside to join imperial armies destined to battle the

1. The Dome of the Rock in Jerusalem, built in 691 during the Umayyad Caliphate.

2. The courtyard of the Suleymaniye Mosque in Istanbul, built by the architect Mimar Sinan in 1558.

3. The Prophet's Mosque in Medina, in which the Prophet Muhammad is buried.

4. The Umayyad Mosque of Damascus. Built in 715, it exhibits strong Byzantine architectural influences.

5. The courtyard of the University of Karaouine, established in 859 by Fatima al-Fihri in Fes, Morocco.

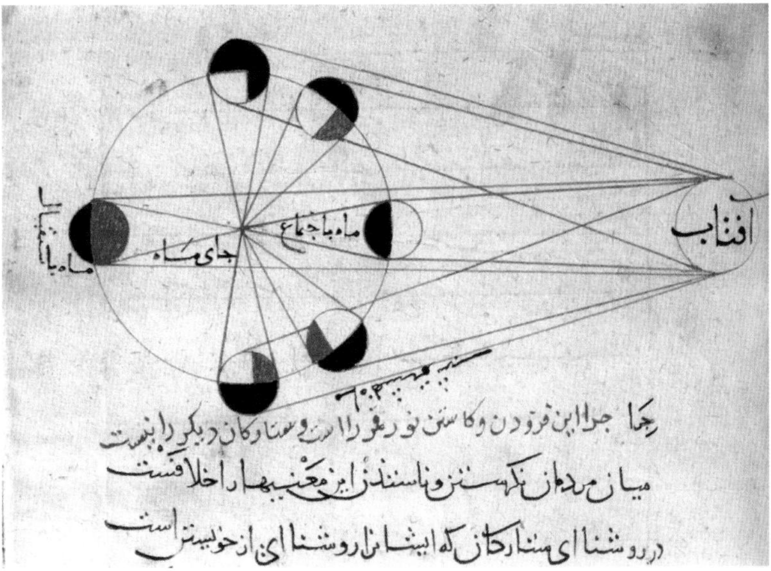

رخا جرا این فرو دن وکا سن نو رعو را اررو سناوکان دیکر را بنرت

میان ردمان یکمسنر و ناسندز این مغینبها دا خلافست

در رو شنا ای سنارکان که ایبشا نر روشنا ای از خویست است

6. A diagram in Persian explaining the science behind lunar eclipses, drawn by al-Biruni in the eleventh century.

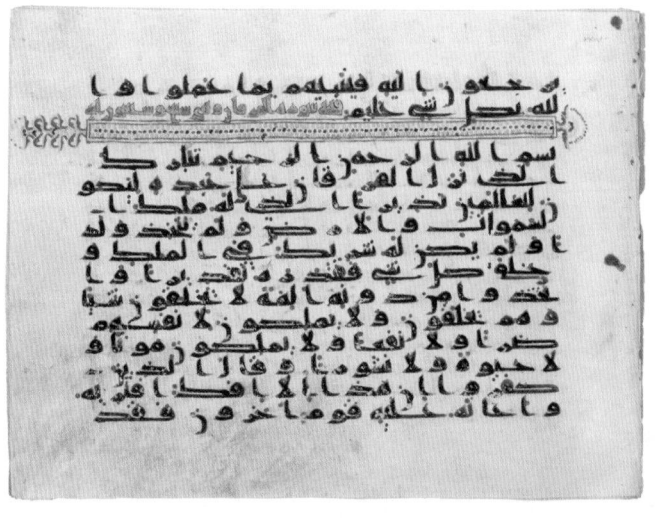

7. An early Quran manuscript written in the angular Kufic script.

8. The Abbasid-era minaret of Samarra.

9. A seventeenth century European engraving depicting Ibn al-Haytham and Galileo as the fathers of science.

10. An Ottoman portrait of Mehmed II, the Conqueror.

11. A portrait of Aurangzeb engaging in *dhikr*, ritual remembrance of God.

12. Mansa Musa depicted in the 1375 Catalan Atlas holding a nugget of gold.

13. Ottoman Sultan Mahmud II, after his clothing reform, which made Ottoman dress more similar to Western European styles.

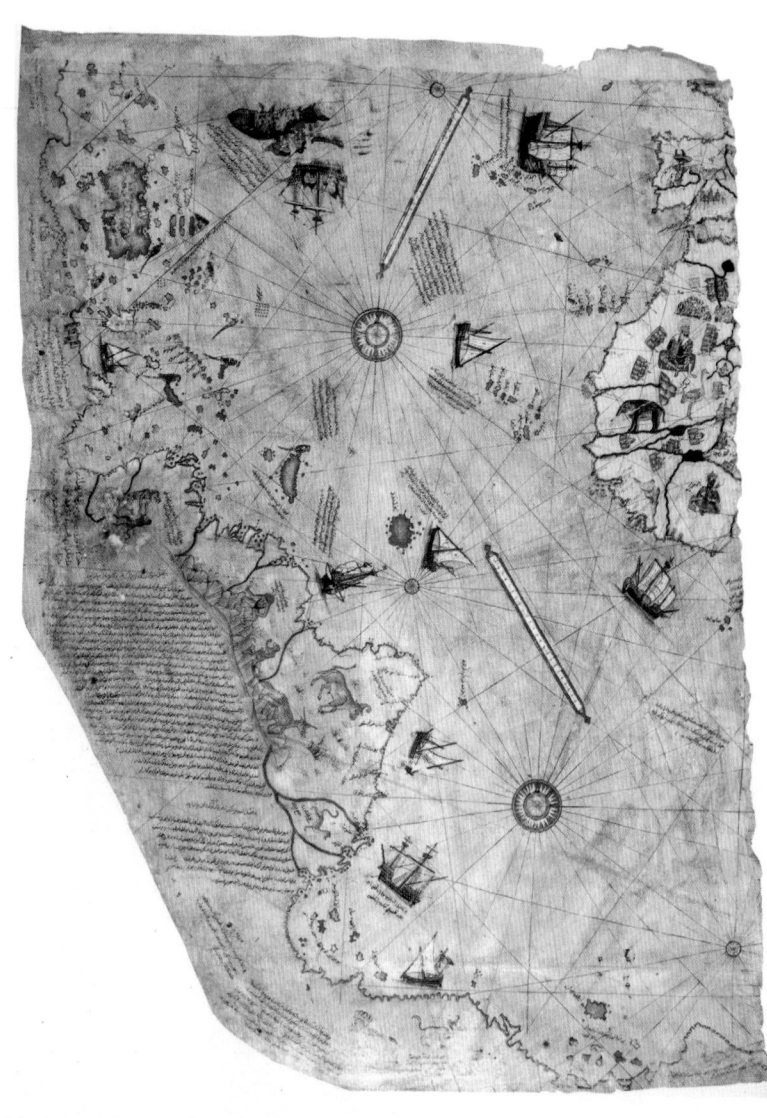

14. A map drawn by Ottoman cartographer Piri Reis in 1513 of the Atlantic Ocean and the South American and African coasts.

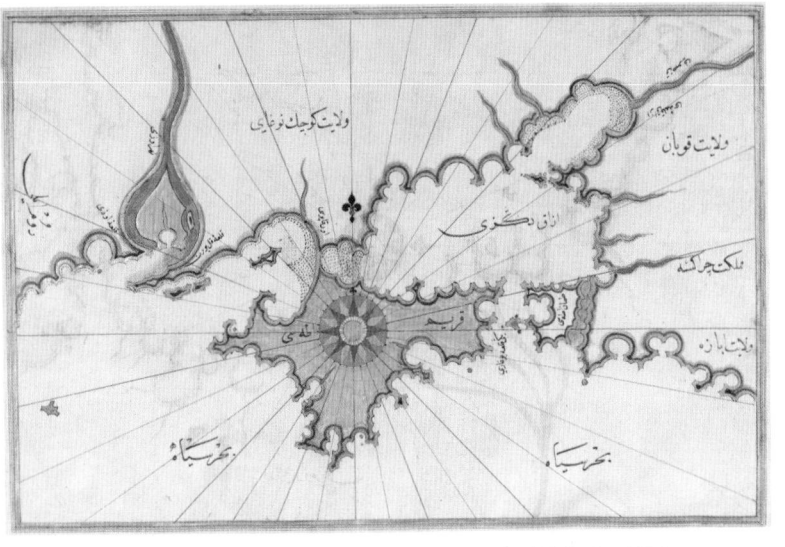

15. A map of Crimea by Piri Reis, from his *Book of Navigation*, 1513.

16. The tughra of Sultan Abdülhamid II, often considered the pinnacle of tughra art.

17. The geometric and calligraphic designs of the Blue Mosque, built by the Ottomans in 1616.

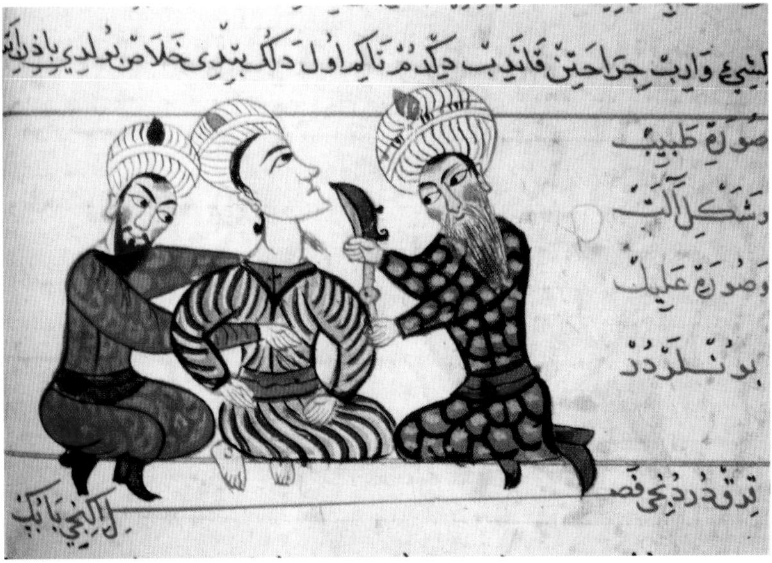

18. A fifteenth-century drawing of a surgical operation from a medical textbook.

19. An eighteenth century Arabic manuscript with interlinear Javanese translation.

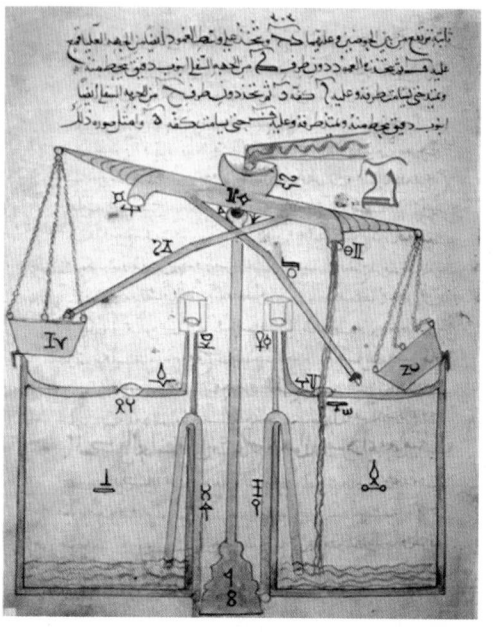

20. A diagram from Al-Jazari's *Book of Ingenious Devices* of a water clock.

21. Al-Azhar Mosque and University in Cairo, established by the Fatimids in the tenth century and converted to a Sunni institution by Salah al-Din.

22. The Qaitbay Mosque in Cairo, exhibiting typical Mamluk architecture.

23. The pillars and arches of the Cordoba Mosque, built by the Umayyads of Al-Andalus.

24. The surrender of the Emirate of Granada to Castille in 1492, the final Muslim state of Iberia.

25. Dolmabahçe Palace, built in 1856 in Istanbul, during the Tanzimat Era, exhibits strong European architectural influences.

26. British general Edmund Allenby entering Jerusalem during World War One in late-1917.

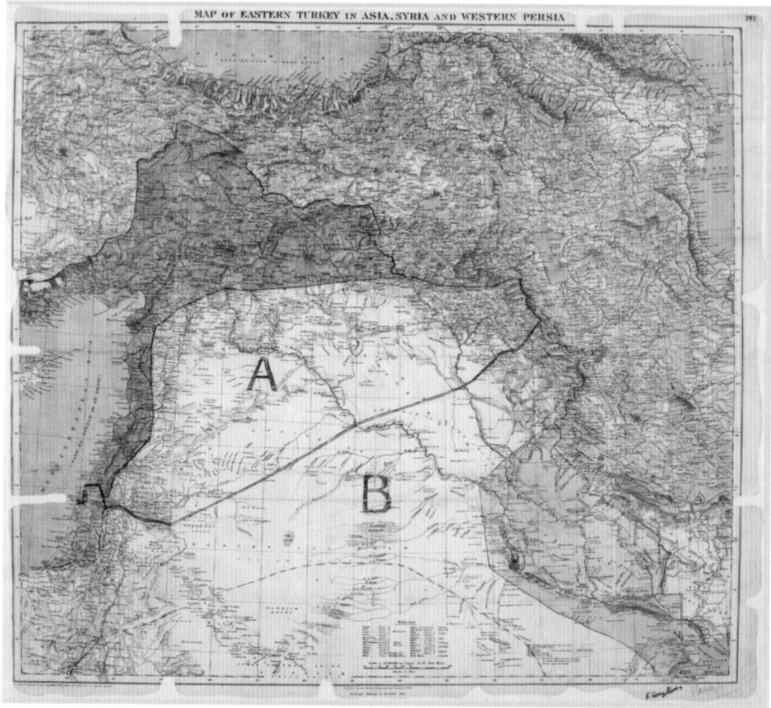

27. A map of the borders demarcated by the Sykes-Picot Agreement of 1916, which divided up the Arab Middle East into zones of British and French control.

28. The remains of Constantinople's Theodosian walls, which held Mehmed II's army at bay for almost two months.

29. A photograph of Hagia Sophia from its time as a mosque in the early twentieth century.

30. A gold coin minted by King Offa of Mercia in the British Isles in the eighth century. It was meant to mimic coins minted by Muslims and even includes the Muslim profession of faith in Arabic.

31. The Great Mosque of Xian, China, which dates to the eighth century.

Christian kingdoms of the north. The Andalusians were content, complacent and unwilling to leave the comfort of their lives for the defense of Muslim Spain. The lethargy of the population crept into the upper-echelons of power. By the early eleventh century, the battle for control among members of the Umayyad family and their supporters was common. Rather than focus on external enemies, the elites aimed their efforts at eliminating rival factions within Cordoba. Groups competing for power were all too eager to enlist Christians from the north and Berbers from Africa to support their causes. In 1009, Suleiman II overthrew another member of the Umayyad clan with an army composed almost entirely of Castilians and Berbers by attacking Cordoba and declaring himself caliph. This led to a reprisal attack on Cordoba the next year by another faction and a reprisal attack for the reprisal attack by Suleiman's supporters the year after that. The tolerant and stable society of tenth-century Cordoba was quickly sinking under the mud of power-struggles and civil war. Throughout the 1010s and 1020s, al-Andalus' political unity dissolved into numerous competing states, with each state known as a *ta'ifa*.

THE TAIFA PERIOD AND BERBER REFORMERS

The Taifa Period of al-Andalus lasted for the majority of the eleventh century. The word *ta'ifa* (plural *tawa'if*) itself comes from the Quran, which exhorts Muslims to make peace between two competing *tawa'if*, or factions, that come to blows. Yet peace was a rare luxury during this period. Ethnic rivalries between Arab, Berber and Iberian Muslims became a focus of conflict as petty kings throughout the peninsula competed to replace the fallen Umayyads. Cities that had once been important pieces of the Umayyad state such as Cordoba, Seville, Toledo, Granada and Zaragoza devolved into small, independent kingdoms constantly at war. Once-prosperous al-Andalus quickly fell into ruin as decades of war ravaged the country. Contemporaries such as Ibn Hazm, a jurist, historian and philosopher, mourned the destruction of country estates and quiet villages by competing armies.

If Muslim *ta'ifa* kings fought to gain power over al-Andalus, the result was regrettably ironic for Islam in Iberia. The only victors of the Taifa Period were the Christian states of the north. Since the original conquest of Iberia in the early 700s, the northernmost reaches of the peninsula eluded Muslim control. Small Christian states were established there in the aftermath of the conquest, protected by the mountainous terrain; they were easily kept at bay when al-Andalus was one united political entity, but when it fractured into competing states, the Christian kings took advantage. Numerous Taifa kings enlisted the help of Christian armies in their conflicts against fellow Muslims. Such actions would have scandalized the early Muslim community and pious contemporaries, but for the Taifa kings, power and control were most important, regardless of ideology. By interfering in inter-Muslim warfare, Christian states such as Castile, Leon and Navarre managed to expand their own wealth and territory at the expense of the Muslims. In one example, the Taifa of Toledo paid an enormous sum to the Kingdom of Navarre to invade Zaragoza, which in turn paid Castile to raid the Toledo countryside, depopulating it and seizing much of its wealth. Muslims paid Christians to attack and weaken other Muslims in this dark chapter of al-Andalus' history. The result was the loss of huge tracts of land throughout the peninsula and the military and economic growth of Spain's Christian states. The fall of Toledo in 1085 to Castile was an important symbolic and strategic loss. Located right in the center of Iberia, its fall meant that Christian power could now directly threaten any of the Taifa states, even in the far south. It was only at this point that the Taifa kings realized they could not hold out against the Christian kings for long, and began to look to the rest of the Muslim world for help. That help came in the form of a puritan movement from Africa known as the Murabitun.

The Murabitun movement was founded in the desert landscape of Morocco, along the trade routes that linked North Africa with the wealthy kingdoms of West Africa. The people there were Berbers who had converted to Islam during the centuries after the Muslim conquest of North Africa in the 600s. By the eleventh century, almost all the Berber tribes were Muslim in name, but many held onto pre-Islamic beliefs and practices. The pre-Islamic tribal alliances were particularly strong and not unlike the pre-Islamic Arab tribal rivalries of the Arabian Peninsula. One Berber theologian, 'Abdullah ibn Yasin, sought to bring Berber society more in line with traditional Islam in the mid-eleventh century. He named his movement the Murabitun, meaning "those who hold fast", alluding to a verse from the Quran requiring that Muslims hold fast to the path of Allah. Spanish and English corrupted the name into the *Almoravid Dynasty*—the name by which they are most known today. The movement was simple in essence, which added to its popularity. Ibn Yasin declared that the Murabitun have three main goals: promoting righteousness, forbidding injustice, and eliminating un-Islamic taxes.

The Murabitun movement grew exponentially throughout the eleventh century, and not by conquest. The basic message and simple lifestyle of the Murabitun was attractive to the Berber tribes. It recalled the simplicity and straightforwardness of the Prophet Muhammad's original message. Similar to how many

Arabs voluntarily accepted Islam in seventh century Arabia, many Berber tribes voluntarily joined the Murabitun confederation. By the 1180s, the movement extended from North Africa to the wealthy territories of Ghana in West Africa. Its rapid growth out of the Sahara Desert meant it was fundamentally different from Muslim Spain. Whereas settled Muslim civilization had existed in al-Andalus for hundreds of years, the Murabitun were untainted by the wealth and luxuries of city life. The Berber warriors were tough and ready to fight, a quality that did not go unnoticed by the petty Taifa kings of al-Andalus.

"And if two factions [tawa'if] among the believers should fight, then make settlement between the two. But if one of them oppresses the other, then fight against the one that oppresses until it returns to the ordinance of Allah."

– Quran (49:9)

When the Christian Reconquista threatened the existence of Muslim Spain, the Taifa kings called on the Murabitun for help. Led by Alfonso VI of Castile in the late 1000s, the Reconquista reached the walls of Seville, a major center of political Islam in Spain. Thus, the Taifa king of Seville, along with some of the other quarreling Muslim leaders in Iberia, sent for the Murabitun in the name of Muslim unity against a common Christian enemy. In 1086, the Murabitun, led by Yusuf ibn Tashfin, crossed the Strait of Gibraltar with 12,000 soldiers. Ibn Ziyad crossed the same strait to bring Iberia under Muslim control 375 years earlier. Now, Ibn Tashfin was doing the same to ensure it remained so, but he made it clear this was not a campaign of conquest. Ibn Tashfin was coming at the request of the existing kings of al-Andalus and seems to have had no interest in annexing the region to the Murabitun Empire. Thus, his army met up with the army of Seville and clashed with Alfonso at the Battle of Zallaqa in October of 1086 near Badajoz. The result was a decisive victory over the Castilians. Alfonso was forced to retreat from his advance on Muslim lands and for the time being, what remained of Muslim Spain was safe. Although Ibn Tashfin had the upper hand, he chose not to follow up his victory with a campaign of conquest in the peninsula. Instead he retreated with the majority of his army back to North Africa, where the political complexities of al-Andalus' Taifas were absent.

Despite being a foreign minority ruling over al-Andalus, the Murabitun were well-accepted early in their reign. Their reliance on local scholars of Islam as government officials and lower tax rates led to widespread support from the general population.

The Murabitun could not stay out of the politics and conflicts to the north. Yusuf ibn Tashfin was called back to al-Andalus in 1088 to aid in another campaign against Alfonso. Ostensibly, this was to be a unified Muslim force bringing together various Taifas and the Murabitun. But ibn Tashfin's experience on this expedition was less than uplifting. The campaign was constantly hampered by rivalries among the Taifa kings, who regularly complained to ibn Tashfin about each other and distrusted anyone but their closest supporters. The campaign resulted in failure and ibn Tashfin returned a second time to Africa, determined not to get involved in Andalusian politics again.

The inherent weakness of Taifa al-Andalus and the rivalries of the kings meant that Alfonso VI would once again become a threat to the continuation of Islam in Iberia, and yet again, ibn Tashfin and the Murabitun were called on to save the day. Upon his third entrance into al-Andalus, ibn Tashfin came armed with a *fatwa* (religious ruling) from none other than Imam al-Ghazali, declaring that the Taifa kings were corrupt, unfit to rule and should be removed from power. In 1090, the Murabitun conquest of al-Andalus commenced, with ibn Tashfin personally leading the campaign to end the Taifa period. The petty Taifa kings were not willing to give up their realms to the Berbers, and some even pledged allegiance to Christian kingdoms in order to resist the Murabitun. Such actions only confirmed the suspicions of the Andalusians and the Islamic scholars that the Taifa kings were concerned only with themselves and their power, and not with the defense of the Muslim world. Popular uprisings in support of the Murabitun erupted throughout al-Andalus led by scholars who demanded the return of past glory. Yusuf ibn Tashfin's takeover of the Muslim territories of al-Andalus thus ended up being relatively bloodless. As Taifa kings were overthrown, they were exiled one by one to North Africa, where their petty disputes could no longer cause division in al-Andalus. Within ten years, all the Taifa states had capitulated to the Murabitun, with the exception of Zaragoza, but even its king was wise enough to acknowledge the superiority of the Berbers and signed an alliance with them. Yusuf ibn Tashfin, with an empire that stretched 3000 kilometers from al-Andalus to Ghana, was one of the most powerful people in the world at the end of the eleventh century.

The Andalusian acceptance of Murabitun control over al-Andalus may initially seem surprising. Nomadic Berber warriors with a strict interpretation of Islam conquering and annexing an almost 400 year-old established and settled civilization would normally be resisted. But here one of the unique repeating themes of Islamic history is seen: when a part of the Muslim world is politically fractured, and external invasion is imminent, rallying around one leader under the banner of Muslim unity is usually the only path to safety. The example of this far-western outpost of Islam was repeated in the unity of Egypt and Syria under Salah al-Din during the Crusades and the absorption of the Turkish *beyliks* in the 1300s by the Ottomans. For the Andalusians, Berber Muslim rulers with their foreign culture, language, and ideas were more tolerable than the encroachment of the Spanish Christians, who seemed determined to stamp out Islam itself in the Iberian Peninsula. Added to this, the simple message of the Murabitun—of getting back to pure Islam as it was intended to be practiced—and removing unfair laws and taxes was certainly attractive to the Andalusians.

Despite their popularity and success in al-Andalus, the Murabitun were not immune to the natural rise and fall of dynasties. Under Yusuf ibn Tashfin they had expanded greatly to absorb most of the Muslim lands of Iberia into an intercontinental empire, but they failed to regain territory previously lost to the Christians. Toledo, the once great Muslim city, was gone forever, and the Christian kingdoms were only halted, not destroyed. Ibn Tashfin's son, ʿAli (r. 1106–1143), lacked the desert upbringing of his father, and although he seems to have been a well-intentioned leader, he did not have the ability to expand the empire through warfare that his father had. When the Murabitun first entered al-Andalus at the end of the eleventh century, their popularity stemmed from the fact that they were capable of finally defeating the encroaching Christian armies. As the military might of the Murabitun declined and Christians began to score major victories against the Muslims once again in the twelfth century, their purpose in al-Andalus was called into question. Rebellion even broke out in Cordoba, the old Umayyad capital, where the people were fed up with the inaccessible and foreign Murabitun who ruled the city.

But the actual fall of the Murabitun would come from North Africa, where they got started. Another Berber Muslim religious movement began to grow in the Atlas Mountains that towered over the Murabitun capital of Marrakesh. They called themselves the Muwahhidun, meaning the monotheists. The leader of this new movement, Ibn Tumart, preached that the Murabitun had strayed from the correct practice of Islam and that the luxuries of al-Andalus had corrupted them and made them complacent. The Muwahhidun Movement also took a very strong theological stance, arguing that religious innovations were rampant throughout al-Andalus and North Africa. Berber tribes that had previously supported the Murabitun switched allegiances and joined with the new Muwahhidun movement throughout the 1120s and 1130s. In 1147, they were powerful enough to challenge the Murabitun in the open, descending from the mountains to successfully attack Marrakesh. Within a year, all of Morocco had succumbed to the Muwahhidun.

The preoccupation of the Murabitun with the growing Muwahhidun Movement in Africa led to al-Andalus being neglected militarily by the Murabitun. That, coupled with the popular discontent of the Andalusian population, led to the emergence of a second Taifa period, starting in 1144. Once again, rival factions arose in the Iberian Peninsula, all seeking to gain power at the expense of other Muslim states. The only winners in this conflict were the Christian kingdoms which were able to take advantage and increase their own territories through war against the Muslims. The general population supported the overthrow of Murabitun rule in al-Andalus, but do not seem to have been able to provide a viable alternative. They were still not willing to pick up arms and join *jihad* armies in any case, so like in the first Taifa Period, the Taifa kings had to rely on military assistance from Christian kingdoms, which came at a cost.

Following in the footsteps of Yusuf ibn Tashfin and Tariq ibn Ziyad, the Muwahhidun, now led by Ibn Tumart's successor, 'Abd al-Mu'min, entered al-Andalus in 1145, seeking to annex the territory just as the Christian Spanish and Portuguese began to advance on the Muslim Taifas. Within a year, Malaga and Seville were annexed. By 1150, Cordoba and Jaen were taken from their Taifa kings. By the time 'Abd al-Mu'min died in 1163, all that remained of Muslim Spain was part of the Muwahhidun Empire. Unfortunately for Spain's Muslims, however, all that remained was the southern part of the peninsula. The central plains of the Iberian Peninsula and the Eastern Coast were firmly under the control of the Christian kingdoms, led by Castile, Portugal, and Aragon. The great achievements and empires built by Spanish Muslims during the Umayyad era were memories that could no longer be replicated. It was clear by now to the Andalusians that the momentum on the peninsula was in favor of the Christians and their main priority would no longer be to build large cities and advance knowledge, but to merely survive in the face of the Christian onslaught.

The arrival of the Muwahhidun spurred an Islamic revival. Andalusians refocused themselves on their practice of Islam. The emergence of numerous scholars in the peninsula at this time testifies to this. Perhaps the most notable among them was ibn Rushd (1126–1198), known as Averroes in the rest of Europe. Reminiscent of earlier Muslim scholars of the Golden Age, he was a polymath who wrote on subjects ranging from philosophy to physics to psychology. His most lasting contribution was his work in *fiqh*. Although he was a follower of the Maliki school of *fiqh* (as were most North Africans and Andalusians), he authored an encyclopedia of comparative *fiqh*, entitled *The Distinguished Jurist's Primer* (*Bidayat Al-Mujtahid Wa Nihayat Al-Muqtasid*). Centuries later, it continues to live on as one of the premier books of *fiqh*, detailing the differences of opinion of the numerous schools of jurisprudence within Islam. Mystics such as Ibn 'Arabi and Abu al-Hasan ash-Shadhili also emerged during the Muwahhidun Dynasty. They sought to spiritually inspire Muslims to improve their relationship with God, no doubt partly as a reaction to the bleak political climate in al-Andalus and North Africa.

The Muwahhidun largely followed the same pattern as the Murabitun. They both emerged out of the harsh desert environment of Morocco. They both sought to fix what they saw as social ills and political weakness in the region. They both halted the Christian Reconquista in Iberia, and they both weakened over time as successive generations lost the drive and willpower that their forefathers cultivated in the deserts of North Africa. The Muwahhidun in al-Andalus declined as family conflicts over power came to the forefront. The late twelfth century saw the emergence of civil war in al-Andalus, coupled with the continued advance of the Christian kingdoms. This time, however, no new Berber religious movement emerged to take their place.

GRANADA

As they had been doing for hundreds of years, the Christians of Spain took advantage of Muslim weakness and division. Pope Innocent III even called for a pan-European Crusade to attack the Muwahhidun, and in 1212, Spanish, Portuguese, French and English knights assembled near the Sierra Morena mountain range that served as the border between Christian and Muslim control in Iberia. Led by Alfonso VIII of Castile, the Crusade made its way through a pass in the mountains to attack the main bulk of the Muwahhidun army. At the Battle of Las Navas de Tolosa, or al-'Uqab as the Muslims called it, the Muslim forces were totally decimated. Over 100,000 casualties for the Muslims meant that the backbone of Muwahhidun power in al-Andalus was broken.

The reasons for the loss of the battle are not as important as the results of the disaster. With no ability to resist the Christians, major Muslim cities began to fall one by one. Between 1228 and 1248, Valencia, Seville, Badajoz, Majorca, Murcia, Jaen, and others all fell to the Christian onslaught. In 1236, Cordoba fell to the Castilians. The historic capital of early Muslim Spain, with its monumental Great Mosque, libraries, palaces and gardens could not resist the Castilian army. The mosque was forcibly turned into a Catholic cathedral, with a giant chapel built in the center of the building. The layout of the building, its niche facing Mecca, and the Quranic inscriptions on the walls all remained, surrounding the Christian chapel, and ironically testifying to its history as a Muslim house of worship. Later, a sixteenth-century Holy Roman Emperor would decry its conversion to a cathedral, remarking that a building so uniquely beautiful was converted into something ordinary and common.

But not all of al-Andalus was lost after the fall of the Muwahhidun. The Emirate of Granada, along the southern coast of

Iberia, remained independent of Christian control. There, an Arab dynasty, the Nasrids, took power and managed to hold on for two more centuries. They traced their descent back to Banu Khazraj, one of the two tribes that welcomed the Prophet in Medina after he was exiled from Mecca in 622. Similarly, the Nasrids welcomed the followers of Muhammad who were exiled from Christian Iberia 600 years after the *hijra*. The *hijra* of Muhammad signaled the beginning of a new Muslim state and a new era of Muslim power in the Arabian Peninsula. The arrival of Muslims in Granada, however, signaled the beginning of the end of Muslim power in the Iberian Peninsula. It was the last remaining Muslim state of al-Andalus.

But the Nasrids of Granada were never truly independent. They only managed to escape annexation by becoming a tributary state to Castile. After the fall of the Muwahhidun, the pattern of messy Taifa politics, which pitted Muslim states against one another in a struggle for survival, had reappeared. With such disunity, it was only because of Granada's utility in the eyes of the Castilians that they managed to escape annexation. They promised military aid to the Castilians along with regular tribute payments of gold, which came from the rich mines of Mali in West Africa. This system continuously strengthened the Spanish Christians of the north while reducing the relative power of the Muslim states throughout al-Andalus and North Africa. In fact, the Nasrids aided some of the Christian conquests of other Andalusian cities in the mid-thirteenth century. Furthermore, outsiders dominated the economy of Granada, as merchants from the rising Italian city-states controlled exports to Europe. Two-way trade with the rest of the Muslim world was almost non-existent. European Christians were the only ones who benefitted as Granada's resources slowly dried up. Such a system was obviously not sustainable for long.

Even as Islam clung to the southern edge of Iberia at the end of the long and tumultuous decline of al-Andalus, the Muslim tradition of grandeur and beauty in architecture managed to erect one last monument to Muslim Spain. The Alhambra was a fortification, located on a cliff overlooking the city of Granada that had been in use as the city's citadel for hundreds of years before the rise of the Nasrids. The emirs of Granada took to expanding and beautifying the fortress as a palace, and, with the influx of Muslims from the rest of al-Andalus, the palace perfectly exemplifies the entire artistic history of Muslim Spain. The famous horseshoe arches of the Umayyads and the geometric patterns of the Murabitun and Muwahhidun, along with new Granadan innovations and Spanish Christian architecture, combined to create a unique capstone. The gardens, fountains and porticos created an environment reminiscent of the great Muslim palaces in fallen Andalusian cities like Cordoba and Seville. But the Alhambra was more than just a replica of earlier monuments: it also created a new style entirely that was in turn imitated in both Europe and the Muslim world. The Alcazar of Seville, built as a royal palace by the Castilians soon after the Alhambra, directly copied the style of the Nasrid palace, including its gardens, courtyards and arches. Schools and mosques throughout North Africa also drew inspiration from the Alhambra, leading to an architectural legacy that spans centuries. Perhaps the most striking feature of the Alhambra is the motto of the Emirate of Granada, which is plastered all over its walls: *Wa la ghalib illallah*, meaning "And there is no victor except God". It was a fitting slogan for a state that represented the only vestige of the once-great Muslim civilization of al-Andalus. Even as enemy forces surrounded the vulnerable Granada, the slogan reminded the faithful of their belief in an Omnipotent God that cannot be defeated, regardless of the political decline in the peninsula. Perhaps most ironically was the fact that the slogan about God's ultimate victory remained on the walls of the palace, even as the victorious Christian kings occupied it after the fall of the city in 1492.

Even as Granada ushered in the final cultural golden age of al-Andalus, its surrounding political environment weakened it over time, leading to its ultimate demise. The perennial threat to the Nasrids from the Castilians in the north remained a problem. The yearly tribute only strengthened the Christian nation while continuing to weaken Granada. Meanwhile, the Berber Marinid Dynasty that ruled over North Africa also emerged as a threat, effectively surrounding Granada with hostile states.

Despite the unfavorable surroundings, Granada could have held steady in the face of the Christian advance. It had a very strong defensive position, being shielded by mountain ranges and numerous fortresses that dotted its territory. It was because of this that the Emirate of Granada managed to escape the conquest that befell the rest of al-Andalus. Yet it was not external invasion that brought about the final end of Muslim Spain, it was internal disagreements. The 1480s was a decade of court intrigue and family conflict, as the emir of Granada, Abul-Hassan, was overthrown and exiled by his son Abu 'Abdallah Muhammad XII in 1482. Muhammad XII (who was known as Boabdil by the Spaniards) was declared a rebel against God by the scholar class of Granada, and indeed his actions led to the continued decline of political Islam in the Iberian Peninsula.

As he rallied armies to fight against his father, the Castilians did not let up their encroachment on Granada. Muslim disunity coupled with advanced artillery in the hands of the Christians led to the quick capture of strategically-important fortresses through-out Granadan territory. Just a few decades after the Ottomans used cannon to conquer Constantinople in 1453 and launch Islam into Eastern Europe, Christian armies used the same technology to eliminate it from Western Europe. Furthermore, throughout the history of al-Andalus, whenever the tide turned in favor of the Christians, North African Muslims would ride to the rescue of their coreligionists. But the late fifteenth century saw no such res-cue. Civil unrest in North Africa meant the rulers were preoccu-pied with their own problems, and Castilian diplomatic efforts effectively kept them out of Andalusian affairs. The Mamluks of Egypt were called upon by the Granadans for help, but were only able to offer symbolic support. Granada had to find a way to hold off the Christians while dealing with internal civil war on their own. In the end, such a momentous task proved impossible.

Muhammad XII's leadership only added to the woes of Granada; the Castilians captured him in 1486, and during his captivity his father was able to retake the throne. After being held captive for a year, Muhammad was released upon his pledge of allegiance to the Christian state. With arms and soldiers supplied by the Castilians, he managed to establish himself once again as the emir of Granada, leading to another round of civil war, this time against his uncle. He promised to stay out of the raging war between the Castilians and his uncle, during which most of the Emirate of Granada was conquered by the Christians. By 1490, Granada was the only Muslim-ruled city left in the Iberian Peninsula. At this point, Muhammad XII's alliance with Castile was irrele-vant. The famous Catholic Monarchs, Ferdinand and Isabella, united the kingdoms of Castile and Aragon, paving the way for modern Spain. They had no interest in allowing Granada to continue as an independent Muslim city in the midst of a united Christian Spain, despite their past aid of Muhammad XII.

In 1490 and 1491, during the lead up to the fall of Granada, the Spanish slowly closed in on the lone city. Resources were cut off, refugees flooded the city, and a sense of despair permeated the population. On its own, and with no help coming from the Muslims of North Africa, it was impossible for Granada to hold out against the numerically and technologically superior Spanish, and Muhammad XII knew it. On 25 November 1491, he sent his vizier to negotiate terms of surrender with the Catholic Monarchs. On 1 January 1492, the city of Granada was officially handed over to the Spanish. Muhammad XII handed over the keys to the city and the Alhambra to the conquerors early that morning, so that when the residents of the city awoke, they saw that the flags declaring "And there is no victor except God" that flew over the Alhambra were lowered for the last time as the Castilian flag took their place. To the Christians, it was the joyous fulfillment of a centuries-long struggle to make the Iberian Peninsula Christian. To the Muslims, it was the end of a long and important chapter of Islamic history, one that saw some of the most enlightened, wealthy, and powerful states the world had ever seen. For the vanquished emir, whose political incompetence directly led to the loss of the last bit of al-Andalus, exile awaited him. Legend has it that on his way out of the city, he looked back at it one last time and began to cry. His mother reproached him, uttering the famous line, "Do not cry like a woman for what you could not defend as a man."

THE MORISCOS

The political history of al-Andalus ended in 1492. But that was not the end of Spain's Muslim population. There were still between

500,000 and 600,000 Muslims (out of a total population of 7–8 million) throughout the Iberian Peninsula, with most of them in the former Emirate of Granada. It would not have been possible for the Catholic Monarchs to expel such a large portion of Spain's population immediately. Many territories throughout the Iberian Peninsula still relied on their Muslim population to run the local economies. Furthermore, the Spanish did not have the human capital to immediately fill up depopulated cities. Instead, Ferdinand and Isabella initially adopted a tolerant approach to the Muslim minority. The Muslims thus lost some social standing now that the rulers were not of their same religion, but they were given freedom to continue to worship as they pleased under the Spanish monarchy.

In 1492, the Spanish government expelled all Jews from their lands. Ottoman Sultan Bayezid II ordered his military and governors to welcome any Jewish refugees from Spain. A sizeable Jewish community descended from these Spanish Jews remained in Istanbul until the twentieth century.

That does not mean that the Christians did not attempt to convert the Muslims to Christianity. Any Muslim that voluntarily chose to convert would be showered with gifts, gold, horses and other valuables. This led to a number of Muslim conversions to Christianity in the years following 1492. To the surprise and disheartenment of the Christians, after collecting their gifts, most of those "converts" would be found soon afterwards worshipping in mosques and reading the Quran again. With Muslims taking advantage of the incentives offered to them and not sincerely converting to Christianity, the Catholic Church decided to take a more hardline approach. Francisco Jiménez de Cisneros, a Catholic archbishop, was appointed in 1499 to speed up the conversion process by harassment of Spain's Muslims, persecution and arbitrary imprisonment of those who chose not to convert. In his own words, he declared, "if the infidels couldn't be attracted to the road to salvation, they had to be dragged to it." The result was an expected rebellion by Spain's Muslims against the oppression. The Muslims of Granada, who had endured eight years of Christian rule but would not endure oppression by the new archbishop, barricaded the narrow streets of Granada and declared their defiance to the efforts of de Cisneros.

The revolt gave the Catholic Monarchs the excuse they needed to admonish Spain's Muslim community. The Muslim rebels were given two options: the death penalty or conversion to Christianity, which would lead to an official pardon. Pragmatic as ever, Granada's Muslims chose conversion, and a huge wave of baptisms in the predominantly Muslim city commenced. Further rebellions flared in the surrounding countryside, but the more powerful Spaniards eventually put them down within a few years. By 1502, when the rebellions were over, the Christian authorities chose to outlaw Islam throughout Spain. All Muslims were given the option to convert, leave Spain or die. Like the people of Granada, Muslims throughout Spain chose conversion, and soon, the Catholic Monarchs could boast that they had converted an entire nation to Christianity within a few years.

The reality, however, was that Islam continued to live on in Spain, but underground. The supposedly former Muslims, known by the Spanish as Moriscos, professed Christianity to avoid continued persecution, while continuing to live as Muslims in the privacy of their own homes. The Spanish authorities, perhaps suspecting that the Moriscos were not sincere in their conversion to Christianity, instituted numerous laws, as part of the Spanish Inquisition, throughout the early 1500s to "cleanse" the Moriscos of their Islamic past. Butchering animals according to Islamic law was banned in 1511 by royal decree. Women were banned from covering their faces in 1513. Muslim-style clothing in general was banned in 1523. Furthermore, Moriscos were banned from using bathhouses or closing the doors to their homes on Fridays in an effort to ensure that no one was secretly practicing Islam. Weddings had to be attended by "Old Christians" to ensure that Islamic nuptials were not being practiced. In 1526, even speaking Arabic was outlawed, and Moriscos were forced to speak Castilian at all times, including when at home. These efforts to rid the Moriscos of both their religious and cultural heritage only pushed them further underground and caused them to cling more vigorously to their beliefs.

Overall, the Inquisition failed to remove Islam from the hearts of most Moriscos; instead, it forced them to be more creative about how they worked around the laws. Numerous Muslim scholars wrote *fatwa*s, allowing Muslims to practice their religion in non-traditional ways to avoid detection by authorities. For example, the famous 1502 *fatwa* by the mufti of Oran, in present-day Algeria, allowed Muslims to perform ritual cleansing before prayer without water by touching a clean wall, to pray at night instead of five times a day, and to eat pork if forced. Religious instruction was restricted to the home, as mosques and schools were closed or converted to Christian churches. But the Arabic language survived behind closed doors, as parents made sure to teach their children Islamic rites and verses of the Quran. Moriscos with Christian names would go to church on Sundays, worship according to Catholic rites, then come home, be referred to by their secret Muslim names and read the Quran and pray according to the Islamic fashion.

The kings of Spain were never fully ignorant of the secret beliefs of the Moriscos. Even one hundred years after the conquest of Granada, it was clear to the Spanish monarchy and the Catholic Church that the attempts to convert the Moriscos to Christianity were failing. More and more Moriscos continued to be caught in the middle of Islamic acts by the Inquisition, and the punishments doled out to those caught did nothing to deter others. King Philip III, heavily influenced by hardline Catholic priests, decided in April 1609 to expel all the Moriscos left in Spain. Despite protests from aristocrats throughout Spain, who saw the expulsion the Moriscos as detrimental to the economy, the royal decree took effect later that year.

Entire Morisco villages were depopulated, with their citizens being forced to the coast where ships from all over Europe waited to take them to North Africa. The Moriscos were allowed to take whatever they could carry with them, but the Spanish confiscated their property. Children under the age of four were exempt from the expulsion, and were taken from their families to be raised as Christians. In the south of Spain, rebellions once again arose. The expulsion meant that Moriscos who had been masquerading as Christians had nothing to lose by coming out as Muslims and leading one final defense of Islam in the peninsula. For the first time in over one hundred years, the Muslim call to prayer rang out in the valleys and hills of Spain. Public communal prayer, unseen since the years after the fall of Granada, was once again convened. The glory days of Islam in Spain were long gone, but the rebels, despite being quickly defeated by the Spanish, managed to revive the memory of al-Andalus and its 800-year history one last time. By 1614, the Moriscos were all gone, and the rebellions all put down. Islam was gone from Spain. There were reports that some Moriscos had managed to somehow stay in the country, and continued practicing Islam in secret for centuries. But this truncated Muslim community was nothing more than a shadow of al-Andalus. Despite its contributions to the history of the Iberian Peninsula and the rest of Europe, Islam was absent from Spain. But as Islam fell in this western outpost, it was just starting to be revived in the East, where the Ottomans would re-introduce Islam to Europe and preside over a new golden age.

9

THE EDGE

Far too often, the "Muslim world" is thought of as the Middle East and nothing beyond it. Islam of course began in the Arabian Peninsula and saw its greatest empires rise in the region between the Nile and Oxus Rivers. But by only focusing on this region, some of the richest history of the Muslim world is neglected. It is in the furthest reaches of Islam, in Sub-Saharan Africa, China and in Southeast Asia that the relationship between Islam the rest of the world can be seen in all its complexity.

WEST AFRICA

When Islam arrived in North Africa in the decades after the death of the Prophet, it generally clung to the coast. Much like the Romans and Byzantines before them, the Muslims chose to settle in cities along the Mediterranean coastline for practical reasons, including the connection to Mediterranean shipping and the fact that further inland the Sahara Desert prevented any major settled civilizations from thriving. The civilization that flourished in

North African cities such as Qayrawan, Tripoli and Tangier was a mix of Arab and Berber influences, brought together under the banner of Islam and closely connected to Muslim civilizations in the Middle East and al-Andalus.

From this urban hub along the Mediterranean coast, Islam slowly began to diffuse southward across the Sahara Desert. In West Africa, the landscape is dominated by the Savannah and the Niger River. Sustainable settled communities are difficult in the rolling grasslands that evolve into the Sahara Desert north of the river, as well as in the dense forests to the south. As a result, most West African kingdoms, before and after the arrival of Islam, tended to cluster around the Niger River, particularly the inland delta that provided rich farmland. A nomadic group of Muslim Berbers, the Tuareg, dominated the trade routes that led from North African cities, across the desert wasteland, and into the West African Savannah. The kingdoms that developed in this region relied heavily on the trans-Sahara trade, which provided a market for their goods, chiefly gold and salt.

That same trade brought more than just wealth to West Africa, it also brought Islam. Muslim merchants who made the trek across the desert began to settle in West Africa, and by the eleventh century, immigrant Muslim communities could be found in many cities and towns across the Savannah. Since the bulk of the Muslims in West Africa were businessmen and not missionaries, Islam spread slowly among the local populations. West Africans would commonly convert to Islam and yet hold on to pre-Islamic beliefs in spirits and sorcerers for generations. Unlike in North Africa, where Islam came in as a strong political force all at once, Islam in West Africa slowly diffused into the local culture, accepting new Muslims without requiring them to adhere to all Islamic beliefs immediately. The only exception to this was the Murabitun movement, which managed to conquer land in West Africa for a brief decade in the eleventh century, but doesn't seem to have had a lasting impact.

The first native Muslim kingdom of West Africa was Mali. It was founded in the 1200s by the mythical character Sundiata Keita, a partially Islamized ruler of the Mandinka people. Nicknamed the Lion King, he was said to have been exiled by an evil ruler, rallied support among the Mandinka people while in exile, came back to take his rightful throne, and took the title *Mansa*, Mandinka for *King of Kings*. The details of the story have probably been blurred through generations of oral storytellers, but what is known for sure is that the empire that Sundiata founded in West Africa in the Inner Niger Delta region soon grew to be one of the wealthiest and most powerful states of the age.

The wealth of Mali is best seen in the reign of Mansa Musa, who ruled from 1312 to 1337. After taking power when his brother, the former mansa sailed west across the Atlantic in search of new lands, Mansa Musa took hold of what was probably one of the wealthiest and most powerful Muslim empires of the day. While the Middle East was dealing with the consequences of the Mongol invasion and al-Andalus was reduced to the Emirate of Granada, Mali rose in the Savannah south of the Sahara Desert to become the premier Muslim political entity. Yet it was far away from the eyes of the rest of the Muslim world, which was relatively unaware of this distant Muslim state. Most of what we know about Mali from this time comes from accounts of Mansa Musa's epic 1324 *hajj* to Mecca, which served to showcase Mali's wealth and power to the rest of the Muslim world.

Mansa Musa's *hajj* caravan departed the West Africa Savannah with an entourage of over 60,000 people. The king was accompanied by 12,000, each dressed in valuable silk robes and carrying two kilograms of gold extracted from Mali's famous gold mines. Camels also carried bags of gold dust, which was distributed to the poor along the route. Numerous towns and cities along the route marveled at the grand procession coming from the unknown West African kingdom. When Mansa Musa reached Egypt, which was then ruled by the Mamluk Dynasty, Mansa Musa left quite an impression on the local Mamluk officials. They recorded that he was exceptionally devout, never missing a prayer and with a mastery of the Quran. In Egypt, Musa was said to have given out so much gold to the cities' locals, that unintended inflation wrecked the economy, and when the famous North African traveler Ibn Battuta visited Egypt ten years later, he noticed that the local economy had still not recovered from the giant influx of the valuable metal.

Perhaps more remarkable than his journey to Mecca was Mansa Musa's return to Mali. Given that Mali was still in the middle of a long process of Islamization and local indigenous beliefs still mixed with Islamic orthodoxy, Mansa Musa saw a need for more qualified Islamic scholarship. Using his considerable wealth as a tool for the advancement of Mali, he paid for some of the best scholars, teachers and artists to accompany him back to West Africa. Arabs, Persians and Andalusians all came to Mali with Mansa Musa in the 1320s, creating an African society with clear influences from the rest of the Muslim world. Furthermore, the huge influx of scholars helped catapult Mali to the forefront of knowledge. Half a century after the Mongol disaster that destroyed Baghdad's House of Wisdom, a new hub of scholarship arose in the West African Savannah.

In the early 1400s, a scholar of *fiqh* from the Hijaz, 'Abd al-Rahman al-Tamimi, traveled to Timbuktu only to realize that the level of scholarship was so high there that he would have to go to Fez first to take prerequisite courses before he could study with Mali's scholars.

The center of Mali's knowledge was Timbuktu. About twenty kilometers north of the Niger River, Timbuktu lies on the edge of the Sahara Desert and was a major stop along the trans-Sahara trade. It came under Mali's control during the reign of Mansa Musa, and immediately benefitted from his importation of scholars. Libraries, mosques, and universities sprung up all over Timbuktu, giving the city a distinctly Islamic character. One of the people Musa brought back with him to Mali, the Andalusian architect Abu Ishaq, was commissioned by the sovereign to build palaces, mosques and schools throughout Timbuktu in the hope that it could rival other, older urban Islamic centers. Musa also sent scholars from Mali north to the more established educational institutes in Morocco to be educated in advanced concepts in Islam so that they could come back and serve the Malian community in Timbuktu. Both Mali and the Songhai Empire, which replaced Mali in the late 1400s, granted special benefits to Islamic scholars, commonly giving them tracts of land and charters of privilege. Through the importation of scholars from the Arab world and the intellectual growth of the native African community of Timbuktu, it became one of the leading centers of Islamic knowledge in the world at a time when Muslim civilization was on the decline in its traditional centers.

EAST AFRICA

The East African coast did not have to wait long to be exposed to Islam. Before Muhammad undertook his *hijra* to Medina, a group of his Companions escaped Meccan persecution and settled in Aksum (modern-day Ethiopia) for a few years, where a Christian king welcomed them. Immigration also went in the opposite direction and Bilal, a Companion of the Prophet who would commonly recite the call to prayer in Medina, was a former slave from Ethiopia. This was not strange considering that before Islam arrived in the seventh century, trade links between the East African Coast and the Arabian Peninsula already existed. As had occurred in West Africa, it was through trade routes that Islam would spread along the Indian Ocean coast of Africa.

In the early nineteenth century, a Muslim slave in America, Bilali Muhammad, wrote a thirteen-page manuscript about Islamic law based on West Africa's educational curriculum to teach fellow slaves on his plantation.

Merchants from the Arabian Peninsula, in particular the region of Hadramawt in Yemen, began to settle in cities along the East African Coast in the centuries following Yemen's conversion to Islam. The earliest artifacts attesting to Islam's presence in East Africa date from the late 700s and early 800s. Evidence shows that Islam was incorporated into East African life first in the northernmost parts of the coast, which were nearest to Arabia. Mosques dating from the tenth century have been excavated in Kenya, about 2500 kilometers south of the birthplace of Islam. By the thirteenth century, Islam had taken root even further along the coast in what is now Tanzania. The main avenue through which

Islam spread in East Africa was commerce. As a rich Indian Ocean trade developed, East African city-states welcomed Muslim merchants. It was through these areas that Islam diffused into the coastal region.

The pattern of conversion along the coast is unique in the Muslim world. East Africa was distant enough that no large-scale population movements occurred, yet accessible enough that a sizeable number of traders were able to regularly visit the coast, and in some cases permanently relocate. Wealthy merchants who settled in the cities along the coast intermarried with local African women, assimilating into the local culture, but with the addition of Islam. These were not settler communities of Arabs and Persians who dominated the local Africans. This was a genuine intermixing of cultures that led to the development of a new hybrid culture, with Islam at its heart. Swahili, a Bantu language native to East Africa, became the lingua franca of the coastal region as merchants travelled from city to city, tying the region together culturally and linguistically. Because of visiting Arab merchants, Swahili adopted many Arabic loanwords, but at its core, it remained a native African language. Similarly, Africans in the port cities adopted aspects of Arab and Persian culture. As has been seen in all parts of the world that adopted Islam, the arrival of the new religion did not mean the elimination of the previous culture and traditions.

As the local populations adopted Islam, powerful Muslim trading states developed along the Swahili coast. The most reliable information about them comes from the same Ibn Batutta who visited West Africa in the fourteenth century. According to him, these city-states along the coast were not just commercial centers, but also religious ones. Ibn Batutta comments that the sultan of Mogadishu (in present-day Somalia) would rely on his religious advisors, the chief of whom was brought from Egypt, in the day-to-day affairs of his state. In Kilwa and Mombassa, he remarks about the religious zeal of their peoples and the large, well-kept mosques in those cities. He is especially praiseful of the Sultan of Kilwa, who would give special treatment to religious scholars and descendants of the Prophet, and regularly ate meals with the city's poor.

Besides anecdotes about the Islamic character of the East African coast, it is important to recognize the assimilation of Islam into the lives of the Swahili. Islam was not seen as an outsider religion imposed on the local Africans by Arab and Persian immigrants; Islam was seen as a native African religion. Stories of the African Companion of the Prophet, Bilal, and the presence of Muslim refugees in Abyssinia were important to the locals as they created a sense of identity that was entirely Islamic and entirely African. There were external cultural influences, chiefly from southern Arabia, Persia and India, brought by traders from those regions. But much like other parts of the Muslim world, a culture developed that was based on the pre-Islamic character of the region, modified to fit in with Islamic law, but not absent of influences from the variety of peoples, all tied together by common faith.

AFRICAN SLAVERY AND THE AMERICAS

The Islamization of Africa would lead to the eventual spread of Islam across the Atlantic Ocean in North and South America. Once the era of European colonization of the New World began with Columbus' voyage across the Atlantic in 1492, a pressing need for labor developed in Europe's American colonies. The original plan of enslaving Native Americans proved inefficient. Native Americans were decimated by European-introduced diseases and died by the millions in the early decades of the 1500s.

European colonists looking for a better solution looked south to Sub-Saharan Africa and its black population for slave labor. European slave-traders arrived at ports along the West African coast looking to buy slaves by the hundreds. They dealt with local African kings who would capture fellow Africans in war and sell them to the Europeans in exchange for more weapons that could be used to capture more slaves. This destructive cycle led to the complete political destruction of the region and the depopulation of large areas of West and Central Africa, whose peoples were forcibly taken across the Atlantic in inhumane conditions to work as slaves in the New World.

Of course, large parts of Black Africa had accepted Islam by the 1500s, and a significant number of the slaves taken to America were Muslims. Estimates vary, but of the 15–20 million Africans brought to America through the slave trade, between three and six million may have been Muslims. Their experience in America was one of humiliation and subjugation to European colonists. There were usually no laws regulating how slaves could be treated, so slave owners were free to beat, abuse or kill their slaves however they saw fit. Slaves generally worked on plantations in the American South, the Caribbean and South America, unprotected from the elements and forced to work long hours. Whippings and other forms of torture were common punishment for slaves who did not work up the expectations of the owners, or defied orders. Furthering the humiliation of the slave population, it was not uncommon for a slave to be given just one set of coarse, tattered clothing, or even be forced to work entirely naked.

While all slaves suffered at the hands of slave owners who refused to see them as equals, Muslim slaves experienced unique difficulties. Breaking from work five times a day for prayer was rarely possible, and travelling to Mecca to perform the *hajj* was totally out of the question. Furthermore, avenues to learn more about Islam were few. Some slaves who already had the Quran memorized before their captivity were able to revise their memorization and teach some parts of the Quran to others, but no educational institutions existed which could help preserve the Islamic tradition. Thus, as the generations went on during the sixteenth through nineteenth centuries, the knowledge of Islam among Muslim slaves and their descendants slowly decreased. Attempts to secure imported Qurans from Europe, bought with money made doing extra work, helped slow the decline of Islamic knowledge, but it was no substitute for the great centers of Islamic learning of West Africa.

In the 1800s in Rio de Janeiro, there was such a high demand from Muslim slaves in Brazil for Arabic Qurans that one bookseller imported over 100 Qurans per year to sell to the local slaves. The slaves would spend years doing extra work to pay for them.

African Muslim slaves also had benefits that other slaves did not. Unique among the slave population in the Americas, Muslim slaves tended to be very well educated, in some cases more so than their owners. The tradition of emphasis on education among Muslims in general and in West Africa specifically led to a class of Muslim slaves in the Americas who were literate, unlike most non-Muslim slaves and even Europeans. While in some cases their higher level of education gave Muslim slaves the opportunity to do less demanding work such as accounting and management for plantations, it also gave them the ability to organize and lead revolts. A notable example occurred in the Brazilian state of Bahia in 1835. Muslim scholars who had been taken to Brazil as slaves used their knowledge and positions of leadership in the sizeable Muslim community of Salvador to plan an organized rebellion against their masters. Notes written in Arabic were passed among slaves, detailing the plan and its objectives. The revolt, which involved about 300 slaves, ended up being unsuccessful as Brazilian soldiers brutally put down the activities of the Muslim slaves. But it did instill enough fear of Muslim slaves among Brazilians that many Muslims throughout Brazil were sent back to Africa in hopes of avoiding another revolt.

The centuries of servitude inflicted on Muslim slaves in the Americas was not without consequence. Throughout Islamic history, regions distant from the Arabian Peninsula almost always had some kind of intellectual or economic connection with the birthplace and central areas of Islam. For Muslims in the Americas before the modern era, however, being so far removed from the rest of Muslim world geographically and intellectually meant the eventual disintegration of that Muslim community. Each successive generation inherited less and less of the original Islamic knowledge and practice that the first generation slaves had. In the United States, by the mid-1800s, there were almost no Muslims left who had knowledge of Islam, and by the 1900s, only a few grandchildren of slaves could recall their ancestors practicing foreign rites different from the mainstream Christianity of most African Americans. A revival of the memory of Islam among the descendants of slaves came about in the twentieth century, however. The Nation of Islam, a syncretic religion bringing together Christian and Islamic rites and beliefs formed as a racial-religious organization aimed at the advancement of America's black community. By the 1960s, however, former Nation of Islam members such as Malcolm X and W.D. Muhammad led thousands of African Americans away from the Nation and back to a more mainstream understanding of Islam, one that had been slowly erased from the lives of their ancestors centuries earlier.

CHINA

After the establishment of Islam during the 600s and 700s in the region that stretched from Spain to India, various cultures beyond the borders of the Islamic empire slowly adopted Islam and eventually became Muslim-majority regions. Examples include East and West Africa, Central Asia and Southeast Asia. Islam also slowly spread into China at around the same time. Unlike those other regions, however, China never wholly adopted Islam, and the Muslim community remained a minority. Despite this, Muslims played an integral part in Chinese history for centuries.

Islam's origins date back to the caliphate of 'Uthman bin 'Affan, who sent another early convert to Islam, Sa'd ibn Abi Waqqas, as an ambassador to the Tang Dynasty of China around the year 650. Muslims were capable of reaching out to the distant Far East just decades after Muhammad led the meteoric rise of the religion in the 600s. But it was not until the 700s when a permanent Muslim presence was felt in China. It was in the 750s when Muslim soldiers were invited by the Tang government to serve in the Chinese military. Groups of Muslim warriors made the trek to China, and joined the military and bureaucratic structure of the Chinese government. Encouraged to intermarry with local women and settle permanently in Chinese cities, Muslims found a stable and prosperous role in Chinese society. Government and military work soon became the niche that Muslims occupied. Muslim pursuit of careers in those fields continues in China to this day.

Despite their role in the upper echelons of Chinese society, there remained many barriers between Muslims in China and native Chinese people. The eastern religions popular in China, namely Buddhism and Confucianism, are a world apart from Islam. While Muslims in Christian areas further west in the Muslim world could relate to others through a shared history about Abraham, Moses and Jesus, the Muslims in China had no such luxury. Thus, Muslim communities tended to be separated from mainstream society. Special enclaves developed that kept Muslims apart from other Chinese, but they also served as portals of Islamic knowledge that connected Chinese Muslims with their distant coreligionists in the Arab and Persian lands. Through such isolated communities in the midst of Chinese cities, Muslims were able to retain their Islamic identity and practices even thousands of kilometers away from the rest of the Muslim world.

But that isolation would end during the Mongol conquests of the thirteenth century. The Mongols' vast empire included Muslim lands in Central Asia and Persia along with China. The destruction of entire cities and regions in the Middle East meant the whole-scale movement of populations. With political unity linking the heartland of the Muslim world with Muslim communities in China, a new avenue for contact between the two regions opened up. Furthermore, mass migrations by Muslims into China meant a huge boost to the Chinese Muslim population. Just as important was the Mongol policy of assimilating Muslims into mainstream Chinese culture. Muslim communities no longer served as isolated enclaves surrounded by non-Muslims. They were instead encouraged to take on more public roles in society, and were especially useful as administrators in a Mongol Empire that encompassed Muslims in its eastern and western ends.

In the 1300s, the Hongwu Emperor wrote the "Hundred-word Eulogy", which praised the characteristics of the Prophet Muhammad. Copies of it were distributed to mosques throughout China.

During Mongol rule over China and the succeeding Ming Dynasty, Chinese Muslims became fully assimilated into Chinese culture. They were no longer seen as foreigners, but rather as Chinese countrymen with their own identity—Hui. The Hui were no different from the Han, China's majority ethnic group, other than when it came to religious identity. Finally considered to be fully a part of Chinese society after living in the country for hundreds of years, Muslims in Ming China were able to assimilate into the local culture, adopting Chinese customs and even names, all the while continuing their tradition of serving the imperial government as civil servants and military leaders.

It was during this time that perhaps the most famous Chinese Muslim, Zheng He (1371–1433), became one of China's greatest explorers. A Hui from the Yunnan region in the south, Zheng He was favored by the Ming government and was given command of a fleet of treasure ships. Commanding hundreds of ships, some large enough to carry all three of Columbus' ships alone, and tens of thousands of sailors, he was given the responsibility of trading with distant lands and establishing diplomatic relations between them and Ming China. His voyages touched dozens of modern-day countries throughout Asia, the Middle East and even Africa, but he is perhaps most fondly remembered in Southeast Asia, where he is revered as a figure who helped spread Islam in the Malay Archipelago. Mosques throughout the region are named after the famed admiral, known locally as Cheng Ho. But Zheng He managed to cross over from being just a notable Muslim figure to one who is celebrated among non-Muslim Chinese as their nation's greatest explorer. Zheng He is emblematic of the nature of Islam in China: fully Chinese yet fully Muslim with no contradiction between the two identities.

INDIA

After Muhammad bin Qasim's expedition into the Indus River Valley in the early 700s, Islam did not penetrate much further politically into the Indian Subcontinent. A foothold was established in Sindh, but due to its distance from the Muslim capital at Damascus and then Baghdad, further military expeditions were impractical and probably financially untenable.

The arrival of the Turks in the Muslim world pushed Muslim power further into India. Of particular note is Mahmud of Ghazni (r. 997–1030), a Turkic sultan who was the first to lead military expeditions deep into India. By establishing himself as the leader of an autonomous state based in Ghazni in the Afghan highlands, he was close enough to India to focus much of his attention on the subcontinent. His seventeen military campaigns into northern India served as the basis of his rule, bringing wealth and power to him and his empire. While his raids were no doubt detrimental to local power and rule in India, he also established major cultural centers and helped spread Persian culture throughout his reign. The legendary Persian poet Firdawsi, who perhaps did more to revive ancient Persian culture than any other person after the country's conversion to Islam, and al-Biruni, a scientist, historian, geologist and physicist, were both mainstays of Mahmud's court. Because of his status as a patron of the arts coupled with his ruthless raids into India, Mahmud of Ghazni's legacy in India today is colored by modern politics as much as anyone else.

In addition to his scientific discoveries, al-Biruni wrote volumes on Indian history and society. Translations of his history of India served as the main source of knowledge about India in Medieval Europe.

Regardless of his legacy, Mahmud and the Ghaznavid Dynasty he founded laid the foundation for Muslim conquest in India. The succeeding dynasty, the Ghurids, also ruled out of Afghanistan, and managed to push their borders even further into India, capturing Delhi in 1192. The Ghurids relied on slave soldiers of Turkic origin who formed the core of their army, much like the contemporary Ayyubids further west in the Muslim world. Like their counterparts in Egypt, who established the Mamluk Sultanate, the slave soldiers in India eventually overthrew their masters and inaugurated their own dynasty: the Delhi Sultanate.

The Delhi Sultanate ruled over parts of India from 1206 until the arrival of the Mughals in 1526. Five separate slave dynasties—the Mamluk, Khilji, Tughlaq, Sayyid and Lodhi—ruled from Delhi during the sultanate's three centuries. The exact political successions and conflicts are not vital enough to mention in detail, but there are important political trends that characterize the Delhi Sultanate. Firstly, the Sultanate was ruled as a Turkic slave dynasty, not unlike the Mamluks of Egypt. Power was rarely passed down from father to son. Instead, when a sultan died, a new general would be elected by notables of the empire to take his place. A sultan could even be recalled and removed from power by his subordinates if he failed to fulfill his duties as head of state. This allowed the sultanate to stave off the culture of complacency that plagues many hereditary dynasties after the first few generations. Furthermore, the vast majority of Delhi's sultans did not claim the title of caliph. They recognized the ultimate authority of the Abbasids as leaders of the Muslim world, and saw themselves as subjects. Even after the destruction of Baghdad and the relegation of the Abbasids to nominal figureheads in Cairo, the Delhi Sultanate regularly sent emissaries to the caliph seeking his approval and permission to rule under his authority. Despite being separated by thousands of kilometers and the high Himalayan and Hindu Kush mountain ranges, the Delhi Sultanate attempted to keep India tied together with the rest of the Muslim world, at least by name.

The Delhi Sultanate era is also notable for the spread of Islam within its domains. Islam had of course been present in India since the early 600s, when Arab merchants appeared in trading ports along the Indian Ocean coast. But it would take patronage from a Muslim political entity to truly spread Islam inland among a large portion of the Indian population. The Delhi Sultanate provided that opportunity. Sufi orders enjoyed royal sponsorship and were able to travel throughout India preaching to all social classes of people. Sufism, with its spiritual focus, found fertile ground in the subcontinent, where a polytheistic native population would have trouble accepting the strict monotheism of Islam without an inward, spiritual dimension. Itinerant scholars, many of whom came directly from Arab and Persian lands, preached spiritual fulfillment and a new connection with God which helped them gain huge followings during their travels. Furthermore, the egalitarian nature of Islam, exemplified best by the Prophet when he declared all believers are equal before the eyes of God, offered an escape from Hinduism's caste system, known for its rigidity and inequality. Exact numbers are impossible to come by, but through the combined preaching of wandering missionaries and the continued Indian Ocean trade that brought merchants to areas such as Gujarat and Bengal, Islam managed to find a solid foothold in Indian society throughout much of the subcontinent, even though the Muslim population never outnumbered the Hindu.

SOUTHEAST ASIA

The influence of travelling merchants and preachers in converting a local population was magnified further east in the Malay Archipelago. This region had long served as the crossroads of trade, connecting merchants based in India with those based in China. The Chinese, with their fixed bureaucracy and imperial traditions, were less capable of spreading their own culture and government ideas in the archipelago than the more flexible Indians. Thus, before the turn of the first millennium, Buddhism and Hinduism, exported from India, held major sway in Southeast Asia. The Buddhist Srivijaya Empire, based on the island of Sumatra and the Medang Kingdom based on Java, were among the numerous kingdoms that spread Indian influence in the region. But once Islam had established itself among India's coastal communities, the opportunity arose for merchants and preachers based in India to spread a new Islamic influence in Southeast Asia.

Once again, commerce played a major role in the spread of Islam in a land far away from the Arabian deserts where Islam was born. Conversion to Islam was attractive to local kings partly because of the economic opportunities it presented. Islam provided the glue that held together an Indian Ocean trade that spanned from East African city-states to Arabia to coastal India. Shared beliefs and Arabic as a lingua franca facilitated trade between regions that would otherwise not have much in common. If a king in Southeast Asia converted to Islam, he could also join this lucrative economic community. Once local rulers in the archipelago began to convert to Islam around the 1100s, powerful Muslim empires arose in the region, built on the economic opportunities that Islam brought.

It was through these rulers that Islam began to spread among the local population of the Malay Archipelago. Traditional stories in the region commonly state that a king was the first to accept Islam, followed by his close advisors and family, and that Islam would trickle down into society from the top. These kings probably provided the opportunity for missionaries from further west, many of whom preached Islam through Sufism, to come and spread their beliefs among the locals, spreading Islam in much the same way as the Delhi Sultanate. A notable difference is that, while in northern India there was a heavy Persian element to the spread of Islam, in Southeast Asia the missionaries tended to come from the Indian Ocean rim, particularly Yemen. Thus, the school of *fiqh* that became most prominent in East Africa, coastal India and Southeast Asia was that of Imam al-Shafiʻi, due to Yemen being a center for Shafiʻi learning as well as a key hub in the Indian Ocean trade. Northern India, on the other hand, was more influenced by the Hanafi school which was popular in Persia and Central Asia.

The Muslim kingdoms that arose during and after the Islamization of Southeast Asia were tied in with the rest of the Muslim world through the Indian Ocean trade network. The first Muslim state, Pasai, located on the island of Sumatra, was converted at least by the 1200s, when Marco Polo visited it and attested to the Islamic character of its port cities. Ibn Battuta commented a century later about the order of the kingdom and the power of its ruler. From Pasai, Islam spread eastward to the Kingdom of Malacca, which was established around 1400. Located on the strait through which virtually all shipping between India and China travels, its location made it one of the most important states in the region. Buoyed by the immense trading wealth from the ships that passed through its waters, Malacca exerted huge influence on the surrounding areas. Its Malay language and customs were adopted throughout nearby kingdoms, culturally linking the entire region including parts of modern Malaysia, Indonesia and the Philippines to the powerful trading empire. Its cultural influence served as a vehicle carrying Islam as well. Malay identity was linked with Muslim identity so much so that when someone converted to Islam, it was said that he or she had *"masuk Melayu"*, meaning "entered this realm of the Malays". This Islamic identity interwoven with culture and ethnicity would spread eastwards from Malacca throughout the Malay Archipelago and survive numerous invasions and occupations, first by the Portuguese and later by the Dutch and English.

REBIRTH

According to the fourteenth century historian and philosopher Ibn Khaldun, dynasties have a natural lifespan. The early years of a dynasty are characterized by expansive growth, a "desert toughness", an ethos of hard work and little desire for worldly luxuries. The second generation of the dynasty continues in the legacy of the founders, but growth slows as leaders begin to place more emphasis on the luxuries of urban palace life than on administration and leadership. By the third generation, the decay of the dynasty is complete as the leaders and viziers are so consumed by luxury and pleasure that the state cannot protect itself from internal or external threats due to the negligence of the rulers. At that point, the cycle begins all over again as a new dynasty rises to replace the old, decrepit one.

In this framework, the Muslim world in the mid- to late-thirteenth century was clearly in the third phase of Ibn Khaldun's dynastic theory. Incompetent leadership, the apathy of the warrior class and excessive wealth and luxury helped contribute to the

Muslim world's inability to defend against external attack. In keeping with Ibn Khaldun's philosophy, a new dynasty arose to replace the old order. The house of Osman, a Turkish warrior in western Anatolia, would rise in the fourteenth and fifteenth centuries to become the premier Muslim power and usher in a new era of stability, growth and cultural magnificence. But contradicting Ibn Khaldun's philosophy, this new empire would last far longer than just three generations. It would continue to be a world power until its fall in the First World War in the early 1900s.

"Son! Be careful about the religious issues before all other duties. The religious precepts build a strong state."

– Osman, speaking to Orhan

OTTOMAN ORIGINS

Due to the Mongol onslaught, families of Turks fled Central Asia to find refuge in the borderlands of the Muslim world. The Turks, being traditional nomads, were capable of quickly and easily adapting to whatever lands they entered, including former Byzantine domains. Ever since the Seljuks defeated the Byzantines at the Battle of Manzikert in 1071, Anatolia had been open to Turkish conquest and settlement. When the Mongols entered the region in the thirteenth century, the remnants of the Seljuk domain were crushed for good, and Anatolia was ruled by numerous Turkish dynasties scattered throughout the peninsula. These small states, known as *beyliks*, were usually based around charismatic military leaders known as *beys*.

One *bey*, Osman, managed a small warrior state on the very edge of the Byzantine Empire. Out of the numerous *beyliks* in Anatolia, his was the one that would rise to become a world power. The reasons for this are difficult to ascertain, but the fact that his *beylik* bordered the crumbling Byzantine state was important. The Byzantines were a shadow of their former selves. The once mighty empire only controlled Constantinople, Greece and parts of the Balkans by the early 1300s. They were still recovering from the disastrous Latin rule of Constantinople from 1204 to 1261, which effectively ended Constantinople's reign as the world's largest and greatest city. Osman was able to take advantage of the Byzantines' weaknesses and aimed at constant expansion of his domain into Byzantine lands. He was further aided in his quest by the fact that refugees from the rest of the Muslim world were fleeing Mongol slaughter, providing a valuable source of manpower to the small *beylik*. In this context, the idea of external *jihad* against the perceived enemies of Islam was revived as Osman led his soldiers in raids against the same enemy whom the Rashidun, Umayyads and Abbasids had fought against centuries before.

The traditional establishment of the Ottoman state ("Ottoman" being a corruption of "*Osmanli*", the Turkish name for Osman's empire) is considered to be 1299, although this date may be arbitrary. As the roaming band of warriors led by Osman and his son Orhan acquired more Byzantine towns, the Ottoman *beylik* began to resemble a stable state more than the territory controlled by a band of nomadic Turks. By the time Osman died in 1326, the Ottomans had captured their first major city, Bursa, which became the first Ottoman capital. Orhan continued in the gazi tradition of his father, leading warriors against the Byzantines all the way up to the shores of the Sea of Marmara, less than 100 kilometers from Constantinople. He also began to adapt the Turks to a more sedentary lifestyle. The Byzantine cities in Anatolia were established urban centers with strong fortifications. The Ottomans could no longer rely on the traditional raiding tactics that had been so beneficial to the Turks for hundreds of years. Instead, they began to lay siege to cities, surrounding them and aiming to squeeze them into surrender. The Byzantines, being preoccupied with civil disturbances in the Balkans in the early 1300s, were unable to protect their last remaining outposts in Asia, and the Ottomans quickly expanded their domain. As the Byzantines weakened, the Ottomans strengthened. In the first few decades of the 1300s, they had gone from a small tribal band of warriors to the most powerful *beylik* in Anatolia, and a serious threat to the continuation of the Byzantine Empire. They were so much of a threat that the Byzantine emperor Adronicus was forced in 1333 to meet with Orhan to discuss tributary payments to the Ottomans in exchange for the safety of some of the last remaining Byzantine fortresses.

As the fourteenth century wore on, the Ottomans continued to expand into territory that had not seen Muslim armies since the Umayyad raids on Constantinople almost 700 years before. In the 1350s, the Ottomans crossed the Dardanelles Straits into Europe for the first time. Taking advantage of Byzantine disunity in the region, Sultan Orhan, and later his son, Murad I, were able to firmly establish Ottoman authority in parts of Thrace. The Turks, with their nomadic history, managed to easily move entire families and tribes into the new European frontier and establish new towns throughout the conquered lands. This huge demographic movement gave the Ottomans stability in an area that would have otherwise been a challenge to manage.

The remarkable growth of the Ottoman state from a tiny Turkish *beylik* to a regional power in the fourteenth century was made possible by the unique intellectual tradition that the Ottomans built on. To the early Ottomans, their war against the Byzantine was a religious duty. The *ghazis* (warriors of the faith) that fought under Osman, Orhan and Murad believed themselves to be continuing in the tradition of centuries of Muslim warriors who picked up arms against the Byzantines. Islam provided a unifying force for the Turks of Anatolia to rally under. By professing to be protectors of the faith, the Ottoman sultans managed to get thousands of Turkish warriors to fight under their command. With the recent (and still ongoing) Mongol disaster in the Middle East fresh on their minds, the promise of being able to bring glory to Islam once again must have been a motivating factor for the Turks. Islam was the only force capable of bringing together a disunited, nomadic and diverse group of people like the frontier Turks of the fourteenth century.

With the Ottomans placing such an emphasis on Islamic tradition, the Muslim rules of war also applied. Back in the 630s, when Caliph Abu Bakr sent an expeditionary force north to face the Byzantines, he gave them strict rules about not harming civilians or private property, and only killing enemy soldiers. That tradition continued under the Ottomans, who seemed to have been remarkably tolerant of non-Muslims under their rule. As the Ottoman armies advanced into Europe, villagers were mostly left alone so long as they did not actively rebel against Ottoman authority. The freedom that the Ottomans gave Orthodox Christians contrasted greatly with the behavior of the Latin Crusaders a century earlier that raped and pillaged Byzantine territory for decades. In comparison, the Ottomans were lenient and fair conquerors. Furthermore, the aristocratic class of southeastern Europe was generally eager to seek help from the Catholics of the West in the face of Ottoman invasion. But the general population was not ready to see Latin domination of their lands once again, and they seem to have supported the Ottomans in many cases, once they received promises of religious toleration. Thus, for both practical and religious purposes, the Ottoman policy of religious tolerance seems to have been the rule as they expanded into Christian Europe.

The greatest period of early Ottoman expansion occurred under the fourth Ottoman sultan, Bayezid I (r. 1389–1402). His soldiers nicknamed him *Yıldırım*, meaning "Thunderbolt", due to his ability to quickly move his army back and forth between Europe and Asia. The yearly migration of his army meant that half the year was spent expanding the empire into Christian Europe while the other half was spent in Asia fighting against rival Turks and the partially Islamized Mongols. In Europe, he added territories that would remain under Ottoman sovereignty until a wave of European nationalism swept through the empire in the 1800s. He conquered Serbia, Bulgaria and, Greece, and was the first Ottoman to cross the River Danube into Wallachia. Constantinople itself was besieged by the Thunderbolt, although the Ottomans had neither the technology nor the numbers to bring that city to its knees yet. Even without that imperial city, the Ottomans were one of the most powerful empires in Europe and the Muslim world.

That power attracted the attention of another Muslim ruler seeking to be the next great world conqueror. Timur, a Mongol ruler whose domain included Central Asia and Persia, sought to re-establish Mongol authority in Anatolia in the face of Ottoman expansion. Although Timur was a Muslim, his actions in war did not differ from his non-Muslim ancestors who had ravaged the region 100 years before. He wanted to bring back the Mongol Empire founded by Genghis, which meant the transcontinental Ottoman state would have to be eliminated. At the Battle of Ankara in 1402, the two great military leaders Bayezid and Timur squared off. The Ottomans, despite being reinforced by soldiers from the Christian vassal states of Europe, were decisively defeated. The great Thunderbolt himself was captured in battle and taken to Timur's capital at Samarkand. The Ottoman realm, meanwhile, was divided between Bayezid's four sons by the victorious Timur, who hoped they would fight each other enough to bring about the end of the Ottoman Empire.

Coffee was first introduced by Yemeni Muslims in the 1400s. When the Ottoman Empire grew to encompass the Arabian Peninsula, coffee spread north to Istanbul, and from there to the rest of Europe.

For the next eleven years, the Ottoman Empire was in a state of constant civil war. Bayezid's sons Isa, Musa, Suleiman and Mehmet raised rival armies and met each other many times in battle in Europe and Asia, each seeking to become the sole inheritor of their father's empire. The Ottoman Interregnum, as it is called, showcases one of the inherent problems in the dynasty. There never existed a formal succession procedure by which sultans can be chosen. The Ottomans seem to have believed that the most able son would always arise somehow to win the throne after his father's death. This would ensure that only the best of the dynasty would become sultans, leading to an eternally powerful state. In practice, however, what this tradition meant was civil war between brothers that commonly erupted after the death of a sultan. This would continue to be a problem until Sultan Ahmad I formulated an official succession policy in the seventeenth century.

In the early 1400s, however, the sons had to fight to the death. By 1413, Mehmet emerged as the victor over his brothers and managed to reunite his father's lands under his control. How he was able to do this militarily is not as important as why the Ottoman Empire was capable of reconstituting itself after eleven years of civil war. The main reason was the institutions that the Ottomans established throughout their realm in the fourteenth century. Above all, the Ottoman emphasis on Islam as a unifying factor helped bring Turkish leaders back under Ottoman control when Mehmet won the civil war. As the protectors of Islam's frontiers, the Muslim population of Anatolia and the Balkans looked up to the Ottomans. The division of the empire among four sons meant that unity and strength in the face of Byzantine power was compromised. When Mehmet emerged as the victor, the Muslims of the region could once again unite, as they had previously, under a strong Islamic state in opposition to the Byzantines and other Christian nations. Furthermore, economically, the Ottomans established a guild system that also made use of the Turks' Islamic identity. Throughout the Ottoman state a loose system of guilds, known as *akhis*, regulated manufacture and business practices. The *akhis* were commonly intertwined with Sufi orders and placed as much emphasis on the spiritual advancement of their members as they did on business and trade. This provided an economic basis from which the Ottoman Empire could reconstitute itself after the Interregnum. Military traditions also played a huge role in the reunification of the empire. During Orhan's reign, an elite corps of soldiers was recruited that served directly under the Ottoman sultan. These troops are known as the janissaries, a corruption of the Turkish *yeniçeri*, meaning "new troops". By the time of Sultan Bayezid, the janissary corps numbered in the thousands, recruited primarily from the Christian populations of the Balkans. Since the janissaries came from diverse ethnic backgrounds but were all incorporated into a unified corps loyal to the Ottoman state, they served to unify the various cultures and backgrounds that lived under Ottoman sovereignty. Greeks, Serbs, Albanians, Bulgarians and others contributed to one of the most prestigious institutions of the Ottoman Empire, something that rarely happened with the Greek Byzantines or Catholic Latins.

In all, once Mehmet had reunited the empire in the 1410s, it continued with little residual hangover from the Interregnum period. Under Sultan Murad II (r. 1421–1444 and 1446–1451), the Ottoman state continued to annex Byzantine territory, until all that was left of it was Constantinople and its environs. Murad attempted to capture Constantinople and finally eliminate the last remnant of the Byzantine Empire, but his siege failed to defeat the city's massive walls. The challenge of conquering the seemingly unconquerable city would fall to his son, Mehmet II, whose name would go down in history as one of Islam's greatest military leaders.

THE TRIUMPH OF THE OTTOMAN EMPIRE

By the time Mehmet II took the throne in 1451 at age nineteen, the Ottoman Empire was by far the premier power in southeastern Europe and Anatolia. It was multi-ethnic, flexible and powerful. There was perhaps no man who better represented that empire than Mehmet. He was fluent in at least six languages that were spoken throughout his domain. Special emphasis was placed on Islam and scholars were greatly prized. The Empire—literally and figuratively—bridged the gap between Europe and Asia, and Mehmet placed much emphasis on bringing together the intellectual legacies of both. During his reign scholars of traditional Islamic sciences were patronized along with European Christian artists. Mehmet was reminiscent of earlier Muslim leaders such as Harun al-Rashid and Salah al-Din, who were masters of knowledge, leadership and military prowess.

But there were two major thorns in Mehmet's side. One was his relative inexperience. He was young when he took the throne, and was thus naturally distrusted by elder statesmen that had served under his father. In fact, Mehmet briefly held power once before, at the age of twelve, when his father abdicated to live a peaceful life of retirement. But that first reign ended when his own grand vizier, who brought back his father, overthrew him. When Mehmet came to power a second time after his father's death, doubts abounded in government and society about his ability to hold onto the throne. In order to prove his worth as sultan of the mighty empire, Mehmet realized he had to rid himself of the second thorn: Constantinople. The city was situated almost exactly in the middle of the empire. Although it was no longer nearly as powerful as it once was, it still had the ability to harass Ottoman trade and military movements. From a practical standpoint, it had to be eliminated. But there was also a religious element to the city. The Prophet Muhammad had predicted 800 years before that Muslims would one day conquer it, and that the leader and the army that did so would be wonderful indeed. Soon after taking power, Mehmet began making preparations to fulfill that prophecy. Doing so would strengthen the Ottoman Empire and his own position as its sultan.

Despite Constantinople's relative weakness, it was still a fortress that had never been breached. Its defenses were seemingly impenetrable. The city was surrounded on three sides by water. Its land-side was defended by the enormous Theodosian Walls, built in the 400s as a set of two walls that were as high as twelve meters and as thick as six meters. In their thousand years, Constantinople's walls had seen countless armies disintegrate in its shadow, including the earliest Umayyad sieges in the late seventh century. More recent attempts by Bayezid I and Murad II also ended in failure. If Mehmet wanted to be the leader that Muhammad had spoken so highly of, he needed new techniques and new armies to get the job done.

A few kilometers north of the city, he built a fortress on the banks of the Bosphorus Strait, across from an earlier one built by his great grandfather Bayezid I. The dual fortresses became a chokehold on the waterway, preventing the Byzantines from seeking reinforcements from the Black Sea region. To combat the city's massive walls, Mehmet commissioned a Hungarian engineer to build the largest canon the world had yet seen. The Ottomans were familiar with gunpowder, which made its way into the Muslim world from China in the previous centuries, but it had never been a decisive element in previous conquests. Mehmet's canon was over 8 meters in length and could launch a 250 kilogram ball 1.5 kilometers. The world's strongest wall needed the world's most powerful canon to bring it down. On top of that, Mehmet recruited an army from Ottoman forces in Europe and Asia that numbered over 100,000 soldiers, including Christians from vassal states in the Balkans. Mehmet was going all in on his gamble. With such preparations, failure to take the city could result in the disintegration of the Ottoman Empire itself.

Within Constantinople, divisions were arising that would play out in favor of the young sultan. The Byzantine Emperor Constantine XI believed they could only survive the coming siege by seeking the help of the Catholic Church. Many in Constantinople however were still bitter at the destruction the city experienced at the hands of Catholic Crusaders in the thirteenth century, and a faction of Orthodox Christians arose that openly opposed any cooperation with the West. Despite the contingents of Italian soldiers that made their way to Constantinople to aid in its defense, the inherent disunity in the city would prove to be one of the reasons for its eventual downfall.

Although he took Constantinople by force, Mehmet did not impose Islam on the city's inhabitants. They were free to continue to practice religion as they did before the conquest.

In April of 1453, Mehmet's army arrived at the walls of the legendary city. The few thousand defenders of the city managed to put up a valiant defense from behind the massive fortifications. But in the end, the constant bombardment, repeated attempts at going over or through the walls, and an ingenious strategy that involved carrying seventy Ottoman ships over two kilometers of land and into the city's harbor all led to eventual capture. On 29 May 1453, a Muslim army finally conquered the legendary city. Mehmet, thereafter known as "the Conqueror", made the city his capital. The Ottoman Empire no longer had a thorn in its side and Mehmet's fame spread throughout the Muslim world as the powerful ruler of an upstart empire that finally fulfilled the 800 year-old prophecy. At this point, there was no doubting the Ottoman Empire's position atop the Muslim world. After the destruction of Baghdad 195 years earlier—which plunged the Muslim world into its deepest lows in history—Muslims had risen again to expand their borders and reach into new frontiers.

The Ottoman conquest of Constantinople was more than a military victory over an old enemy. It also symbolized the resurgence of the Muslim world as an imperial and multicultural force. It had been centuries since the conquests of the Rashidun and the Umayyads opened up new lands to Islam. In those early years, as Muslims conquered ancient cities such as Damascus, Ctesiphon, and Toledo they created a new amalgamated culture, which brought together Islam and local traditions. The Ottomans in Constantinople, which became popularly known as Istanbul, brought that practice back. In the new Ottoman capital, the cultural traditions of the Byzantines, Romans and Greeks found new life in an Islamic context. A prime example of these cultures mixing remains visible today in Istanbul's skyline. The ancient Hagia Sophia Church, built in the 500s by Byzantine emperor Justinian, was for centuries a symbol of Christian Byzantine power. After the Ottoman conquest, it was converted into a mosque, but remained the centerpiece of the city, with its gigantic dome serving as an inspiration and a model for Ottoman architects. Imperial mosques commissioned by sultans such as Mehmet II, Suleiman, and Ahmed I all borrowed the motif of a giant central dome, although adapted for Islamic use with tall, thin minarets and Arabic calligraphy inside instead of Christian figural art. Like in earlier Islamic history, conquest did not mean the replacement of one civilization with another, but the creation of a new one based on the cultures of both.

THE OTTOMAN GOLDEN AGE

The Conqueror continued to expand the Ottoman realm militarily. Soon, the Ottoman flag flew over more territories in Serbia,

Bosnia, Moldova and Albania. In his last years, an expeditionary force was sent to Italy, with the aim of taking Rome itself, although this plan was aborted upon news of his death in 1481. Military and economic expansion continued under his successors, sultans Bayezid II and Selim I. During the brief, eight-year reign of Selim from 1512 to 1520, the Ottomans defeated the new Safavid Dynasty of Persia and annexed the entire Mamluk Sultanate of Egypt. The traditional heartland of the Muslim world, including Syria, Egypt and the Holy Cities, came under Ottoman control. As such, the dynasty took on an increasingly religious role. Protection of Mecca, Medina and Jerusalem fell to the Ottoman sultans. Furthermore, the Abbasid caliphate, which existed in name only under Mamluk protection in Cairo, officially came to an end as Sultan Selim I inherited the title as the first Ottoman caliph. Although Ottoman sovereigns used the title sparingly, the implications of being the most powerful state coupled with the seat of the caliphate meant the Ottomans were expected to take on the role of protector of Islam. As such, the Ottomans aided Muslims combating growing European power as far away as North Africa and Indonesia throughout the sixteenth and seventeenth centuries.

The nature of the Ottoman Empire as a Muslim state did not mean oppression and subjugation of non-Muslims. In keeping with Islamic law, non-Muslims were allowed to practice their religion freely, but the Ottomans also went a step further and allowed Christians and Jews within the empire to form semi-autonomous communities. In what they called the millet system, non-Muslims were allowed to elect their own leaders to represent them in the Ottoman government. These leaders served as intermediaries between the Ottoman sultans and the various faith communities within the empire. Eventually, dozens of millets were formed to represent the numerous Christian churches present in the Ottoman realm. For an empire that had a non-Muslim majority, including and integrating that population was of the utmost importance. Unlike many other European empires of the time, ethnic and religious homogeneity within its borders was not a pre-requisite for stability and power. In fact, part of what made the empire so great was its ability to host various peoples and benefit from what each could provide for the empire.

The golden age of the Ottoman state was no doubt during the illustrious forty-six-year reign of Sultan Suleiman from 1520 to 1566. During his time, the Ottoman Empire reached its maximum size. The Balkan Peninsula, the Arab world including the Arabian Peninsula and North Africa, and parts of the Caucas Mountains and Persia fell under Ottoman control. The energetic sultan personally led assaults on previously unconquerable strongholds in Rhodes and Belgrade, but failed in a 1526 siege of Vienna, which set the border between Christian and Muslim Europe during the sixteenth and seventeenth centuries. Continued expansion meant further spoils of war, fueling an already strong economy based on lucrative trade routes through the empire. The immense economic power of the empire also led to great cultural achievements.

As part of his administrative reforms, Suleiman lowered taxes on peasants in his empire. This led to immigration of Christian peasants who left the rest of Europe to live and work in the Ottoman Empire.

With unrivaled political, military and economic power, Suleiman was able to make major changes to the legal system of the Ottoman state. With his grand mufti Ebussuud Efendi, the highest legal official in the empire, he rewrote the entire law book of the empire. As in almost all previous Muslim states, the highest set of laws remained the unchanging *shari'ah*, the Islamic laws based on the Quran and *hadith*. But the empire's secular laws, instituted by previous sultans, had to be examined to make sure they did not conflict with each other or with the *shari'ah*. Outdated, contradictory or un-Islamic laws were eliminated. The result was a streamlined and straightforward legal code that would serve the Ottoman Empire for hundreds of years. For this, his subjects affectionately knew him as *Kanuni*—"the lawgiver".

When Suleiman died in 1566, power went to Selim II. Unlike the first Selim, Suleiman's favorite son was not nearly as effective as an administrator or military leader. An ill-advised invasion of Cyprus in 1571 prompted a united Christian front against the Ottoman Empire. At the Battle of Lepanto in that same year, Christian Europe finally won a decisive victory over the Turks, and Ottoman navel supremacy in the Mediterranean was forever gone. But the Ottoman Empire was not a feeble house of cards in mortal danger after a single loss. It remained a major European power for hundreds of years after Selim's reign. However, the age of Ottoman conquests was over by the late sixteenth century. Europe was finally catching up with the Muslim world both technologically and socially, just as the Ottomans were learning what the limits of their military and political power were. It would take another few centuries before the balance of power would fully shift, but the long, slow decline of the Ottoman state had begun.

THE SAFAVIDS

Soon after the meteoric rise of the Ottoman state in the fifteenth century, a new empire formed in the east as a rival to the Turks.

The Safavid Empire's origins are similar to the Ottomans' in many ways, but the worldview it espoused and its religious structure were fundamentally different. The conflict between the two great empires in the sixteenth through eighteenth centuries helped define the Middle East's religious makeup for centuries, the results of which are still visible today.

As early as the eleventh century, windmills in Persia were used to pump water for irrigation.

After the decline and fall of Timur's empire in the 1400s, Persia entered a period of political anarchy. No one group was able to exercise control over the entire region, and various petty principalities appeared, seemingly always in conflict with each other. With no central authority, diverse and sometimes unorthodox ideas were free to flourish. Although Persia had been mostly Sunni since its conquest in the 600s, a Shi'a movement began to flourish in the north, led by a Turkic Sufi order known as the Safavids. The order traced its origins to the chaotic period after the Mongol invasion in the 1200s, and over time became more mystical and more hereditary than other Sufi paths. Eventually, it adopted the Twelver branch of Shi'ism as its official creed. Shi'a empires had come before the Safavids, but they had never been Twelvers. This was because a core belief of the Twelver branch is that the Twelfth Imam is in hiding and will only come back at the end of times as the savior of humanity. Most Twelvers thus believed that political activism should be halted until the Imam returns. The Safavids got around this by implying that the leaders of the group were descendants of 'Ali and were in contact with the Hidden Imam himself, giving them legitimacy as a hereditary Shi'a political group.

With such a fusion of political and religious legitimacy, the Safavids went about creating an empire in the late 1400s. Much like Osman and his descendants, the Safavids led armed incursions into Christian-dominated lands, particularly the Caucasus, north of their base in Azerbaijan. The growing power of the Safavids in the late 1400s coupled with their heterodox religious views led to opposition and oppression from the Sunni princes of Persia. In 1488, the leader of the Safavids was killed, and control of the group went to a two-year old boy called Isma'il. Throughout his childhood, he was in hiding, protected by a group of warriors loyal to him known as the Qizilbash (Turkish for redheads, referring to the distinctive red hats they wore). When Isma'il eventually came of age, he proved to be an able military commander as he led the Qizilbash to victory over the Turkish princes of Azerbaijan, eventually capturing the city of Tabriz, which would serve as his capital, in 1501. The following years brought more victories, and by 1510, most of Persia was under his control.

Isma'il's expansion of the Safavid domain is due to more than just his military capabilities and Persia's relative disunity. Isma'il also tapped into a long-dormant but powerful sense of Persian nationalism that lay just under the surface of Persian society. Since the Muslim conquest in the 600s, Persia had not had a native Persian government. The Arabs and later the Turks and Mongols dominated the region, even while the general population clung to their pre-Islamic Persian identity. Isma'il brought that identity back to the forefront. He declared himself Shah, a pre-Islamic term meaning king that brought back memories of the great Persian Empires of the past. Persian became the lingua franca of the government and the people. To make the Empire even more uniform, Isma'il joined together Persian nationalism with Twelver Shi'ism. His branch of the Shi'a movement became the official religion of the empire and was harshly imposed on the population. Sunni Islam was outlawed, and the population was given the choice to convert, flee or die. Shi'a scholars were brought in from outside the empire, notably Iraq and Lebanon, to educate the masses in their new beliefs and eradicate the legacy of Sunni intellectualism. The land of great Sunni scholars such as Abu Hanifa, Ibn Sina and al-Bukhari quickly became the center of the Shi'a movement. But Isma'il was not content controlling only the beliefs of Persians and hoped to not only convert people inside his borders to Shi'ism, but outside of it as well. Missionaries were sent into Anatolia to encourage the people to adopt Shi'ism and rise up against the Sunni Ottomans.

Unluckily for Isma'il, the Ottoman sultan in power during the 1510s when this missionary work was going on was Selim I, whose nickname, *Yavuz*, meant grim. Needless to say, Yavuz Selim was not one to sit idly by as outsiders interfered in his empire, especially when they promoted an unorthodox version of Islam. In 1514, Selim invaded the Safavid domain, seeking to crush Isma'il and his army. The two sides met at Chaldiran, near the capital, Tabriz. In a fight that pitted Ottoman canons and guns against Safavid religious fervor, the Ottomans came out on top. Isma'il fled, with his supernatural aura forever tainted. He supposedly lived the rest of his life in depression and alcoholism, never having gotten over his defeat at the hands of the powerful Sunni empire. His empire remained intact, though. Selim was unable to annex Safavid territory, and the battle served more to formalize the border between the Sunni Ottomans and the Shi'a Safavids than to end the dynasty. That border remained generally unchanged through the centuries and lives on today as the border between Sunni Turkey and Shi'a Iran.

The empire of Isma'il reached its zenith under his great grandson Shah Abbas I, who ruled from 1587 to 1629. When the border with the Ottomans became more concrete and warfare less common, the Safavids were able to focus more on a real revival of Persian culture. Painting human figures, which was generally discouraged by Sunni scholars, flourished in Safavid Persia. The Persian miniature became the dominant form of artistic expression and heavily influenced art in neighboring Muslim states as well. Unlike works of the contemporary European Renaissance, with its focus on realism in painting, Persian miniatures were not meant to depict realistic scenes. They were usually used to illustrate illuminated manuscripts, and thus served to supplement a given story. Along with the miniatures, the art of Persian story telling experienced a revival as well. The old pre-Islamic epics found new life alongside newer works telling the story of the Persian people. The *Shahnama*, a ninth century epic poem telling the history of pre-Islamic Persia achieved special notoriety as it encouraged people under Safavid control to embrace their Persian culture and history. The greatest testament to Safavid power and culture came in the form of Persian architecture and urban planning. In Isfahan, Shah Abbas I's capital, elaborate public buildings and mosques were constructed. Supplemented by vast open gardens and complex geometric mosaics and calligraphy, the structures in the imperial city stand as a testament to the wealth and power of seventeenth-century Safavid Iran. Safavid architecture of the era was so enchanting that a common phrase developed to spur on the city's fame: "Isfahan is half the world".

THE MUGHALS

The third great Muslim gunpowder empire came about in the East, in India. Here, the Delhi Sultanate had ruled over the northern part of the Indian subcontinent since the early 1200s. The fusion of Arab, Persian and Turkic cultures with native Indian cultures slowly forged a new and unique Indian Muslim civilization. By the early 1500s, Muslim political power in India was waning, but enough of the population had become Muslim—and accustomed to Muslim culture—that a new Muslim dynasty would be able to easily take hold in the subcontinent.

The Mughal Empire was founded by a Turkic conqueror from Central Asia, Babur (1483–1530). He claimed to be a direct descendant of Genghis Khan and Timur, and believed that his genealogy was a sign that he too would lead a great empire. However, his early years as ruler of his father's small state in modern-day Uzbekistan proved to be relatively unsuccessful. He lost control of the major city of Samarkand, along with his ancestral homeland in the Fergana Valley, and was forced into exile with a small band of followers. He eventually established himself as the ruler of the city of Kabul, in the Afghan highlands, by taking advantage of disunity and anarchy in the region. From this base he attempted on many occasions to conquer his homeland in Central Asia, at times with Safavid help, but was ultimately unsuccessful. Instead, he turned his attention across the Hindu Kush Mountains and into India. In 1524, he attacked the Delhi Sultanate, at the time under the control of the Lodhi Dynasty. At the Battle of Panipat in 1526, Babur decisively defeated India's lone Muslim state and enthroned himself in Delhi. As the sixteenth century wore on, the Mughal Empire extended its reach over most of the Indian Subcontinent. In many cases, local rulers were left in place in return for nominal loyalty to the Mughals.

In a land as diverse and disjointed as India, such a political arrangement was necessary to the stability of the imperial state.

Urdu, a language common among India's Muslims, exhibits Arabic, Persian, Turkic and Indian influences. Its name derives from the Turkic word "*ordu*", meaning army, since it was at the Turkic army camps that these four languages intermingled.

Unlike his ancestor Timur, who raided into India but never established a lasting empire, Babur's state in the subcontinent would last for centuries. It was called the Mughal Empire, a reference to Babur's supposed Mongol heritage, but Mongol culture and tradition played a relatively small role. Instead, the Mughal Empire served as a fusion point for Arabs, Turks, Persians and Indians. Much like the contemporary Ottoman Empire, the Mughal Empire brought together diverse peoples and traditions. It was not uncommon for a Hindu in the Mughal Empire to read and write in Persian—the literary language of much of the Muslim world—or for a Persian Muslim architect to be inspired by local Indian Hindu buildings. A student of the great Ottoman architect Mimar Sinan travelled to the Mughal Empire to take part in the construction of the legendary Taj Mahal. India was particularly attractive to Muslim religious scholars from other parts of the Muslim world who saw in India an opportunity to spread Islam through missionary work.

The atmosphere of mixing cultures and ideas reached its peak during the time of Mughal Emperor Akbar (r. 1556–1605). Considering himself a patron of the arts and an intellectual, he was keen to support scholars regardless of their cultural or religious background. He was known for hosting debates and discussions at his court between scholars of various faiths. Hindus, Buddhists, Christians, and Jews were all invited to discuss their varying concepts of God and religion with Muslim scholars. Eventually, Akbar went on to formulate his own religious theories, which in his mind bridged the gaps between the various traditions. He called his new religion *Din-e Ilahi*, meaning "Religion of God". Monotheistic Islam and polytheistic Hinduism are not naturally compatible theologies. As a result, Akbar's religion tended to focus on personal behavior rather than divinity. Traditional Muslim scholars were scandalized by Akbar's actions, declaring them blasphemy and beyond the borders of Islam. In the end, *Din-e Ilahi* was never particularly popular. Adherents seem to have followed it simply to gain favor with the emperor, and the new religion did not last after Akbar. Its short-lived existence testifies to the high level of cultural, social and even religious mixing present in a diverse Mughal India.

The succeeding emperors charted a path back to traditional Islam. This culminated with Aurangzeb (r. 1658–1707), the sixth Mughal Emperor, and the one who ruled over its apogee. His imperial title was Alamgir, the World Conqueror, on account of his military expeditions all over India. His forty-nine-year reign can be characterized by the increasing military activities of the Mughal Empire and his personal piety and sponsorship of Islamic knowledge. He famously disagreed with his father Shah Jahan's construction of the Taj Mahal, an elaborate (and expensive) tomb for his mother, which Aurangzeb saw as wasteful and against the spirit of what Prophet Muhammad had preached. He also felt that a comprehensive guide for Islamic law tailored to the needs of Indian Muslims was needed, and thus brought together hundreds of scholars of Islamic law to work out a solution. The result was the monumental *Fatawa-e Alamgiri* (the *Religious Decrees of Alamgir*), a collection of religious decrees based on the Hanafi school of Islamic law, which he used as the official legal code for the empire. Hearkening back to that first Muslim state in Medina, Aurangzeb thus established Islamic *shariʻah* as the law of India. This ended up increasing his popularity with his subjects throughout India, as previously-established taxes not in line with Islamic law were abolished, lightening the financial load on his subjects.

With regards to relations with non-Muslims, Emperor Aurangzeb has achieved a modern reputation as a bigot ted and intolerant sovereign. His legacy is indicative of the impact that modern politics has on how people understand the past. Worthy of particular scrutiny is the fact that numerous Hindu temples across India were destroyed during his reign. That historical fact, coupled with his intense devotion to Islam, has led many historians and writers in the modern era to refer to him as an intolerant and oppressive ruler. But the reasons behind his destruction of Hindu temples must be analyzed to understand what kind of a ruler he was, and more generally, the nature of Mughal rule itself. During the seventeenth century, temples in India were commonly used as political centers as well as places of worship. Temple leaders regularly served the Mughal Empire as political officers in their respective jurisdictions, helping maintain order and imperial control. The temples destroyed by Aurangzeb correspond to political revolts against Mughal rule led by temple officials, a trend that increased during his reign, especially with the creation of the Maratha Confederacy that arose in the late 1600s. Thus, in the eyes of the Mughal Empire in the seventeenth century, destroying a temple was not an act of religious oppression, but of political survival. In fact, during Aurangzeb's reign, numerous new temples were built throughout India, and many of his top advisors were Hindus. One of the dangers of a superficial study of history that has to be avoided in today's politically-charged world is the imposition of modern political conflicts onto the legacy of ancient figures.

THE THREE GUNPOWDER EMPIRES

Together, the Ottoman, Safavid and Mughal Empires are known as the Gunpowder Empires. They reigned over a new order in the Muslim world. Born out of the ashes of the devastating Mongol invasion, they represented the rebirth of the Muslim world. Despite spanning vastly different regions, having opposing political goals, and the occasionally difficult religious difference between them, they shared a common core culture based on Islam that made the three empires more alike than different. They all shared a religion that originated in the Arab lands, a court bureaucracy and culture based on the Persian model, and Turkic ancestry. A Muslim could conceivably travel in the 1600s from the Balkan Peninsula, through the Arab heartland into the Iranian highlands, and across the Hindu Kush into the Indian subcontinent without feeling particularly out of place. A new cultural unity developed that tied together a larger part of the world than the ancient Greek and Roman Empires ever did. Furthermore, there was a high degree of technical cooperation between them. The Ottomans were the first to adopt the use of gunpowder and canon on a wide scale, and the Safavids and Mughals soon followed. The degree of scientific and technical achievement was certainly not on the level of the Abbasid golden age of science, but this time marked the final era of Muslim technical superiority. Soon the

European nations would gain the upper hand, eventually decimating all three empires in the eighteenth and nineteenth centuries.

Most significantly for the modern Muslim world, the idea of pan-Islamic unity was seen as no longer feasible. The Umayyads and Abbasids had ruled over an empire that stretched from Spain to India, but that political model no longer seemed feasible. The caliphate was in the hands of the Ottomans, but some scholars of Islamic law floated around the idea of each region having its own caliph. There were even times when letters from the Ottoman sultans addressed the Mughal Emperors by the caliphal title, *Amir al-Mu'mineen*, meaning "Commander of the Faithful". There were later attempts at a symbolic pan-Islamic unity, most notably during the reign of Ottoman Sultan Abdülhamid II in the late nineteenth century, but by the time the gunpowder empires rose, the practicality of a pan-Islamic empire was all but gone.

DECLINE

PROBLEMS WITH THE OTTOMAN EMPIRE

Islamic history seems to go in cycles. In the seventh and eighth centuries, Islam sprung from the deserts of Arabia to create empires that were some of the most powerful in the world. The devastating period of invasion from the eleventh to thirteenth centuries reversed that, leaving the Muslim world politically, economically, and socially disjointed. The rise of the Ottoman, Safavid, and Mughal Empires in the fifteenth and sixteenth centuries signaled the rise, once again, of Muslim power on the world stage. The Ottomans, by the 1520s, had managed to even touch the edge of central Europe at Vienna, and although they failed to take that city, they were Europe's premier empire.

The Ottoman Empire's rapid rise was followed by a long, slow stagnation and decline. The beginning of this stagnation can be said to have started at the end of Sultan Suleiman's reign in 1566. Although the Ottomans were still the most powerful European empire at the time of his death, and would continue to be so for at least a few decades, several factors played into the oncoming decline of the Ottoman state. Coinciding with the decline of the Ottoman Empire was the rise of Western European states, particularly France and England, which soon filled the power vacuum left by the Ottomans as they retreated from the world stage.

The first and most obvious reason for Ottoman decline was that it was no longer able to win decisively on the battlefield. Early in its history, the Ottoman Empire had a clear technological advantage over its enemies, being the first to employ large cannons to knock down city walls (like those of Constantinople), as well as smaller, more portable weapons that would later evolve into rifles. It did not take long for the rest of Europe to adopt the similar technology, taking away the advantage the Ottomans had on the battlefield. In conjunction with this, the zealous warrior attitude that Osman built his small-scale *beylik* on faded away as the empire got bigger and more stable. The janissary corps, which had proven instrumental in many victories early on, succumbed to corruption and bureaucracy, and ceased to be an effective fighting force by the 1600s.

More importantly for the empire, however, was that it had reached its natural maximum size. The tradition of yearly campaigns that set out from Istanbul every spring meant that Ottoman armies were most effective in areas they could reach before the onset of the coming fall, especially in more northern areas of the empire that got colder faster. A prime example of this was the 1529 siege of Vienna. Ottoman armies left Istanbul in May and trekked across the Balkans throughout the summer, reaching Vienna's walls in late September which gave Suleiman only a few weeks to conduct his siege before returning to Istanbul. This logistical problem meant that Ottoman armies could not advance any further than Hungary, leaving the German-speaking lands of Central Europe out of Ottoman hands permanently. Another attempt at Vienna in 1683 similarly ended in failure.

The limits of Ottoman military ability became clear with the Treaty of Karlowitz in 1699. After a devastating fourteen-year war that pitted the Ottoman Empire against much of Europe, the Ottomans were forced to concede territory through a treaty for the first time in their history. Hungary, where Suleiman had marched victorious Ottoman armies in the 1500s, was ceded to the Austrians along with Transylvania. Parts of Ukraine inhabited by the Crimean Tatars, Muslim vassals of the Ottomans, were taken by Poland. Even the city-state of Venice made gains, acquiring Ottoman lands in southern Greece and along the Adriatic coast in the Balkans. Most significantly for later Ottoman history, the Ottoman sultan was forced by the treaty to recognize and protect Christians in the empire. The Ottomans had already been doing so in accordance with Islamic law and the millet system. What was important about this stipulation was that the protection of Christians was being forced upon the empire by outside powers. During the 1700s and 1800s, European nations would use this same concept to further disintegrate the Ottoman realm as it tumbled towards its final dissolution.

The inability of the Ottomans to succeed militarily had huge ramifications for other aspects of the empire. At its core, the Ottoman Empire was a military state. Conquest brought in more wealth, people and territory that would strengthen the empire and help it launch further military campaigns. During the unrestrained growth of the empire from 1300 to the mid-1500s, the militaristic nature of the Ottoman state paid huge dividends economically and socially, creating a pan-ethnic empire that benefitted from huge spoils of war. With the end of conquest, the Ottoman government would have to find new foundations on which to build the Ottoman economy. Such a fundamental change in the nature of an empire would always be difficult to manage, but compounding the problem was the decline in the quality of leadership that the empire experienced.

From the time of Osman in the early 1300s to the Golden Age of the empire under Suleiman in the mid-1500s, the Ottoman sultan was the ultimate executive of the Ottoman government. The sultan was expected to guide the Ottoman army in battle, lead the government through numerous viziers, dictate the empire's relations with other states and defend Islam as the caliph of the Muslim world. After Suleiman, however, there was a definite change in the nature of the sultanate itself and the role the sultan played in the government. Starting with Selim II, Suleiman's son, many sultans preferred to spend time enjoying the luxuries of the palace instead of engaging in the governance of the empire itself. Sultans once led the armies in battle and fought alongside their troops, boosting morale as the Ottoman soldiers marched through Anatolia, the Balkans, and the deserts of the Middle East. Beginning in the late 1500s, however, sultans would appoint deputies to lead the troops while they enjoyed the comforts of Istanbul.

Sultan Ahmed I (r. 1603–1617) cemented the lethargy of the sultanate. He officially ended the 300 year-old Ottoman tradition of princes fighting for the throne. Whereas previously sultans could not allow their brothers to live lest there be an insurrection against their rule (as occurred during the reign of Bayezid II), now all members of the Ottoman family were allowed to survive, but were forced to live in seclusion in the palace's harem. When a sultan died, government officials would go into the harem complex and simply pick the oldest surviving member of the Ottoman family to sit on the throne. Many of these sultans only came out of seclusion well into their adult lives, and had residual effects of spending decades alone in gilded rooms. Without any prior training in governance, sultans were incapable of effectively leading such a large and complex empire. Administration thus fell to the viziers and other government workers, who held effective power, albeit in the name of the sultan. In the 1600s and 1700s, the fortunes of the empire did not rely on the ability of the sultans, but of the grand viziers. Ahmed I's intention may have been to protect the dynasty from costly civil wars, but the results of his reform effectively prevented the Ottoman dynasty from producing any capable or effective sultans during the 1600s and 1700s.

Further exasperating the military and political problems of the Ottoman Empire during its decline was the economic situation of Europe starting in the 1500s. Western European nations such as Spain, Portugal, France, and England took the lead in exploring the New World, and exploiting its resources in a mercantile system that emphasized the amassing of huge amounts of gold and silver. The mines of Central and South America, in particular, provided shiploads of silver that made its way into European markets through Spain. When this huge influx of silver hit the Ottoman economy, the Ottoman currency was greatly devalued and inflation increased. The Ottoman economy was thus hit on two fronts: there were no further wars of conquest that brought in booty and the rise of Western Europe weakened the Ottoman Empire by comparison.

Intellectually the empire stagnated in the 1600s and 1700s. After centuries of Muslim advances in science. While Europe struggled through the Dark Ages, Ottoman scholars exhibited a certain amount of disdain for European intellectual progress. They could hardly be blamed for this, as Europe struggled to produce scientific or intellectual capital since the fall of the Roman Empire. The reality was that in the 1600s the Dark Ages were over. The Renaissance and subsequent Enlightenment ushered in a new era of European intellectualism which was ironically spurred by the translation of centuries-old Muslim works in major European cities. Most Ottoman scholars failed to recognize this shift, and European advances were disregarded as heathen innovations. Earlier in its history, the Ottoman Empire had sought to bridge the intellectual gap between Christian Europe and the Muslim world. European painters, scholar, and linguists could be found in the court of Mehmet II. But by the time Europe began to take a dominant role in world politics, the Ottoman Empire's mistrust of its Christian neighbors led to an anti-intellectualism that prevented its continued growth.

The huge influx of American silver caused runaway inflation in the Ottoman Empire. In 1580, one gold coin could be bought for sixty silver ones. Ten years later, in 1590, it would take 120 silver coins to buy one gold. In 1640, it took 250 silver coins.

Despite all these factors working against the Ottoman Empire, it remained one of the premier empires in Europe and the Middle East in the 1600s and 1700s. The incredible growth of the empire in its first 300 years was so great that the military, economic, political and intellectual challenges it faced in its stagnation could not completely undo what had brought the Ottomans to such dizzying heights. The fundamental nature of the empire had to change and adapt to new geopolitical realities. Most important was the relationship between the Ottoman state and the rest of Europe. Viziers were pragmatic enough to recognize that unending conflict with their Western neighbors would end in disaster. The antagonistic relationship between the Ottomans and the rest of Europe thus began to fade as Ottoman viziers recognized the era of expansion was over by the 1600s.

Nowhere was this clearer than during the Tulip Period that lasted from 1718 to 1730. During this time, the grand vizier of the Ottoman Empire, Nevşehirli Damat Ibrahim Pasha, charted a new course with Europe that was characterized by trade relations and cultural borrowing. European artistic styles, particularly Baroque, were adopted by the Ottomans and fused with traditional Islamic styles to create a new, distinctive look. Tulips (popular in the early eighteenth century in Western Europe) featured strongly in the art of this period. Despite the cultural flourishing of the Tulip Period, a more significant trend began to emerge in the relationship between the Ottoman Empire and Western Europe.

The stagnation and faltering of the Ottomans in the 1600s led to a precipitous fall in the 1700s. The aforementioned Treaty of Karlowitz of 1699 brought to light Ottoman weakness. But the subsequent wars and treaties of the 1700s made the decline of the Ottoman state clear for the world to see. An Ottoman attempt to regain Southern Greece led to a full-fledged war with Austria in the 1710s that ended with the Treaty of Passarowitz, which ceded Serbia to the Austrian Empire in 1718. An attempt to regain land that led to the further loss of territory was wholly indicative of the situation the Ottoman Empire was in. A few decades of relative peace were followed by a disastrous war with the Russians from 1768 to 1774. The Russians managed to gain control over the Crimea and the Northern Caucasus, and received vague assurances that Christians in the Ottoman realm would be protected. Complete partition of the empire in the late 1700s was only prevented by eruption of the French Revolution and Europe's preoccupation with it. By the end of the eighteenth century, the Ottoman Empire had lost huge amounts of territory in Europe. The tide had turned in Christian Europe's favor for good.

The economic and political concessions they were forced to make were just as destructive as Ottoman military defeats. In what were known as capitulations, the Ottoman government gave up effective control over huge swaths of its own economy and society to Western Europe as it declined. Sultans as early as Selim I had signed agreements with France, which gave the French special trading privileges within the empire. These early capitulations were mutually beneficial, as they strengthened the trading ties between two of Europe's largest economies. As the Ottomans declined, the capitulations took on a new character. In exchange for dearly needed diplomatic support, the Ottomans agreed to give up jurisdiction over French citizens within their own borders. This meant that Frenchmen were effectively immune from any kind of prosecution or control by the Ottoman government. By the mid-1700s, the French managed to get all Catholics within Ottoman borders recognized as French subjects, and thus under French law. Furthermore, they had the right to extend French law to any Ottoman subject they wanted. The result of this was that Christians in the empire were given a huge economic boost; they were given preferential treatment by the French, who covered them politically with the capitulations and then chose to trade exclusively with them. The majority of Ottoman overseas trade was now completely out of its control, and worse yet, the capitulations had to be renewed or even strengthened throughout the 1700s as the Ottomans continued to need French diplomatic support in order to avoid partition at the hands of Austria and Russia. The fact that the Ottoman Empire was willing to give up sovereignty within its own lands is indicative of how the empire had weakened by the eighteenth century.

Sultan Abdulmecid I's construction of extravagant palaces coupled with the disastrous Crimean War led to a depleted Ottoman treasury. In response, foreign loans were taken out at very high interest rates, further worsening the financial situation of the empire.

LIBERAL REFORMS

By 1800 it was clear the Ottoman Empire had to reform in order to survive. A series of sultans came to power in the nineteenth century that sought to reclaim some control of administration from the grand viziers as well as reform the empire along European lines. Mahmud II (r. 1808–1839) was the first of the reforming sultans. He reorganized Ottoman government to function in a more European style. Instead of competing viziers and their complex palace intrigues and bureaucracy, ministries were established to oversee foreign affairs, domestic affairs, justice, education, and other government departments. The janissary corps was ended in a bloody battle on the streets of Istanbul, as Mahmud established his *Nizam-i Cedid* (The New System), which followed European military practices. Education was brought in line with European standards and French was taught alongside Turkish in schools. Even clothing was reformed: the traditional turban and robe that government workers had worn for centuries were abolished in favor of trousers, military jackets and leather boots. The fez became the ubiquitous headgear among government workers and regular citizens alike. As Mahmud implemented his reforms, the expected opposition came from the religious scholars who opposed such cultural borrowing from Europe as religious innovation.

They were sidelined by the new, more powerful central government, which also began to exercise power in distant provinces, much to the chagrin of governors that had long experienced relative autonomy.

The reforms continued and accelerated under Mahmud's sons, Abdülmecid I (r. 1839–1861) and Abdülaziz (r. 1861–1876). Abdülmecid's reign ushered in an era known as the Tanzimat, Turkish for reorganization. Almost no aspect of Ottoman governance and social life was left untouched by the Tanzimat. European nation-states were seen as a worthy model to emulate, and experts were brought in from the rest of Europe to dictate changes that they believed were necessary for the Ottoman Empire. The changes of the Tanzimat Era included a modern postal system, a national bank, a census, tax reform, a proto-parliament and an Ottoman national anthem. The education system was overhauled along French lines. According to the ideals of the West, secular scientific education was promoted over the religion-based education that had been the norm throughout Islamic history. Earlier in Islamic history, scientific and religious research was seen as the same enterprise, and even the Prophet had promoted the advancement of knowledge. But with the imposition of French secular attitudes, scientific and religious knowledge were separated, with science considered more valuable. As a result, the new generation of Ottomans prized careers in engineering and medicine over the liberal arts and Islamic studies, a cultural norm that continues in much of the Muslim world today. According to the reformers and their supporters, these were all organizational reforms that were necessary for the Ottoman Empire to function effectively in the 1800s.

But more significantly, the Tanzimat was a fundamental change in the way the Ottoman Empire functioned legally. The old legal

---

The smallpox vaccination was developed in the Ottoman Empire. The
vaccine subsequently made its way to England through the wife of an
English ambassador who observed the practice in Istanbul.

---

law code established by Suleiman and his grand mufti in the 1500s
was replaced with a new one based on the French system, which
prized Enlightenment-inspired natural rights as the basis for the
relationship between citizens and their government. No longer
was the Islamic *shari'ah* the basis for law in the Ottoman Empire.
This infusion of secularism into the Ottoman state was met with
opposition from more conservative elements. Since their earliest
days, the Ottomans had prided themselves on being representatives and protectors of Islam. Osman managed to become a popular *ghazi* by leading the Islamic charge against the Christian
Byzantine Empire. Mehmet II fulfilled the Prophet's prediction of
an Islamized Constantinople. Selim I had brought the caliphate to
Istanbul. Now the Empire was shedding away that Islamic tradition in favor of a liberal, secular, Western approach that it borrowed from Europe. Throughout Islamic history, empires had
based their rule on the Islamic *shari'ah*; whether or not they actually followed it was a separate issue, but never before had a Muslim empire nominally recognized secularism as legitimate policy.
According to the sultan and his advisors, the reality of the times
dictated it, and change was necessary in order to appease Christian Europe.

Along with the rise of secular thought that came with the
Enlightenment, nationalism became a powerful intellectual force
in the nineteenth century. Europeans across the continent began

to shun the idea of traditional pan-ethnic empires in favor of nation-states that were dominated by ethnic or linguistic groups. For the Ottoman Empire, with its Turks, Arabs, Kurds, Armenians, Jews, Serbs, Bosnians, Greeks and multitude of other ethnicities, the concept of nationalism was problematic. When the Greeks managed to become independent of the Ottomans (with help from the rest of Christian Europe) in 1830, the threat of nationalism became real. Other ethnic groups within the empire could similarly seek independence, leading to the complete dismantling of the empire itself.

To combat nationalism, new concepts of identity and belonging had to evolve within the borders of the Ottoman Empire. Some officials, particularly ones educated in Western Europe and influenced by nationalism, attempted to bind all Ottoman citizens around the idea of Ottomanism. Under this idea, all Ottoman citizens, regardless of religious or ethnic affiliation, were considered equal. The Tanzimat Era's legal reforms had already guaranteed that, but now all ethnic and religious groups of the empire were encouraged to identify as Ottomans above anything else. In reality, however, Ottomanism failed to unite the empire's people around one identity. Capitulation to European states still meant that Christians had a huge economic advantage that most Muslims did not have. Now Muslims did not even have any kind of legal or social advantages either. Tensions between Muslims and Christians rose throughout the empire, as Muslims realized they were falling behind as Christians were becoming more powerful and influential. In the end, this attempt at uniting all Ottomans as one people only served to increase tension and agitation between religious and ethnic groups.

The Tanzimat Era lasted until 1876. The reforms of the period failed to slow the decline of the Ottoman state. Ottoman finances were still in disarray. Uprisings among the many ethnic groups of the Balkans became more and more frequent. Ottomanism and reorganization of the provinces failed to quell nationalistic feeling. Meanwhile, Western European powers continued to grow in power and influence as a new era of imperialism and colonialism commenced. Some Western-educated government officials, known as the Young Ottomans, believed the Tanzimat failed because they were not liberal enough. They encouraged more European secularism and further limiting of the sultan's powers. This powerful faction deposed Sultan Abdülaziz in 1876 and replaced with his nephew, Murad V. The new sultan was even more incompetent than his predecessor, and had a nervous breakdown after just a few months in power. He was similarly removed and replaced by his brother Abdülhamid II (r. 1876–1909). This shuffling of the sultanate by the viziers was meant to bring forth leaders who would continue the liberal reforms of the Tanzimat Era. Abdülhamid II's reign, however, did not go according to plan.

In 1908, Abdülhamid II established an Islamic university in Beijing, China, to serve China's Hui Muslims.

PAN-ISLAMISM

Abdülhamid was probably one of the most well-prepared sultans the Ottoman Empire had had in centuries. The system of royal imprisonment inaugurated by Ahmed I had faded by the nineteenth century, and, as a prince, Abdülhamid was able to travel Europe as part of diplomatic delegations and was reasonably well educated. In the mold of the classical era of Ottoman sultans, he was well-rounded and was an accomplished poet, a wrestler, and even fashioned most of his own furniture. Furthermore, unlike his extravagant predecessors, he shunned the luxury of the new, expensive palaces along the Bosphorus in favor of more humble accommodation at the smaller and more remote Yıldız Palace.

A capable leader was desperately needed when he came to the throne. The disastrous Russo-Turkish War of 1877–78 ended in the independence of Romania, Serbia and Montenegro, and the autonomy of Bulgaria within the Ottoman Empire. What was left of Ottoman control in the Balkans was slowly slipping away. Support from Britain in the 1870s held the Ottoman Empire together, which saw it as an effective buffer against Russian imperialism. Furthermore, the Ottomans had already declared bankruptcy in 1875 and a large portion of the budget was allocated to paying interest on the huge foreign debt the empire had accrued during its decline.

Although he had come to power promising to continue the liberal Tanzimat reforms of his predecessors, Abdülhamid took the empire in a new direction. The reforms that attempted to limit the power of the sultan in favor of an Ottoman parliament were abandoned as Abdülhamid sought to bring back the traditional power of the sultanate. The constitution written and implemented by his liberal grand vizier at the beginning of his reign in 1876 was suspended indefinitely in 1878, ostensibly because of the war with Russia. For the first time since the heyday of Ottoman power in the 1500s, the sultan was truly in power.

Along with the power of the sultan, Abdülhamid brought back another forgotten aspect of the Ottoman dynasty: the caliphate. The Ottomans had held the title of caliph since Selim I conquered Egypt in 1517, but it was seldom used. To Abdülhamid, however, his position as the inheritor of the office that started with Abu Bakr was of upmost importance. It was especially significant because with the loss of so much Christian Balkan territory, the Ottoman Empire was now a Muslim-majority state. The Turks, Arabs, Albanians and other Muslim groups within the empire were joined by Muslim refugees who were expelled by Christian powers in Europe—including the Circassians, who were ethnically cleansed from southern Russia in the 1860s. Getting his subjects to unify around their Islamic identity and allegiance to the caliphate was easier than the invented identity Ottomanism promoted. Furthermore, with so many Muslims living under European imperial domination in India, Africa and Southeast Asia, he could use his position as the spiritual leader of the world's Muslims as leverage when dealing with European imperial powers. Pan-Islamism was heavily promoted during his reign as he hoped it would breathe new energy into an Ottoman Empire on its last wind.

Hoping to unite Muslims around the idea of Pan-Islamism, Abdülhamid undertook a series of projects aimed at bringing back the orthodox Islamic nature of the Ottoman Empire which had faded during the Tanzimat years. Railways were laid across the empire, but of special importance was the Hijaz railway, which stretched from Istanbul to Medina. Logistically, it made sense to link the Ottoman Empire with its farthest provinces, and to make the arduous *hajj* journey easier for pilgrims traversing the Arabian Desert. The railway also served as a spiritual link between the Ottoman caliphate in Istanbul and the location of the first Muslim state, ruled by the Prophet. Delegations were sent to Muslim communities outside Ottoman borders, as far away as Sub-Saharan Africa and China. Loyalty from the world's Muslims could be useful to a sultan dealing with the growing power of Europe. In one particularly impressive act of Islamic bravado, he famously turned down Theodor Herzl and the Zionist movement, which offered to buy Palestine in exchange for paying down some of the empire's looming foreign debts.

Abdülhamid's goal of pan-Islamism coincided with the non-secular aspects of the Tanzimat, and reforms aimed at strengthening the empire continued. Grand viziers were appointed with the goal of reorganizing government bureaucracy in the hopes of becoming more efficient and competitive with European powers. Revenues increased during his reign and corruption subsided slowly. German military advisors were brought in to modernize and train the Ottoman army, while new naval ships were ordered from Britain, France and the United States. Education was expanded throughout the empire, as elementary and secondary schools were established to compete with the foreign schools funded by Christian missionary schools. By 1895, over a million students across the empire were enrolled in public schools, leading to a jump in the literacy rate.

Despite his efforts at modernizing the empire while maintaining its Islamic and monarchical nature, Abdülhamid was unable to stop the spread of liberalism and secularism within his domain. The European-educated elites never stopped hoping for a new Ottoman state based on the ideals of Western Europe, and in 1909, Abdülhamid was deposed by a secret society known as the Young Turks. Supported by Ottoman Christians and inspired by European secular liberalism, the Young Turks managed to end Abdülhamid's thirty-three-year reign and its Islamic-oriented administration. They chose not to end the sultanate, however. For the next thirteen years, two more sultans would reign, but only as puppets with no authority. Real power for the rest of Ottoman history was in the hands of the Young Turks.

INDIA

After the apogee of Mughal rule in India that occurred during the reign of Aurangzeb, the centralized nature of the empire began to unravel. Since its earliest days, the Mughal Empire had efficiently managed to turn other sovereign rulers into subordinates rather than eliminate them outright, as the Ottomans tended to do. Even in its heyday, the Mughal Empire was an amalgamation of various kings and governors owing allegiance to the Mughal emperor. This allegiance began to wane in the years after Aurangzeb's death. The main reason for this was the destabilizing wars of succession that wracked the empire. His son Azam Shah ruled for only three months before being killed by his half-brother, Bahadur Shah, in 1707, who in turn only ruled for five years before his own death. More ineffective leaders followed. In all, five emperors ruled in the twelve years after Aurangzeb.

With central authority descending into instability, local leaders began to act as independent sovereigns. They still nominally accepted the authority of the Mughal state as their overlords, but in practical matters, the Mughals had little to do with what happened in the provinces. Even when Emperor Muhammad Shah (r. 1719–1748) managed to provide stability and rule the empire for almost thirty years, local rulers had little use for the Mughal government. The fragmentation of the Mughal Empire had already begun.

In the early eighteenth century, India owned twenty-five per cent of the world's wealth.

As the empire as a whole began to unravel and break up into effectively independent states throughout the 1700s, instability reigned. Echoing the Taifa period of al-Andalus, petty kingdoms ruled by Muslims and Hindus arose, seeking to become the new dominant power in the Indian Subcontinent. Pashtuns, Bengalis, Sikhs, Hindu Marathas and even the British were active in the struggle for power in post-Aurangzeb India. The Pashtuns in the north, led by Ahmad Shah Durrani, managed to establish an independent kingdom that would later evolve into modern Afghanistan by taking land from the declining Safavid and Mughal Empires. Sikhs, who strongly resented Mughal authority after the death of Akbar, managed to exercise more autonomy through militaristic domination of the Punjab region. The Marathas, a confederacy of Hindus in the Western Deccan were one of the biggest threats to the Mughal Empire's continued existence. They managed to conquer most of northern and central India by the mid-1700s, only to be eventually marginalized by the Afghans and Safavids in the North, and the independent state of Mysore in the south.

As states rose and fell in their quest for power in eighteenth century India, Britain entered the fray. The British East India Company, a trading entity that had been doing business in India since the early 1600s, used disunity throughout India to expand its own control in the subcontinent. Beginning in the 1740s, the British company began to get involved in the wars in the Deccan, offering financial support and troops in exchange for exclusive trading privileges from local rulers. From the British perspective, this had the double benefit of expanding their own economic opportunities in India, while simultaneously pushing French merchants out. Within decades, the British managed to leverage their position in India to obtain trading rights throughout much of the country as well as authority as tax collectors and government advisors along much of the Indian Ocean coast. The British even managed to install their own favored government in Bengal in 1757 by using party politics in the region to their advantage. By the late eighteenth century, the British East India Company had risen from being one power among many in a disjointed India to the leading political force, with its own independent administration, military, economic and political goals.

Several factors made the East India Company's period of rule one that was disastrous for India, particularly the subcontinent's Muslims. Firstly, the purpose of any company is not to rule according to law and order, but rather to make money for stock-holders. Thus company rule in India was horribly exploitative, even by the standards European governments were establishing in the eighteenth century throughout the world. British free trade rights devastated economic competition from local merchants, leading to monopolies over many goods and crafts wherein the British could exploit local populations for revenue. The Company was especially disastrous for Muslims. The British, keen to make sure that the Mughals remained unable to rise again as a major power, tended to favor Hindu middlemen over Muslim ones. Hindus thus had huge advantages open to them that Muslims were generally excluded from. Furthermore, the Muslim-ruled areas in the north were fertile ground on which British power could grow, in contrast to the Hindu south, where Mysore managed to hold off British advances in the 1700s.

Just like in the Ottoman Empire, the nineteenth century saw the complete domination of India by Western powers, namely Britain. Officially, the East India Company did not have real sovereignty over most of India, and only exercised control through the myriad local rulers for whom they served as advisors and tax collectors. That changed when Indian soldiers serving in the Company army, known as sepoys, mutinied in 1857. The spark that lit the Sepoy Rebellion was their discovery that the gunpowder cartridges they had to bite on to open were greased with pig and cow fat, which was objectionable to both Muslim and Hindu soldiers. The rebellion exhibited a deep-seated resentment of the British, who were plundering India as part of their global empire. In any case, the rebellion ended in failure for the Indians, but it also precipitated in the end of the East India Company's rule over the subcontinent. The British government chose to confiscate company lands and rule India as an imperial entity known as the British Raj. Although both Muslims and Hindus participated in the revolt, Muslims were given most of the blame, and their social status in India continued to sink as a result. Furthermore, the Mughal Empire, which at this point only existed as a nominal entity under the British, was officially abolished as punishment for Emperor Bahadur Shah II's support for the rebellion. It would not be until 1947 and the establishment of Pakistan that Muslims would once again rule in the Indian Subcontinent.

AFRICA, CENTRAL AND SOUTHEAST ASIA

European imperialism managed to take a more direct role in the lands further away from the traditional centers of Muslim power in Istanbul and Delhi. The Ottoman and Mughal Empires managed to retain autonomy for a while because of their once-great power, but smaller, independent states on the edges of the Muslim world stood no chance in the face of the oncoming European onslaught. Britain, France, Russia and the Netherlands managed to conquer Muslim populations and add them to their expanding imperial domains.

The Mediterranean coast of North Africa had been nominally Ottoman since the sixteenth century. Its influence and control here never matched what it exercised in the Balkans, Anatolia and most of the Middle East, but local governors still owed their allegiance to the Ottoman sultanate, especially since Ottoman navies had helped defend North Africa from Spanish encroachment in the 1500s. In the subsequent centuries, a tradition of raids and counter raids existed in the Mediterranean between the Muslims of North Africa and the growing naval powers of Europe. The Europeans viewed the North African raiders, based in port cities such as Algiers, Tunis and Tripoli, as uncouth pirates who preyed on European shipping (the word barbarian even derives from the native people of North Africa, the Berbers), while the Muslim sailors viewed themselves as defenders of the Islamic domain and the Europeans as uncivilized war folk. In any case, by the late 1700s, the tide had turned in Europe's favor. European navies, buoyed by their overseas empires obtained the upper hand over the North Africans, who survived mostly on seizing European ships. Thus Europeans were finally able to reach the mainland of North Africa, bombarding its major cities such as Algiers and Tripoli. Even the newly-established United States of America got in on the action, attacking Tripoli in 1805.

It did not take long for North Africa to fall to its perennial enemies. The French attacked Algiers and its surrounding territory in 1830, carving out the colony of French Algeria. Unlike other French overseas territories, Algeria was a short hop across the Mediterranean Sea. Thus, Algeria was not seen as a colony, but as a part of France itself. Hundreds of thousands of French people moved to Algeria, dominating its local economy and culture while its native inhabitants were reduced to second-class citizens. Tunisia was similarly invaded and conquered in 1881. In 1911, the newly-unified Kingdom of Italy declared war on the Ottoman Empire and managed to wrest the provinces of Tripolitania, Cyrenaica and Fezzan, which it merged into one colony: Libya. Morocco, in the far west of North Africa, managed to remain nominally independent, but was carved into zones of influence, and later protectorates, by Spain and France. Muslim self-rule over the Maghreb, which had been unbroken since 'Uqba ibn Nafi' swept the region in the 600s, was over in the nineteenth century as European nations scrambled to claim territory as their own.

Egypt was a unique case, separate from its western neighbors. As a lucrative agricultural land, the French had their eyes on it well before the rest of North Africa. Napoleon invaded the Ottoman-controlled land in 1798 in an effort to protect French and disrupt British trade in the region. The campaign ended in failure, and in the power vacuum that followed the invasion, an Ottoman military commander, Mehmet Ali, managed to seize power for himself in Egypt. While remaining officially loyal to the Ottoman sultanate, Mehmet Ali ruled Egypt as an independent monarch. He undertook reforms aimed at modernizing Egypt along European lines well before the Ottomans got into the Tanzimat Era, thus leading to huge European influence in the ancient land. Mehmet Ali's successors continued his lean towards Europe, and Europeans reciprocated by investing heavily in the region, culminating with the construction of the Suez Canal in 1869, financed by the French. The growing role of European nations in shaping Egypt led to popular demonstrations in favor of Egyptian nationalism and against the ruling dynasty in the 1880s. Using the excuse of protecting their financial investments, the British and French governments invaded Egypt in 1882, defeated the nationalists and propping up the Mehmet Ali dynasty. From then on, Egypt was under military occupation by the British, although it officially remained an Ottoman territory until 1914.

On 27 August 1896, Britain defeated Zanzibar in the shortest war in history, lasting only forty minutes. The impetus for the war was the succession to the Zanzibari throne of a sultan who wanted to move Zanzibar out of Britain's sphere of influence.

European colonialism was not limited to the north of Africa. Remote West African Muslim states and the trade-based states of the East African coast also fell to European encroachment. West Africa, already heavily depopulated because of the Atlantic slave trade that began soon after European colonization of the New World in the sixteenth century, was by this time incapable of resisting invasion. The coastal areas, where Islam had not penetrated very deeply, were by the nineteenth century dependent on European traders in the major port cities. From theses bases, the French quickly moved inland in the late 1800s. The Muslim states of the Niger River Valley, long protected by the vast Sahara to the north and the dense forests to the south, were unprepared for the French onslaught. By 1895, the greater part of West Africa was brought under French control. The Europeans plundered the great cities that were once centers of Islamic knowledge, in particular Timbuktu. The wealth and power of medieval Mali became no more than a memory as West Africa was incorporated into the colonized world dominated by competing European powers.

In East Africa, the British took the imperial lead. The Swahili coast was vital to British plans to control Africa along a north-south axis from Egypt to South Africa. But since the early 1700s, Oman, a country along the southeastern coast of Arabia, controlled a maritime empire that stretched along the East African coast. Its main base was the city of Zanzibar, in what is now Tanzania. From here, the Omanis controlled coastal trade and exerted considerable influence over inland regions. By this time the Indian Ocean trade routes were not nearly as important as the Atlantic ones dominated by Europe. The Omanis were thus forced to deal with the British, who gained influence over the Omani government throughout the 1800s. When a succession crisis arose in 1856, the British forced the separation of Oman and Zanzibar into two states, thus weakening both. Furthermore, the British banned the inland slave trade, upon which the government relied for wealth, further weakening Muslim control in East Africa. When the Zanzibari government could not control its territories effectively, the British took the opportunity to establish a protectorate over the entire region. The system of divide and conquer, which worked so well for European imperial powers, proved its effectiveness in reducing the once-wealthy and powerful East African coast to just another European dependency.

In Central Asia, the Russians took the leading role in conquering Muslim lands. Russia had conquered the Tatar Muslims of the Volga region as early as the 1500s, along with their traditional capital at Kazan. Despite centuries of oppressive policies imposed by Russia's tsars, the Tatars re-emerged as a powerful economic force by the nineteenth century. They served as middlemen in the trade between Christian Russia, of which they were citizens, and the Turkish lands of Central Asia, where they could meet as equals with their Muslim brothers. The Turks were, by this time, divided into numerous petty states scattered throughout the deserts of Central Asia. Despite being home to some of the greatest centers of knowledge in Islamic history, such as Samarkand and Bukhara, the home of Imam al-Bukhari, Central Asia was geographically separated from the rest of the Sunni world by Persia. An island of their own, surrounded by the Persians and encroaching British in the south, China to the east, and Russia to the north, the Turks of Central Asia were in no position to hold off Russian influence. The Russians, using their economic ties with the region as an excuse to become more politically involved, began to annex lands in Central Asia in the 1800s, aided greatly by new railroads that linked the region with the center of Russian power further west. The Russian advance alarmed the British who ruled over India, prompting their incursion into Afghanistan, seeking to counter the Russians. The entire conflict and rivalry between the two powers dividing up Muslim Central Asia between them became known as the Great Game. By the end of the century, the Russians managed to conquer the entirety of the Turkish lands all the way up to Persian-dominated Khurasan, while the Afghan highlands formed a buffer against Russian imperialism to the south.

While neither the Russians nor the British managed to conquer Persia outright, they both exerted considerable influence in the country. The Qajar Dynasty, successors to the Safavids since the late 1700s, increasingly fell under the influence of the Russians, who pressed upon its northern borders. Russia negotiated "treaties" with Persia that gave them special political and economic privileges, much like the capitulations of the Ottomans. The Russians held sway in Tehran, but the British, through their systems of protectorates over Arab sheikhdoms along the Persian Gulf coast, exercised a sphere of influence over the southern part of Persia. Political and economic independence in the Persian homeland was effectively over by the end of the nineteenth century as Russia and Britain competed to take advantage of the country and its resources.

The trend of European colonialism taking advantage of weak Muslim states continued in the most easterly of Muslim lands in the Malay Archipelago. Here, the Dutch extended their trading empire in much the same way as the British did in India. The Dutch East India Company established bases throughout Southeast Asia from which they traded spices with the local Muslim kingdoms. The commercial colonizers did not hesitate to use military might to extend commercial opportunities. In 1641, the Dutch forced the Portuguese out of the important port of Malacca, which they had occupied since 1511. In 1621, the Dutch in the Banda Islands massacred over 10,000 people in an effort to solidify Dutch control over the nutmeg crop in the region. Using such brutality, the Dutch quickly managed to conquer most of the Malay Archipelago in the nineteenth century. Local Muslim sultanates in Java and Sumatra did not go peacefully, and revolts against Dutch rule were a constant thorn in the side of colonial control. The vast economic resources of the Dutch, combined with their superior technology and the lack of help from the rest of the Muslim world, led to a Dutch empire in Southeast Asia that lasted until after the Second World War.

In the sixteenth century, the Ottomans sent naval expeditions to the Sultanate of Aceh to aid local resistance to Dutch imperialism.

Overall, the nineteenth century saw the loss of Muslim political power across the Muslim world. Britain, France, Holland, Russia, and others all took advantage of Europe's growing power relative. There is no doubt that in many cases Europeans believed themselves to be worthy of ruling the world due to their "enlightened" governments, economic power, and organized and powerful militaries. Conquering the world and teaching native peoples how to live in a Western fashion was the "white man's burden", as Rudyard Kipling so famously wrote. With this sense of cultural and civilizational superiority, European colonizers obviously did not care much for local traditions or customs. This was not due to an ignorance of Islamic history. In fact, the nineteenth century was when European fascination with the East reached a high tide. Books on the Prophet, Islamic history and Muslim beliefs were published in all the major cities of Europe.

It was perhaps because of this recognition of Islamic history and the potential political and cultural power of Muslims that Europeans insisted on there being no native control over Muslim lands. The concept of "divide and conquer" was effective during the first outburst of European imperialism in the New World in the 1500s. In the 1800s it was used again, this time to fracture a Muslim world that had experienced immense power during times of unity under the Umayyads, Abbasids and Ottomans. Arbitrary borders were drawn by Europeans which did not take into account local identities or political histories in an effort to divide up Muslim political capital and make the conquered territories easier to subjugate and rule. Piece by piece, the Muslim world was taken by Europe, so that by the outbreak of the First World War in 1914, the vast majority of Muslims were under foreign occupation. Major questions arose among Muslims during this time about how God could allow this to happen and what this meant for the future of Islam in the modern world. The people trying to answer these questions would spearhead an attempt at an Islamic revival, aimed at pushing back the European tide and reasserting the dominance of the Muslim world.

12

OLD AND NEW IDEAS

One of the central themes of Islam is its finality and perfection. So many people abandoned pagan beliefs and followed the Prophet Muhammad because they believed he was inspired by God and brought to humanity a true religion that would revolutionize the world. The early generations of Muslims believed that Islam's early history verified the truth of Islam. The first hundred years after the death of the Prophet saw the spread of Muslim political control from southern France to India, despite competition from established and powerful empires. When military expansion ended, Muslims led the world in advancing science to new frontiers, influencing scientific history throughout the known world. The setbacks of the Crusades and Mongol invasions proved to be nothing more than a thorn in the side of Islamic history, as they were followed by the rise of even more powerful empires. To many Muslims, the proof of Islam's truth was its historical record, and the miraculous nature of Islamic history.

But then the decline of Muslim civilization and its subsequent conquest by Europe could be theologically problematic. If Muslims were indeed following a true religion, and its history was proof of that, then what could be made of the seemingly final triumph of Europe over the Muslim world? Throughout the eighteenth through twentieth centuries, Muslim scholars would rise up to answer that question by trying to revive Islam, in an effort to bring back those glory days that had solidified the faith of generations. No matter their location, these revivers had one theme in common: a return to Islamic practice was necessary for an Islamic revival. If Muslims would just practice Islam as the early generations had, then God would reward them with success.

On the other hand, however, a new class of scholars arose that disagreed with the traditionalist view of those revivers. Intellectuals influenced by modern European ideas like secularism and nationalism argued that Muslims should emulate the West. Europe had gone from the Dark Ages to world conquerors, so they must be doing something right, they reasoned. In their minds, the Muslim world had fallen so far behind precisely because it was so focused on religion and bringing back the glory days of early Islamic history, instead of modernizing according to new ideas and philosophies. These two contradicting approaches to revitalizing Muslim civilization battled each other intellectually (and sometimes physically) throughout the twentieth century, and continue to affect the way Muslims think today.

THE WESTERN APPROACH

As the West continued to consolidate its control over Muslim lands (and the rest of the world in general), not all who were subjugated by its imperial policies looked back to Islam's early days to find a model to emulate. Some looked towards Western ideas and philosophies to find a path to independence and self-determination.

The major philosophical trends popular in Europe in the nineteenth and twentieth centuries, namely nationalism and secularism, were adopted by many in the Muslim world who hoped to copy Europe's rise to power over the rest of the world.

The rise of new political ideas coincided with a change in the social lives of Muslims under European control. In the early twentieth century, the cities that had once served as the centers of Muslim social and political life—Cairo, Damascus and Baghdad—served as meeting places between centuries-old Muslim and post-Enlightenment European societies. European tourists, government officials and missionaries mixed freely with Muslim civilians, who were clearly affected by this exposure to Western culture. Everything from European architecture to music permeated Arab society. Muslims in high positions in government already dressed like Westerners since Mahmud II's reforms a century earlier, but now they also talked, acted and lived like Westerners. European-style orchestras played Western scores, cinemas screened Western movies, and dance clubs opened. If something could be found in Paris or London, it could also be found in Cairo and Beirut. Even in the confines of the home, life changed. Speaking English or French with the family was considered a sign of high class. Consumption of alcohol—banned according to the Quran and culturally taboo for centuries—became more widespread.

The emphasis on Western modernism led to the establishment of numerous publishing houses which used printing presses in Cairo. As a result, Egypt became a nexus of Arab culture, a position it maintained into the twentieth century.

It is interesting to note that while Muslims, particularly in the Arab lands, adopted Western culture, Westerners living among them for decades rarely adopted aspects of Arab culture. Throughout Islamic history, the cities had always been the meeting places of cultures, traditions and ideas. Abbasid Baghdad and Ottoman Istanbul in particular owed part of their greatness to the diverse peoples living within their walls. But the twentieth century interaction between East and West was different. The two sides were not meeting on an equal footing. Western society and culture (the conquerors) were associated with power and influence. Traditional Muslim society and culture (the conquered) were now associated with backwardness and impotence. The political reality of the era trumped the former greatness of Muslim civilization in the minds of many city-dwellers. It was only natural for them to adopt Western culture and norms in an attempt to emulate the power of their occupiers. With the adoption of new social ideas came the adoption of Western ideas about politics and government.

The main avenue for the entrance of these ideas into the Arab Muslim world was through Arab Christians. Due to the capitulation agreements that the Ottomans had with European nations, Christian communities within the empire had extensive contact with Western European powers. European merchants, missionaries and diplomats working in the Ottoman Empire brought Christians intellectually in line with the West just as Europe was shedding its religiously-based past in favor of liberal governments, nationalism and secular philosophies. This was coupled with an awakening of Arab intellectual and literary history, as Arab thinkers, especially in Beirut and Cairo, capitalized on the desire among Arabs to achieve the former greatness of their Umayyad and Abbasid ancestors who led the world in everything from military expansion to scientific inquiry. The religious dimensions of those earlier empires were downplayed in favor of their Arab language and identity. In the view of the leaders of this Arab awakening, if the Arabs wanted to re-establish the glory days, they needed to band together as Arabs, not as Muslims, and unite. Furthermore, for the Arab Christians who led this movement in the nineteenth and twentieth centuries, the demise of the Islamic identity in favor of secular nationalism would lead to their own social elevation, as there would be no differentiating between Muslim and Christian.

The pan-Islamic focus of Sultan Abdülhamid II in the late 1800s stifled any sense of popular Arab nationalism. Christian Arabs could not convince fellow Arabs of their ideas so long as the caliph was promising to reclaim the historic glory of the Islamic empires in the name of Islam and not nationalism. When Abdül-hamid was overthrown in 1909, the Ottoman government fell into the hands of the Young Turks and their nationalistic, secular focus. As the pan-Islamism of Abdülhamid faded away in favor of Turkish nationalism, the line between Turk and Arab became painfully obvious among subjects of the Ottoman Empire. Arabs already had a tough time establishing themselves politically in the overwhelmingly Turkish empire, and the rise of the Young Turks only made them feel more alienated. Thus the nationalistic ideas of Christian Arabs began to be adopted by Arab Muslims as well. Ottoman Syria became a hub for this Arab nationalism. Secret societies in Damascus, aimed at establishing an Arab state, flourished under the noses of Ottoman officials. By the 1910s, they were in contact with Western European powers who were eager to finally dismember the Ottoman Empire that had been the bane of European powers for centuries.

TRADITIONAL REVIVALISTS

The first to try to revive traditional Islam as he saw it was Muhammad ibn 'Abd al-Wahhab (1703–1792). Belonging to an Arab tribe from the deserts of the Arabian Peninsula, he lived a lifestyle probably not too different from the lifestyles of the Arabs during the life of the Prophet 1100 years before. He followed in the Hanbali tradition of Ahmad ibn Hanbal and Ibn Taymiyyah that stressed the superiority of authentic prophetic traditions over all else. Despite the fact that he lived beyond the borders of the Ottoman Empire's control, ibn 'Abd al-Wahhab was probably aware of the stagnation and decline of the empire and the rise of the West. In his eyes, this was due to Muslims having lost their way and no longer practicing Islam as the Prophet and his companions practiced it. He railed against Sufis, Shi'as, modernists and others that, according to him, had brought un-Islamic innovations into mainstream Muslim life. Like the Kharijis of the 600s, ibn 'Abd al-Wahhab and his followers argued that the vast majority of Muslims had fallen into disbelief. To redeem themselves, they must all go back to following a pristine, unchanged form of Islam identical to how the early generations of Muslims, the *salaf* (meaning "predecessors"), practiced. The movement evolved into what is known as Salafism, the idea that Muslims should constantly be trying to emulate the early generations of Muslims in all aspects of their lives.

Ibn 'Abd al-Wahhab found a follower in Muhammad ibn Sa'ud, a leader of a small settlement in the Arabian Desert. In exchange for ibn 'Abd al-Wahhab's support, ibn Sa'ud agreed to promote his puritan ideas about Islam throughout his growing kingdom. The pact remained in place after their deaths, with ibn 'Abd al-Wahhab's descendants providing religious legitimacy and ibn Sa'ud's descendants providing political power for the Saudi state. The Salafi movement may not have had much of an impact outside the deserts of Arabia had it not been for the meteoric growth of the Saudi state. By the early 1800s, the Saudis had managed to conquer huge tracts of the Arabian Peninsula, including Mecca and Medina. Despite being expelled from the holy cities less than twenty years later, Saudi control over the pilgrimage sites allowed them to spread their ideas to pilgrims from all over the world. It would take centuries before ibn 'Abd al-Wahhab's movement gained real, lasting power in the 1900s with the establishment of modern Saudi Arabia. While very few fully adopted the Salafi movement, the idea of an Islamic revival based on the early generations of Muslims greatly influenced Islamic thinkers around the world, especially in light of the coming Western deluge.

Further east, in an unstable and disunited post-Aurangzeb India, another reformer attempted to bring back traditional Islam in a changing society. Shah Waliullah (1703–1762) was a scholar of Islam who feared that the disunity of India's Muslims, coupled with the resurgence of its Hindu population, would lead to the breakdown of traditional society. His focus was on the social aspects of the *shari'ah* and how it was necessary to prevent the complete collapse of Islam in the subcontinent. A keen student of history, he recognized that if Mughal India continued along a path of disunity and civil war, others would rise to power in their place. Much like ibn 'Abd al-Wahhab, he advocated for the revival of Islamic tradition, but unlike his contemporary, he did not lead a call to arms against all Muslims he disagreed with. Muslims were, after all, the minority in India, and disunity among them could lead to their ultimate end, as it had in Al-Andalus 200 years previously. Instead he advocated a broad unity, bringing together various traditions, ethnicities, and ideas under the banner of Islam to at least slow down the decline of Islamic political power. While the Mughals did end up falling by the next century, the Islamically-oriented social philosophy of Shah Waliullah played a huge intellectual role in the Indian subcontinent. It was commonly called upon in opposition to the increasing westernization of India's upper classes and the rise of Hindu political power.

Not all reformers totally opposed all Western ideas. Some in fact tried to reconcile what they considered to be beneficial from the West with traditional Islam. During the British occupation in the late-1800s and early-1900s, Egypt was at the front line between Islamic tradition and Western imperialism. Al-Azhar University in Cairo had been one of the main centers of Islamic thought since its conversion into a Sunni school by Salah al-Din in the twelfth century. But it no longer dominated Egyptian intellectualism. Increasing European influence—both political and social—permeated throughout Egyptian society, especially due to the reforms of Mehmet Ali and his descendants. An Egyptian schoolteacher, Hassan al-Banna (1906–1949), sought to bring together Western modernism with traditional Islamic values. The Muslim Brotherhood—Al-Banna's organization—attempted to join Arab nationalism with Islamic values and social activism. Schools, hospitals and social welfare organizations were established by the Brotherhood in an effort to reach all levels of Egyptian society and encourage them to reform their lives in accordance with Islam. Western sciences and organizational ideas were adopted by the Brotherhood, but secularism was not. This middle ground approach proved immensely popular among Egyptians, but the rise of strict secular nationalism in the Arab world and in Egypt specifically would lead to decades of persecution for the Brotherhood.

THE PARTITION

Ultimately it would not be native Arab or Turkish nationalism that would lead to a new political order in the Middle East. In 1914, Archduke Franz Ferdinand of Austria-Hungary was assassinated in Sarajevo, and Europe was plunged into the First World War. The Ottoman government, led by three influential Young Turks (Isma'il Enver, Mehmet Talaat and Ahmed Djemel) known as the Three Pashas, joined the war on the side of Germany, against Britain, France and Russia. The Germans had been military advisors for the Ottomans for decades, and the Ottomans hoped to use the war to reclaim some of its lost territories (namely Egypt) and win the forgiveness of its huge foreign debts.

The Ottomans were in no position to make gains. Their military was hopelessly outdated and lacked effective leadership. Ethnic tensions in the empire—including the back-and-forth conflict between Turks and Armenians—prevented the empire from drawing on public support for the war effort. Furthermore, by the time the Ottomans joined the war in October of 1914, it was clear that their allies, the Germans, had no hope of succeeding in their conquest of France. Finally, backdoor scheming would lead to three agreements regarding rebellion within the empire and a post-Ottoman Middle East. Engineered by the British, these created a political mess that even they were not capable of handling. All this would lead to an eventual Ottoman loss in World War One that had reverberations in the Muslim world that are still felt today.

The ethnic tensions and strains of nationalism within the Ottoman Empire were well known to European powers, who hoped to exploit them. As early as 1915, the British were in contact with Sharif Husayn, the Ottoman governor of Mecca, in an effort to encourage a general Arab revolt. The British promised Husayn a united Arab kingdom throughout the Arabian Peninsula and the Fertile Crescent in exchange for his military support and rebellion against the Ottomans. Husayn, dreaming of being the king of the Arabs, was not difficult to convince, and neither were the Arabs of the Hijaz, who no doubt felt threatened by the Turkish nationalist rhetoric of the Ottoman government. Buoyed by British arms and gold, Sharif Husayn led the Arab Revolt, which swept up the western side of the Arabian peninsula, taking cities such as Medina, Amman and Damascus from the Ottomans and enabling the British to defend Egypt and go on to conquer Jerusalem, which fell into non-Muslim hands for the first time since the Crusades. In the 1910s, it seemed that Arab nationalism had finally become triumphant over the decaying Ottoman Empire. Arab self-determination and power under the kingship of Husayn seemed to be close at hand.

But they had no intention of allowing native Muslim rule, if the imperial policy of the British around the world was any indication. Almost as soon as they concluded an agreement with Sharif Husayn, the British entered into secret negotiations with their French allies, seeking to determine the shape of the post-Ottoman Middle East. The same lands that were promised to Husayn were secretly divided up between the British and the French. France was promised control over the northern part of Syria, including the Christian-dominated Lebanon. The British were to gain control of Mesopotamia and Palestine. The Sykes-Picot Agreement, as it was called, left no room for the pan-Arab kingdom promised to Husayn. The Arabs, after all, were in no position to make demands from the powerful Western European nations, especially ones known for regularly breaking their word. The conflicting agreements did not end here.

In 1917, the Foreign Secretary of the United Kingdom, Arthur Balfour, sent a letter to Baron Rothschild, an influential Jewish

---

The British designed a flag for the Arab rebels with three horizontal
bars and a triangle to the left. It served as the basis for numerous Arab
flags in the twentieth century including the Egyptian, Jordanian, Syrian,
and Palestinian flags.

---

banker, promising to support the establishment of a "national
home for the Jewish people" in Palestine. The letter was sent more
broadly to the Zionist Movement as a whole. Since the late 1800s,
Jews across Europe had been seeking to escape anti-Semitism by
founding a Jewish homeland. Their desired location was Palestine,
where the Jews had lived before being expelled in 70 CE by the
Romans. The Balfour Declaration pledged to support that quest,
despite contradicting the pre-existing agreements that promised
that same land to the Arabs and the British themselves. Jews would
use it in subsequent decades as proof of the legitimacy of their
settlement in that land and the eventual state of Israel, while
Arabs rejected it from the start, insisting the land was promised to
them in the British correspondence with Husayn. The quagmire
that the British created would dominate Middle Eastern politics
throughout the twentieth century.

THE RISE OF NATION-STATES

World War One brought about the final demise of Muslim political
control. The Ottomans were decisively defeated; their land conquered and occupied by the victorious British, French, Russians
and Italians. The Arabs, expecting their own kingdom, were left
with broken promises and European control over their "indepen-

dence". It was a collapse and conquest even more complete than the Crusades and the Mongols. More important than the military conquest was the intellectual environment of the post-war period. The rise of Arab and Turkish nationalism coupled with the arbitrary borders drawn by the victorious Europeans led to the rise of nation-states throughout the Muslim world that imposed European nationalism on a population wholly foreign to it. In Medina, Muhammad preached the unity of all Muslims, regardless of language or ethnic identification. He had paired up Meccan and Medinese Muslims as brothers to encourage this unity. His followers had identified themselves as Muslims above all else throughout the centuries. Now the Muslim world, particularly the Middle East, began to identify according to new nationalistic labels.

"I thank God that abandoning politics prevented me from reducing the Qur'an's diamond-like truths to pieces of glass under the accusation of exploiting them for political ends."

– Said Nusri, twentieth-century Turkish scholar

The most radical jump into the new era of nation-states occurred in the former Ottoman heartland dominated by the Turks. After the war, the British, French, Italians, and Greeks occupied Anatolia. The Ottoman sultanate remained intact but powerless in an Istanbul controlled by the Allied forces. To resist the foreign occupation, Mustafa Kemal, an Ottoman army officer rallied together fellow Turks who had served in World War One and managed to expel the occupiers between 1919 and 1922. At the end of this War of Independence, Mustafa Kemal announced the creation of a new state, Turkey, to replace the Ottoman Empire. The Ottoman sultanate was abolished 623 years after Osman founded it along the border of the Byzantine Empire. In his new nation of Turkey, Kemal hoped to establish a secular, Western-minded nation state, free from the recent Ottoman past marked by weakness, corruption, and conquest.

Kemal, as the leader of the Turkish War of Independence and the founder of Turkey, was affectionately called Atatürk, meaning "father of the Turks". To him, Turkish identity was very important, more so than any other qualifier. According to him, the Turks were a powerful nation even before they became Muslim. If anything, their conversion to Islam in the 900s and the subsequent mixing between Turks, Arabs, Persians and others weakened the Turks. The new Turkey was to be rid of this messy Islamic past as he saw it. One of his first actions was to rid Turkey of the caliphate, which had been in Ottoman hands since 1517. In 1924, the final caliph, Abdülmecid II was forced to abdicate and go into exile in Europe. Later, he would ban the *hijab* and fez, close Sufi orders, officially outlaw the *shari'ah* and ban the *adhan* (Arabic call to prayer) that rang out from mosque towers. Atatürk thus made clear that Turkey would no longer be tied with the rest of the Muslim world. He also instituted language reform, which would rid the Turks of the Arabic alphabet they had been using to write Turkish for centuries. Instead, the Latin alphabet of Europe was adopted, both for its ease of use and connection with Europe. Even vocabulary was changed: Arabic and Persian loanwords were abolished and replaced with old Turkic words from Central Asia. The language reforms of the 1920s and 1930s under Atatürk completely cut off modern Turks from their Islamic history. No longer could the Turks read the calligraphic inscriptions in old imperial mosques or any books published in the Ottoman era. Neither could they easily travel to and do business with the Arabs and Persians. In Atatürk's West-focused Turkey, there was no room for the relationships with others based on Islam that characterized the Ottoman Empire. Furthermore, other ethnic groups were not welcome. Greeks, Arabs, Kurds and Armenians within Turkey's borders were all oppressed by the new Turkish government, which sought to base its power on Turkish identity alone. Non-Turkish ethnic groups threatened this and were not afforded the same freedoms as their Turkish neighbors. The secular, nationalist focus of Turkey remained in place for decades. Any attempts to bring Islam back into public life were usually met with opposition and even coups from the military throughout the twentieth century.

To the south, in the Arab-dominated lands of the Fertile Crescent, the First World War led to the rise of various states, carved out by the victorious Allies. Trying to mediate between the three competing agreements they had made, the British and French divided up the region into mandates, generally along the lines of the Sykes-Picot Agreement. Out of Ottoman Syria and Mesopotamia came the new nations Syria, Iraq, Lebanon, Jordan and Palestine, all with new, arbitrary borders drawn at the whim of the winning powers. Jews were allowed to settle in the Mandate of Palestine as stated in the Balfour Declaration, much to the antagonism of the people already living there. Sharif Husayn and his children were given dominion (under British control) over the newly-created states of Syria, Jordan and Iraq, but only managed to hold onto Jordan in the long term. The political problems and conflict that erupted from the European division of Arab lands into arbitrary states are still being felt today. Iraq's borders were drawn such that Sunni Arabs, Sunni Kurds and Shi'a Arabs all constituted about one-third of the population. With no one group dominating, its history in the twentieth century was marked by ethnic and religious conflict and warfare. A similar situation occurred in Lebanon, a nation with no natural borders. The original idea of a Christian majority envisioned by the French in the 1800s never materialized. Religious conflict in the tiny Mediterranean state has prevented it from ever experiencing extended periods of peace and stability, despite the intellectual and cultural importance of Beirut to the Arab world in general.

The most disastrous British experiment turned out to be Palestine. Zionist Jews were allowed by the British to settle almost unrestricted in Palestine during the mandate period. In 1918, there were approximately 60,000 Jews within the newly-drawn borders of Palestine. By 1939, there were 460,000, mostly due to immigration from Europe. That number jumped during the Second World War, as Jews fleeing Nazi persecution hoped to find peace in a future Jewish homeland. Needless to say, this demographic shift in Palestine was unwelcomed by the Arabs living there, the Palestinians. Riots erupted throughout the 1930s. Arabs viewed the British and the Jews as enemies to the Arab nature of the region. The Jews, in turn, saw the conflict as one of self-defense, colored by their history of oppression in Europe. In 1948, the Jewish population of Palestine was large enough that they were capable of establishing a new state, Israel, as the British ended their mandate over the country. A coalition of Arab nations was unable to defeat the Israelis, who added even more land to their new state. Furthermore, newly established Israel used the war as an excuse to expel most of the Arab population within its borders. In 1948 and 1949, over 700,000 Arab Muslims and Christians were forced out of their land and made refugees in neighboring Jordan, Egypt, Syria and Lebanon.

As a Jewish state, Israel had to recalibrate the demographics to be in their favor. The only way to do that was to force the majority of Arabs into exile. The expulsion, called the Nakba, or "Catastrophe", was a disaster. It led to serious soul-searching among the Arabs, who had not only endured European colonization, but also the establishment of a foreign state in their midst. The conflict between the Israelis and the Arabs brought into focus the complete political failure of the Muslim world in the twentieth century.

The Indian Subcontinent also saw the rise of nation states as the British retreated. After the Sepoy Rebellion in 1857 and the subsequent tightening of British control over India, resistance to imperialism shifted to political and non-violent processes. An Indian National Congress was formed in the late 1800s to push for greater political power in the face of British occupation. Hindus dominated the congress, which was not surprising considering that Muslims were a minority. Thus for Muslims, the Indian independence movement in the early 1900s posed a problem. If India achieved independence from Britain, it would surely be Hindu-dominated. Hundreds of years of Muslim rule in the subcontinent was favorable for the Muslims, who could always count on their fellow believers in the Delhi Sultanate or Mughal Empire for protection. But with Muslim rule in India officially extinguished by the late 1800s, and the demographics of the region clearly not in their favor, the Muslim community of the subcontinent had to look to an alternative view of post-British India.

The favored approach was a partition of the subcontinent into separate Muslim and Hindu majority states. India's leading Muslim intellectuals, including the politician Muhammad Ali Jinnah and the poet philosopher Muhammad Iqbal, led what became known as the Pakistan Movement. Their goal was the establishment of a sovereign

Muslim state free from any potential harassment by a future Hindu government of India. The movement gained support throughout the 1930s and 1940s as its leaders presented the idea to the general Muslim population through declarations, resolutions and speeches. The region of India targeted for the new Muslim state was the Indus Valley, where Muslim political control first appeared with Muhammad bin Qasim in the 700s. Leaders of the Indian National Congress, particularly Mohandas Gandhi, generally did not favor an independent Muslim state in India, seeing it as weakening Indian power overall. But Muslim fears of Hindu control proved too strong in the end, and in 1947 the subcontinent was partitioned when the British ended their direct control over the region. Pakistan, comprising the Northwest (Sindh, Punjab and Balochistan) and East (Bengal), emerged as the new Muslim state of Pakistan, successor to India's great Muslim empires of the past. Muslims, in what became the Republic of India, thus became an even smaller minority, which ended up being ruled by the Indian National Congress. Pakistan was not the only Muslim nation to gain independence in the years after the Second World War, but uniquely, it was one of the few to base its foundation on its Islamic character rather than ethnic heritage or loyalty to a royal family.

After the decline of Muslim civilization in the eighteenth century and its subsequent conquest by Europe in the nineteenth, the twentieth century saw the nominal independence of Muslim nation-states around the world. Egypt's Revolution of 1952 ended the British occupation that had been in place since 1882 and brought the country under the control of the Egyptian military. Algeria, under French occupation since the early 1800s, finally achieved independence in 1962 after a brutal and devastating war. The 1960s saw the independence of nations across sub-Saharan Africa, including Nigeria, Mali,

Mauritania, Kenya and Tanzania. In Southeast Asia, independence movements struggled against British and Dutch imperialism. Indonesia emerged after a long and brutal war against the Dutch Empire in 1949. To the northwest, the British-ruled areas on the Malay Peninsula and the island of Borneo became Malaysia in 1963. Despite sharing a common language, culture and religion, Indonesia and Malaysia became separate states based on the borders established by the British and Dutch. Muslim nations became free of European control through the 1900s, but were still bounded by the borders drawn by their former colonizers.

The name "Pakistan" was formed as an acronym of Muslim-majority regions in India: Punjab, Afghania Province, Kashmir, Sindh, and Baluchistan.

ISLAM AND SECULARISM

It would seem at this point that the Muslim world had once again overcome a threatening political power. The cyclical nature of Islamic history dictated that after a period of weakness and invasion, a new, powerful Muslim empire would arise, reclaiming the glory of the old Islamic states. After the rise of Christian states in al-Andalus, the Murabitun and Muwahhidun arose in the eleventh and twelfth centuries to unite Iberia and North Africa. After the Crusader invasion in the twelfth century, Salah al-Din's Ayyubid Empire and its successor, the Mamluks, united Egypt, Syria, and the Hijaz under their powerful rule. The Mongol invasion in the thirteenth century would lead to the rise of the Ottomans and their tri-continental empire that knocked on the doors of Central Europe. Now it seemed that in the twentieth century, the tide of European imperialism had finally turned and the time was ripe for a new, world-dominating Muslim empire.

Fazulr Khan, a Bengali Muslim, designed the Sears Tower in Chicago. It was the world's tallest building when it opened in 1973.

This time, the traditional Muslim empire would not come. Dozens of Muslim states dotted the world map, disunited by arbitrary borders—a legacy of European colonization. This disunity proved fatal to the Muslim world. In the Middle East, the inability of Egypt, Jordan, Syria and Lebanon to function effectively together meant that Israel, a nation founded by poor settlers fleeing European oppression, was able to defeat them all militarily and further establish itself in wars in 1967 and 1973. In South Asia, East Pakistan broke away to become Bangladesh in 1971, splitting a nation that had the potential to serve as a counter-balance to India's power. In West Africa, the numerous disunited states were all economically weak and continued to rely on the French well after independence. Without unity, the relative political power of the Muslim world remained generally unchanged after independence. Small, competing states, reminiscent of al-Andalus' Taifa period and the decentralization of the Abbasid Empire, were incapable of creating a powerful Muslim realm.

A big part of that failure was a decisive ideological shift in Muslim politics. Throughout Islamic history, upstart empires had based their right to rule on Islam itself. Even in empires whose actions can probably be judged to be against Islamic law, the primacy of Islam itself as a unifying force was always a given. In the twentieth century, however, newly-independent Muslim states generally did not look back at a glorious Islamic past and try to recreate it. Instead they almost always had a secular and nationalist outlook. These concepts were entirely foreign to the Muslim world for its first 1200 years. But with European imperialism, these ideas were implanted into the minds of the upper classes of Muslim society, which ended up leading post-independence governments. The European formula of Enlightenment and subsequent neglect of traditional religion and government was thus adopted on some level in almost every Muslim country. The most extreme example was Turkey, which officially outlawed the *shari'ah*, abolished the caliphate, and proclaimed itself to be a wholly secular state. Led by Egypt, the Arab world adopted socialism and nationalism as a means to create powerful nation-states. Iran, despite its history as a fundamentally Shi'a nation, was led by a secular government aligned with the West until 1979. There were exceptions, of course, the most prominent being Saudi Arabia, which functioned as an absolute monarchy, not unlike Arab tribal states centuries ago, and derived its legitimacy to rule from the Salafi ideology of Muhammad ibn 'Abd al-Wahhab. Overall, however, Muslim countries left behind the idea of political Islam in favor of secular ideologies promoted by the West.

The Muslim world has yet to fully reconcile its Islamic-oriented past with its secular-dominated present. There exist today traditionalists who demand that the Muslim world return to those lost days when Islam and politics were intertwined. The extreme among them forcefully advocate a return to Islamic rule. Others take a more moderate approach, believing that education, action within existing political frameworks, and community service can precipitate to the return of political Islam. On the other end of the spectrum are those who argue that the days of Islam playing a role in political life are over. They advocate a break from tradition in favor of new ideas, mostly originating in the West, about government, society and politics.

"America needs to understand Islam, because this is the one religion that erases from its society the race problem."

– Malcolm X

Muslim society remains split over the role of Islam today. Most recently, the Arab Spring and subsequent upheaval in Egypt, Tunisia and Syria has brought to light the seeming incompatibility of these two competing sides. Turkey is once again at a crossroads between secularism and political Islam, as an Islamic-oriented government attempts to reverse decades of state secularism. This dichotomy exists throughout the Muslim world. How it is solved will dictate its direction in the coming decades and centuries. Whether Islam once again plays a major role, whether nationalism and secularism will be the new driving ideologies, or whether a balance between the two sides will be found that appeals to all, remains to be determined. Those who answer these pertinent questions will dictate a new era for the Muslim world; one that surely cannot be detached from the 1400 years of Islamic history that came before it.

BIBLIOGRAPHY

Ajram, K. (1992), *The Miracle of Islamic Science*, Cedar Rapids, IA: Knowledge House.

Al-Azami, Muhammad Mustafa (2003), *The History of the Quranic Text: From Revelation to Compilation*, Leicester: UK Islamic Academy.

Al-Hassani, Salim T. S. (2012), *1001 Inventions: The Enduring Legacy of Muslim Civilization*, Washington, D.C.: National Geographic Museum.

Armstrong, Karen (1996), *Jerusalem: One City, Three Faiths*, New York: Alfred A. Knopf.

——— (2000), *Islam: A Short History*, New York: Modern Library.

Carr, Matthew (2009), *Blood and Faith: The Purging of Muslim Spain*, New York, NY: New Press.

Diouf, Sylviane A. (1998), *Servants of Allah: African Muslims Enslaved in the Americas*, New York: New York University Press.

Dirks, Jerald (2006), *Muslims in American History: A Forgotten Legacy*, Beltsville, MD: Amana Publications.

Eaton, Richard (2000), 'Temple Desecration and Indo-Muslim States,' *Journal of Islamic Studies* 11(3), pp. 283–319.

El-Ashker, Ahmed Abdel-Fattah, and Rodney Wilson (2006), *Islamic Economics: A Short History*, Leiden: Brill.

Esposito, John L. (1999), *The Oxford History of Islam*, New York, NY: Oxford University Press.

Finkel, Caroline (2006), *Osman's Dream: The Story of the Ottoman Empire, 1300–1923*, New York, NY: Basic Books.

Freely, John (1998), *Istanbul: The Imperial City*, London: Penguin.

——— (2009), *The Grand Turk: Sultan Mehmet II—Conqueror of Constantinople, Master of an Empire*, London: I B Tauris & Co Ltd.

Gross, Jo-Ann (1992), *Muslims in Central Asia: Expressions of Identity and Change*, Durham, NC: Duke University Press.

Hamdun, Said, and Noel King (1994), *Ibn Battuta in Black Africa*, Princeton, NJ: Marcus Wiener.

Hawting, G. R (2000), *The First Dynasty of Islam: The Umayyad Caliphate AD 661–750*, London: Routledge.

Hodgson, Marshall G. S. (1974), *The Venture of Islam: Conscience and History in a World Civilization*, Chicago, IL: University of Chicago Press.

Holt, P. M., Ann K. S. Lambton, and Bernard Lewis (1970), *The Cambridge History of Islam*, Cambridge: Cambridge University Press.

Hourani, Albert (1991), *A History of the Arab Peoples*, Cambridge, MA: Belknap of Harvard University Press.

Inalcik, Halil (1973), *The Ottoman Empire: The Classical Age 1300–1600*, London: Phoenix Press.

Itzkowitz, Norman (1980), *Ottoman Empire and Islamic Tradition*. Chicago, IL: University of Chicago, Press.

Kennedy, Hugh (1986), *The Prophet and the Age of the Caliphates: The Islamic Near East from the Sixth to the Eleventh Century*, London: Longman.

——— (1996), *Muslim Spain and Portugal: A Political History of Al-Andalus*, Harlow: Pearson Education Limited.

——— (2005), *When Baghdad Ruled the Muslim World: The Rise and Fall of Islam's Greatest Dynasty*, Cambridge, MA: Da Capo Press.

——— (2008), *The Great Arab Conquests: How the Spread of Islam Changed the World We Live In*, Cambridge, MA: Da Capo Press.

Khaldūn, Ibn (1969), *The Muqaddimah, an Introduction to History*, Translated from the Arabic by Franz Rosenthal, and N. J. Dawood (ed.), Princeton, NJ: Princeton University Press.

Levtzion, Nehemia, and Randall L. Pouwels (2000), *The History of Islam in Africa*, Athens, OH: Ohio University Press.

Lewis, Bernard (1984), *The Jews of Islam*, Princeton, NJ: Princeton University Press.

Lewis, David L. (2008), *God's Crucible: Islam and the Making of Europe, 570 to 1215*, New York, NY: W.W. Norton.

Lindsay, James E. (2005), *Daily Life in the Medieval Islamic World*, Westport, CN: Greenwood.

Lings, Martin (1983), *Muhammad: His Life Based on the Earliest Sources*, New York, NY: Inner Traditions International.

Maalouf, Amin (1985), *The Crusades through Arab Eyes*, New York, NY: Schocken.

Masood, Ehsan. *Science and Islam: A History*. London: Icon, 2009.

Māwardī, Abu'l-Hasan (1996), *Al-Ahkam As-Sultaniyyah: The Laws of Islamic Governance*, Translated from the Arabic by Asadullah Yate, London: Ta-Ha.

McNeill, William Hardy, and Marilyn Robinson Waldman (1983), *The Islamic World*, Chicago, IL: University of Chicago Press.

Montefiore, Simon Sebag (2011), *Jerusalem: The Biography*, New York, NY: Random House Inc.

Morgan, Michael Hamilton (2007), *Lost History: The Enduring Legacy of Muslim Scientists, Thinkers, and Artists*, Washington, D.C.: National Geographic.

Ochsenwald, William, and Sydney Fisher (2003), *The Middle East: A History*, 6th edition, New York, NY: McGraw-Hill.

Peters, F. E. (1994), *A Reader on Classical Islam*, Princeton, NJ: Princeton University Press.

Ramadan, Tariq (2007), *In the Footsteps of the Prophet: Lessons from the Life of Muhammad*, New York, NY: Oxford University Press.

Saunders, John Joseph (1965), *A History of Medieval Islam*, London: Routledge.

Schroeder, Eric (2002), *Muhammad's People: An Anthology of Muslim Civilization*, Mineola, NY: Dover Publications.

Siddiqi, Muhammad Zubair (1993), *Ḥadīth Literature: Its Origin, Development and Special Features*, Cambridge: Islamic Texts Society.

INDEX